Formation
of the
Bible

SECOND EDITION

Formation
of the
Bible

The Story of the Church's Canon

LEE MARTIN McDONALD

an imprint of Hendrickson Publishing Group

Formation of the Bible: The Story of the Church's Biblical Canon
Second Edition

© 2012, 2023 by Lee Martin McDonald
First edition 2012. Second edition 2023

Published by Hendrickson Publishers
an imprint of Hendrickson Publishing Group
Hendrickson Publishers, LLC
P. O. Box 3473
Peabody, Massachusetts 01961-3473
www.hendricksonpublishinggroup.com

ISBN: 978-1-4964-8484-0

All rights reserved. No part of this book may be reproduced or transmitted in any form or by any means, electronic or mechanical, including photocopying, recording, or by any information storage and retrieval system, without permission in writing from the publisher.

Scripture quotations marked (NRSVue) are taken from the New Revised Standard Version Updated Edition. Copyright © 2021 National Council of Churches of Christ in the United States of America. Used by permission. All rights reserved worldwide.

Printed in the United States of America

First Printing Second Edition — October 2023

Cover art: The portion of 1 Corinthians 14:21–23 from the *Codex Sinaiticus* is reproduced courtesy of the British Library. Manuscript illustration of Emperor Constantine and the Council of Nicaea, drawing on vellum from Biblioteca Capitolare, Vercelli, ca. 825, Illustrator Anonymous, Public Domain.

Library of Congress Cataloging-in-Publication Data

McDonald, Lee Martin, 1942–
    Formation of the Bible: the story of the church's canon / Lee Martin McDonald.
       p. cm.
    Includes bibliographical references.
    ISBN 978-1-59856-838-7 (alk. paper)
    1. Bible—Canon. I. Title.
    BS465.M375 2012
    220.1'2—dc23
                      2012028196

To
Bruce G. Laverman

A dear servant of Christ from whom I have learned much
and whose friendship has enriched my life.

Table of Contents

List of Tables	viii
List of Illustrations	ix
Preface to the Second Edition	xi
Preface to the First Edition	xiii
Abbreviations	xv
Introduction	1
1. What is the Bible? An Overview	15
2. The Origin of the Old Testament Scriptures	37
3. The Closing of the Old Testament Scriptures	68
4. The First Scriptures of the Earliest Christians	83
5. How the New Testament Came to Be	94
6. What the Ancient Manuscripts Tell Us	116
7. Councils, Catalogues, and Canons	152
8. The Question of Authorship and Pseudepigrapha in Antiquity	168
9. Epilogue	187
Glossary of Terms Related to the Formation of the Canon	195
Select Bibliography	203

List of Tables

Summary of Timeline for Canonization of the Bible	10
Old Testament Timeline	12
New Testament Timeline	13
Table 1: Lost Ancient Books Mentioned in the Bible	74
Table 2: Jewish Religious Books Not in the Christian Scriptures	75
Table 3: The Names and Sequences of Books in the Hebrew Bible and Christian Old Testaments	79
Table 4: Old Testament Catalogues of Scriptures	88
Table 5: The New Testament Apocrypha	113
Table 6: Early Lists of Scriptural books	158

List of Illustrations

The Parthenon in Athens	16
The Temple of Artemis at Sardis	17
Ionic capital from a column at Sardis	17
The Temple of Zeus in Athens	18
Site of the Pergamum library	24
Ruins at Qumran	43
Replicas of jars at Qumran	44
Replica of a Dead Sea Scroll	44
View toward the ruins of Qumran and the Dead Sea	45
Cave 4 at Qumran	46
Cave 11 at Qumran	47
Fragment of the Temple Scroll	48
Dead Sea Scroll copy of Joshua 1:7–12; 2:2–3	48
A water canal coming from the wadi at Qumran	49
Actual clay jar	50
Isaiah 53 in Codex Sinaiticus	60
Inscriptions on a stone wall in ancient Delphi	117
A clay tablet (ca. 1950–1835 BC)	117
A stone tablet dating from approximately 2000 BC	118

Early Greek ostracon	119
Codex Zacynthius	120
Papyrus sheet used for writing	121
Codex Vaticanus (ca. AD 350)	124
Statue of Johann Gutenberg from Mainz	126
Photo of replica of the famous Gutenberg printing press	127
An example of moveable type used in printing	128
A page of the Gutenberg Bible	129
Families of manuscript copies	137
A portion of 1 Cor in Codex Sinaiticus	138
Locations of the various manuscript families	140
Desiderius Erasmus of Rotterdam (1466–1536)	142
$\mathfrak{P}^{52}$ (ca. AD 125) fragment of John 18:31–33	144
John Wycliffe (1329–1384)	146
William Tyndale (1494–1536)	147

Preface to the Second Edition

I am pleased to be invited to write a new edition of *Formation of the Bible*. In the last dozen years since I wrote the first edition, which has been welcomed in many churches and undergraduate classes, scholarship has produced more information that warrants being addressed in this introductory volume. I am grateful for the invitation of Hendrickson's Marco Resendes to produce this new edition. I am also grateful to Phil Frank, who typeset the book, and Tyler Comer, who helped in the editing and proofreading of the updates. They have been most helpful and encouraging. This update includes charts with more precise dating, interactions with recent scholarship that elucidates the historical context of the relevant ancient literature, and a new chapter on ancient pseudepigrapha in Judaism and early Christianity. I have bolstered the bibliography with new and helpful resources for further study of canon formation.

My idea for writing this book, as noted in the first edition, came from Kathy Sakenfeld, professor of Old Testament Studies at Princeton Theological Seminary, who asked me over lunch why I had not written something that would be useful in the church. She was right since most of what I had written earlier was for scholars and graduate students. Following her advice, I decided to provide a book for interested laypeople. However, since its publication several undergraduate schools have also used it as an introduction to canon formation for their students.

I am grateful for the continuing interest in this work. Biblical scholars have seldom agreed on how the Bible was formed, largely because no one in antiquity told this story or answered many modern questions. But many scholars now agree on several important facts that I have presented in this edition. Hopefully, this will make this small volume more useful both in churches and in some university and seminary classes.

Once again, I dedicate this volume to the Rev. Bruce Laverman, who has been my close friend for more than forty years now.

Lee Martin McDonald
December 2022

Preface to the First Edition

No book in history has had more of an impact on Christians, and on the Western world as well, than the Bible. For Christians, the Bible is their most important collection of religious writings that gives them meaning and direction in life. Christians, of course, are aware that the Bible did not fall out of heaven fully bound and with gilded edges, but few of them know much about the origin of the Bible or what historical factors were involved in the collection and transmission or distribution of their Scriptures. The story of how the various books of the Bible came to be placed in a fixed collection of sacred Scriptures is still largely unknown.

The aim of this volume is to help readers fill in some of the important background information on the formation of the Bible and to answer some of the more important questions that emerge from such an investigation. While I do not minimize or ignore the role of God in this process, there is a considerable amount of information about the origin of the Bible that can be known from historical research and that can have an important impact on our understanding of the Bible.

Christians may well ask why we need to spend any time on the origin of the Bible; wouldn't it be better simply to read and use it to advance the mission of the church? What difference does a background study make now, and why are we focusing on the Bible of the *early* churches? The Bible today is a complete entity that will not likely change, so why trouble believers about it? Such questions are not unfamiliar to those who attempt to tell the story of the origin of the Bible. However, if the Bible conveys the Word of God and clarifies to us who God is, what the will of God is for us, who we are as the people of God, and what our mission in this world is, then the question cannot be unimportant for Christian faith. Further, what we learn from such a study can significantly affect our understanding of the origin of the Bible. Given the current skepticism of many contemporary scholars about the origin of the Bible and its faith claims, it is important to answer recent challenges to the Bible and to aid those who recognize the Bible as a sacred book, but who do not regularly deal with its origins.

This volume was written to fill an important need in churches. There are other studies written by and for biblical scholars and those in advanced biblical studies at universities and seminaries, but there is also an important need for the whole church to understand the origin and development of its Bible. Hopefully, this small volume will bring greater understanding for those in the church who are interested in this very important subject.

As an ordained Christian minister who has served for many years as a pastor and also as a professor of biblical studies, I have led many discussions on the subjects discussed in this book both in various churches and small Christian groups and also in more public venues such as service clubs, academic institutions, and theological seminaries. I am also aware of the lack of reliable information available to the laity in our churches as well as the hesitancy of some clergy to discuss such matters with their church members.

Not long ago when I was a visiting scholar and professor at Princeton Theological Seminary, I was asked by one of the biblical professors if I knew of any book on this subject that was written for laypersons. Her question has stayed with me, and I have decided to address it in this volume. At that time, there was nothing that I could point to that was well informed and responsibly written for the church that could also address some of the critical questions related to the origin of the Bible. Hopefully, this small volume will aid in bridging the gap between biblical scholars who engage in such discussions and those in the churches who read their Bibles as a source of inspiration and spiritual direction. I have not used the usual footnotes or many technical words, though occasionally in the glossary toward the end of this book, I introduce a few terms that are important for clarifying this subject.

I owe special thanks for this book to Dr. Allan Emery and his colleagues at Hendrickson Publishers for undertaking this project. Allan was the first to contact me to see if I would be willing to write such a volume, and I was both honored and pleased to accept the invitation.

I have also dedicated the volume to my dear friend, the Rev. Bruce Laverman. He and I were introduced many years ago when we were fellow pastors in Nebraska. One of his church members, a JAG officer (a military lawyer), served with me in the same unit where I served as a chaplain. He was sure that his pastor and I would get along well. Richard Payant took us both to lunch, introduced us, and was right: Bruce and I became very good friends. I was immediately impressed with Bruce's knowledge of the church and how it operates, and I was always impressed with his commitment to evangelism and his effectiveness in Christian ministry. I learned much from him in those years and ever since. More times than I can remember when I was a pastor, he pointed me in important and helpful directions. We have been close friends for more than thirty years now, and I am pleased to dedicate this small volume to him.

Lee Martin McDonald
January 2012

Abbreviations

General

AD	*anno domini* (year of our Lord)
ANF	*Ante-Nicene Fathers*
BC	Before Christ
c.	century (on charts only)
ca.	*circa* (about)
LCL	Loeb Classical Library
NPNF	*Nicene and Post-Nicene Fathers*
pl.	plural
p(p).	page(s)
Rev.	revised, Reverend
v(v).	verse(s)

List of Biblical books

Old Testament

Gen	Genesis
Exod	Exodus
Lev	Leviticus
Num	Numbers
Deut	Deuteronomy
Josh	Joshua
Judg	Judges
1–2 Sam	1–2 Samuel
1–2 Kgdms	1–2 Kingdoms
1–2 Kgs	1–2 Kings
3–4 Kgdms	3–4 Kingdoms
1–2 Chr	1–2 Chronicles
Neh	Nehemiah
Ps(s)	Psalm(s)
Prov	Proverbs
Eccl	Ecclesiastes

Song	Song of Songs/Song of Solomon
Isa	Isaiah
Jer	Jeremiah
Lam	Lamentations
Ezek	Ezekiel
Dan	Daniel

New Testament

Matt	Matthew
Rom	Romans
1–2 Cor	1–2 Corinthians
Gal	Galatians
Eph	Ephesians
Phil	Philippians
Col	Colossians
1–2 Thess	1–2 Thessalonians
1–2 Tim	1–2 Timothy
Phlm	Philemon
Heb	Hebrews
1–2 Pet	1–2 Peter
Rev	Revelation

Apocrypha, Pseudepigrapha, and Dead Sea Scrolls

Apos. Con.	Apostolic Constitutions and Canons
Bar	Baruch
Ep Jer	Epistle of Jeremiah
1 En.	1 Enoch
1–2 Esd	1–2 Esdras
1–4 Macc	1–4 Maccabees
Pr Azar	Prayer of Azariah
Wis	Wisdom of Solomon
Gos. Heb.	Gospel of the Hebrews
Gos. Pet.	Gospel of Peter
Gos. Thom.	Gospel of Thomas
CD	Damascus Document
QS	Rule of the Community

Introduction

The Bible is without question the church's most important sacred book, and throughout church history countless millions of Christians have given an enormous amount of their time to study and interpret its message. Contrary to popular media hype, there is no concerted effort in the church to cover up any part of the history of the Bible and its formation. Some of the media and public presentations about the church and its Bible have had a positive impact on biblical scholarship because they have led many scholars to ask fresh questions about the origin of the books that comprise their Bible. Not infrequently, new questions are asked about why certain books were included in the Bible and others excluded: Who made those decisions, how and when were they made, and especially why? The media influence in this regard has been helpful because it has prompted scholars to do more diligent homework than what was done before. The downside of the new inquiry is that much of it has not yet reached the wider church audience in an accessible manner.

Readers may be surprised that there are no ancient documents that tell us how the Bible came to be or provide the answer to many of our questions, nor that describe the formation of the Christian Bible! Bible scholars make their inferences about the origin and fixing of the books of the Bible from a limited amount of data in order to piece together this complex puzzle that we call *canon formation*; that is, what books form the Bible and how the Bible came to be in its current condition. As a result, biblical scholars often disagree on how to interpret the scant surviving data. Fortunately, we are not left completely in the dark on the matter, but care is still needed to sift through the various pieces of this historical story. The good news is that much more important information has come to light that was not available when this volume first came out in 2012.

Assessing Questions, Claims, and Sources

The early Christians showed relatively little interest in the origins of their Bible, and there has been little interest in this subject until modern times. But there has been no concerted effort to conceal any of the factors that led to the forming of the Christian Bible. As Christians still do today, the early followers of Jesus employed the Old Testament Scriptures to articulate their faith and to advance their mission in the world. That was more significant to them than questions about the origin and stabilization of their Scriptures. There is no evidence that such questions about the origin and formation of their Scriptures existed at the earliest stages of the church's development. Before the Bible was present in the churches, the primary beliefs circulated through teaching, creedal summaries of those beliefs, hymns, and baptismal and eucharistic (communion) affirmations. The absence of any written statement on the accepted books of the Bible may have been because everyone already knew the answers to the questions we raise today. At that time, there was no need to ask or write anything about which of the circulating texts were authoritative within the churches. However, it is more likely that the early Christians were concerned with other more pressing problems facing the church, such as persecution and theological divisions.

When I was in seminary in the mid-1960s, questions about the origin of the Bible did not appear to be important topics of discussion, though students were asked to read about ten or so pages on the subject in our Old and New Testament introduction courses. Those pages were generally summarizing statements rather than well-argued positions. There was little in those pages of much consequence, and so students did not focus on most of the issues that have subsequently emerged in recent research on the formation of the Bible. We were taught what were believed to be the basic outlines of the formation of the Bible: the Old Testament Scriptures were formed and "fixed" long before the time of Jesus, who passed them on to his followers; the formation of the New Testament was essentially over by the end of the second century AD. Most of us then, including the well-intentioned professors who simply shared such things with us, knew relatively little of the formation of the Bible, and consequently very little was shared in our churches.

Years later when I was a pastor of a Baptist church in Nebraska, a young student came home at Christmas break from his university. He had just taken a religion course and learned about ancient religious books that did not make it into the Bible. In a mid-week Bible study class, he asked me about those books and why they were rejected and who made those decisions. I responded to him by passing on information I had received in my seminary training, but my responses were clearly inadequate. I asked him for more time so I could respond more appropriately to his thoughtful questions. I soon realized that almost everything that I told him was inaccurate, and so I began a more serious study that led to several publications on the question.

His questions and those of many others have been of special interest to a number of Christians who take their faith seriously and affirm the importance of the Bible in their spiritual journeys. As one who has taught in undergraduate and graduate classes over the years, I realize how important it is to make this information about the origin of the Bible available to the broader Christian community. Certainly, most Christians who take their Bible reading seriously can understand and appreciate the important factors in how we got our Bible if we take the time to explain them.

In recent years, discussions of the formation of the Bible have focused mostly on the date of the origin of both Old and New Testament canons and the factors or criteria that were involved in the selection process. Why were some ancient books rejected but others accepted by the early Christians? In order to address this broader issue, it is helpful to consider some of the situations and discoveries that have prompted many of our questions about canonical formation.

Many have read or heard about Dan Brown's widely published fictional book *The Da Vinci Code* or the earlier *Holy Blood and Holy Grail* by Michael Baigent and Richard Leigh. The claim that the respective stories were based on legitimate ancient sources, especially in Brown's book, took many Christians by surprise; quite reasonably, many of them asked their church leaders why they had not heard of those sources. The obvious questions that came thereafter focused on why the church rejected such books and if the church was trying to cover something up in the process of recognizing the books that made up the Bible. Similarly, since special television programs often flood the airwaves in the weeks before Christmas and Easter, it is not unusual in these media programs to hear the producers or authors claim that their information is based on important ancient documents. Such declarations carry the inference that since the ancient books mentioned were not included in the church's Bible, then there is something that the church is trying to hide from those who are interested in the history of Christianity and the books that comprise the Bible.

Not long ago, I was contacted several times by a publisher to see if I would write a popular "airport" type book on the origins of the Bible, which I was certainly willing to do, but the publisher wanted me to write it from the perspective of "what the church does not want you to know." I declined the invitation and told the publisher that I do not know of anything that the church does not want us to know or that it is trying to hide from the public. That invitation illustrates how unfounded sensationalism continues; it also underscores that sensationalism often "sells" better than the simple truth about matters related to the church and its Bible.

On a positive note, those who make such fanciful claims have often initiated considerable popular interest in the origins of the Bible, and subsequent scholarly investigations have brought clarity to many of the questions that have been raised about the Bible or the core teachings about Jesus. A number of biblical scholars have responded to the challenge of researching the origins of the Bible and making useful information available to students of the Bible. It is therefore especially important to make the results of such research available to a wider audience, especially to those who read the Bible faithfully and seek to live in accordance with its teachings today.

It is encouraging to see a growing interest in how the church got its Bible, but also often disheartening to discover how few Christians know anything about the Bible's origins. Most would not say that the Bible "fell out of heaven with gold edges," but little is known about it among Christians. What ancient books were written and why are the books in our Bibles the only ones that were selected? Such questions and many more are the focus in the following study.

We will mention here another significant source of information that has provoked similar questions about biblical origins, a source to which we will return in more detail later in the book. One of the most influential discoveries of the twentieth century was the discovery and publication of the famed Dead Sea Scrolls. Quite by accident, some Bedouin shepherds found these ancient Jewish religious texts in the vicinity of the northwestern shores of the Dead Sea, at a place now called Qumran. These ancient scrolls contain many religious texts that were likely copied and preserved by a small Jewish sect known as the Essenes who lived mostly in Judea from roughly 170 BC to AD 68. As we will note later, of the estimated 960 scrolls discovered at Qumran, around 200 of them are copies or partial copies of Old Testament books, but more than 700 of the manuscripts are of nonbiblical books. It is perhaps widely known that these scrolls included all of the books of the Bible except Esther and Nehemiah, but seldom do we hear that many other books that circulated in the land of Israel in the first centuries BC and AD were not later included in the Jewish Bible.

Some of the so-called nonbiblical scrolls discovered among the Dead Sea Scrolls later informed the faith of some of the early Christian churches, but they were eventually excluded from both the Jewish and Christian Bibles. These nonbiblical scrolls were produced from the end of the fourth century BC to the middle of the first century AD, and several of them had widespread influence in the land of Israel, both before and during the time of Jesus.

Some readers will remember the considerable media hype about these ancient documents when they first came to public attention. There were several scholars at the time who claimed that the church was somehow trying to hide their contents out of fear that they could damage the church's teachings. This underlying suggestion sold several popular books, but all such allegations have been shown to be without foundation and essentially nonsense. Jewish and Christian scholars have investigated the Dead Sea Scrolls carefully and in considerable detail for more than seventy years now, and their research has shown that those sensational claims have no factual basis. Most, if not all, of the Dead Sea Scrolls predate the ministry of Jesus and the beginning of the church; they also provide no threat to the teachings of the New Testament, although they have added considerably to a better understanding of several Old and New Testament passages and helped clarify the context of early Christianity. In our investigation of the Old Testament, we will look more carefully at the positive benefits for the church that can be gleaned from the Dead Sea Scrolls and also how they significantly affect our understanding of the closing and formation of the Old Testament.

At this point, we should take a moment to introduce some of the specific questions that pertain to Old and New Testament canonical composition. Some of the biblical books were obvious candidates for inclusion in the Scriptures: for instance, especially the books of the Law (or Pentateuch), the Prophets, the Psalms, the Gospels, and several of the letters in the New Testament. On the other hand, it is less clear why some other books were included, like Esther, which never mentions the name of God; Ecclesiastes, which gives a fatalistic and pessimistic view of life; and the Song of Songs, essentially a love story that both Jews and Christians have allegorized or spiritualized in order to make it more relevant for believing communities. Likewise, Jude cites a non-biblical book as Scripture, and interpreting the book of Revelation poses a special challenge to both scholars and laypersons alike.

As we will see later on, the popularity of a given book can be an important factor in its inclusion or exclusion from the Bible. Some Jewish religious books were very popular among Jews and subsequently among Christians, and were frequently cited as Christian Scripture, such as Sirach (or Ecclesiasticus [not Ecclesiastes!]), the Wisdom of Solomon, and 1 and 2 Maccabees. By contrast, the most popular, canonical Old Testament books among both Jews and Christians in the first century were Deuteronomy, the Psalms, and Isaiah. I have chosen to use the word "Jew" (and "Jewish") in this book to identify those people (and their Scriptures, ideas, religion, and culture) who were worshipers of the God of Israel during and since the Babylonian diaspora. One must recall that Jesus was born, raised, and died a Jew and that his Scriptures were the Jewish Scriptures. His followers, who would soon also be termed "Christians," for a number of years were predominantly Jews (hence my reference frequently to their relationship as [religious] "siblings").

In regard to Christian books, the early Christians widely read the Gospels, especially the Gospel of Matthew, and the letters of Paul, but seldom spent much time reading or citing Hebrews (except for a few favorite texts), 2 Peter, Jude, or Revelation. On the other hand, the most popular nonbiblical Christian books that were copied and read in churches for several centuries included the Shepherd of Hermas, the Didache, the Letters of Ignatius, and 1 and 2 Clement. These books often circulated in many churches and were more widely read in Christian worship than some of the New Testament books. For example, there are more surviving copies of the Shepherd of Hermas in the first few centuries than all of the other New Testament books except for the Gospels of Matthew and John.

This book was also included in a well-known copy of the church's complete Scriptures (Codex Sinaiticus) in the late fourth century AD.

But why were some books included and others that were more popular among the Christians excluded? Questions about the scope of the Bible often lead to other important questions, such as whether the church should still be open to the possibility of including additional books into its biblical canon, or whether some other books that are no longer a part of the Christian's sacred Scriptures should be included now. Since none of the books that make up our Bibles say that the age of inspiration is over, or that only a select collection of books should be read in the churches, should the church be open to adding new books that are influential in the church's witness and ministry? Some church leaders have suggested that possibility, and I will address it below.

Likewise, as some Christians have already proposed, should we exclude books or passages that no longer seem as relevant to the church's needs, or those that appear to some to pose some embarrassment? For example, what should we do today with biblical passages that deal with slavery (Eph 6:5–9; 1 Cor 7:21–24), or a woman's submission to her husband (1 Cor 14:33b–36; Eph 5:22–33; and 1 Tim 2:8–14)? Should a woman follow the biblical mandate during her menstrual cycle as commanded in the book of Leviticus (12:1–8; 15:19–30)? Some have asked whether biblical mandates about divorce are still relevant, given the high incidence of divorce in the Western world and the large acceptance of it even among leaders in modern churches. Should modern Christians make exceptions for biblical concerns or mandates that no longer affect them? These are not easy questions but nonetheless require responses for those who still accept the Bible as the Word of God for our generation.

There was a time during the formative years of the church when decisions were made about which books to welcome as sacred Scripture and which ones to reject. The circumstances facing the early churches varied, and it is seldom possible to know what criteria they used to determine the scope of their Scriptures. The churches that made such decisions did not use the same criteria, and the criteria that *were* used were not *consistently* used. For example, if only books written by apostles could be included in the New Testament, that of course does not account for the Gospels of Mark and Luke, Hebrews, and possibly others.

By the fourth century and following, books were generally rejected if churches discovered that the purported author did not write them. We know that many more books were written than those that survived antiquity, so what should we do if someone should discover them? Should we now include them in the Bible? If someone should find some lost letters that the apostle Paul wrote that are mentioned in the New Testament, as in the case of Paul's earlier letter to the Corinthian Christians (see 1 Cor 5:9) or a letter that he wrote to the Christians at Laodicea (Col 4:16), what should we do with them? Could we ignore either letter if someone found them? Likewise, the teachings of Jesus were clearly at the core of the authoritative base of the early churches: if Jesus said it, that settles it, since he is the final authority of the church (Matt 28:19; Rom 10:9). So what if other authentic sayings of Jesus were discovered that are not in the Gospels or in the rest of the New Testament? What would we do with those?

As it happens, a number of sayings of Jesus *were* circulating in the early churches that were not eventually included in the New Testament. Some of them survived in ancient biblical manuscripts or circulated in the oral traditions of the church, and are cited by a number of the early church fathers. These sayings are generally called the "Agrapha," and while most scholars concede that most of them are false (Jesus did not say them), they agree that some of them may likely come from Jesus. What should the church do with these sayings if they are authentic? Should they be read as Scripture in worship? Of the more than two hundred of these sayings, only between eight and sixteen of them are considered authentic: Jesus likely said these things. All of these questions are about the "canon" of the Bible; that is, the story of how the Bible came to be and what that means today. Depending on how we answer them, there are important implications for the church to consider.

Today there are more challenges against the validity of the current biblical canon, or whether there should *be* a biblical canon, than at any time in the last four hundred years. Some recent scholars have encouraged changes in the biblical canon, but what difference would that make? What would be lost or gained in the process, and how many Christians would agree with those changes? What changes in the Bible would make a difference in the church's statement about its identity, community life, or mission? These, too, are questions about canon, and they focus on the sacred books that Christians around the world believe are foundational to their faith, conduct, and mission.

Do we have answers for all of the many questions about the origins of the Bible? By no means! As readers will soon discover, the origin and formation of the Bible is a complex, remarkably detailed inquiry, and those seeking quick and simplistic answers will likely be disappointed that there are still some places of ambiguity in our understanding of the many questions related to the origin of the Bible. Because of continuing advances in scholarly research, however, we know much more now than was possible in previous generations. Also, what we know now is worth sharing with those who are a part of the church and have a deep reverence for their sacred Scriptures.

If the Bible is critically important for knowing who God is, what the will of God is, who Jesus is, who the people of God are, and such like matters, then its origin and development cannot be unimportant. At the end of this study, I will ask whether the ancient churches got it right; that is, did they make the right selection of books for inclusion in our Bible? I will respond positively to that question and indicate why I do so, but I will also draw attention to some of the important implications that this response presents.

About the Design and Audience of This Book

Before I present some final notes on the structure and intended audience of this book, I should add that I am occasionally asked why I do not spend more time on the role of the Holy Spirit in the canonical process. The answer is that we do not know much about that matter except that Christians regularly acknowledge that God was involved in the origin and process of the development of the Scriptures. That is a matter of faith, and faith is not unimportant, but in this volume we will focus on the historical activities that were involved in the canonization of the Bible. Many of those features are not only clearer to us now, but they are also important for understanding the importance of the biblical message itself.

In the following chapters, I will present a summary of the most important issues related to the formation of the Christian Bible, which will offer readers an understanding of the story of the origin and canonization of the Bible. It is hoped that this brief study will be useful in church classes for laypersons and others who are *beginning* their study of the Bible and even those more advanced in their understanding of it. I will occasionally draw attention to the similarities and differences between Jewish and Christian collections of sacred books, and also those issues that are most important in determining when and where the Christian writings were recognized as sacred Scripture. Hopefully, this study will also facilitate better communication among various communities of faith on the origins of their Bibles.

In several chapters, I will include lists of collections or catalogues of early Christian and Jewish collections of Scriptures. These lists tell a very important story and allow us to see the widespread agreement in the ancient churches on most of the books that now comprise our Bible, but also some of the differences about others. This information is most helpful in shedding light on the origin and development of the Bible. There are, of course, a number of more detailed books on this subject, which are listed in the Select Bibliography at the end of this volume. Those resources will enable readers to pursue a more thorough investigation of these matters.

This volume is *not* for biblical scholars who have access to many ancient and relevant resources and who regularly engage in critical discussions and dialogues on the topic of the Bible's formation. This book is an *introduction* to the formation of the Bible, written for those in the church and beginning students who would like to know more about the formation of their Bible. One of the aims of this volume is to provide an account of recent scholarly research on the subject, presented in a way that is understandable to most of those who attend church classes on the Bible but have little or no training in historical, linguistic, or biblical inquiry. I hope that this small volume will shed some light on an often dimly lit corridor in our thinking about the Bible.

Having begun this study by reflecting upon some important questions that are helpful in understanding the discussion of biblical formation, we turn first to a timeline that will show in a brief visual and summarizing format the birth and formation of the church's Bible. After that, we will focus first on the Old Testament formation and then the New Testament and conclude by addressing several of the important issues related to our understanding of the notion of a biblical canon.

Summary of Timeline for Canonization of the Bible

Key Developments in the Canonization of the Old Testament (OT) Scriptures:

1. Recognition of some sacred writings/inscriptions (ca. 1400–1300 BC).

2. Early stages of writing the Law/Torah and Israel's sacred story (1300–1200 BC).

3. Recognition of collections of sacred writings (700–619 BC, mostly Law).

4. Recognition of *some* of the Former and Latter Prophets (500–200 BC).

5. Beginning of the use of the term "scripture" for sacred Jewish writings (130–100 BC).

6. Production, use, and recognition of several nonbiblical books (mostly 200 BC–AD 100).

7. Widespread recognition of most, if not all, of the OT books along with some Apocryphal and Pseudepigraphal books circulating among the Christians (first to fourth centuries AD).

Key Developments in the Origin of the New Testament (NT) Scriptures:

1. Jesus as canon (authority) and Lord of the church (ca. AD 26–30 and first century).

2. Recognition of the value of Christian writings (Gospels and Paul, ca. AD 50–100).

3. Use of Gospels ("Memoirs of the Apostles") like Scripture alongside OT Scriptures (AD 150–160).

4. Acknowledgment of Christian writings as Scripture (AD 130–200).

5. Delimitation (or de-selection) of Christian writings from use in churches (AD 175–500).

6. Early Translations: Syriac and Latin (ca. AD 200–400).

7. Initial catalogues or lists of NT writings (AD 330–400 and AD 400–850).

8. Widespread recognition of Christian writings both as Scripture and the NT along with limiting the selection to the NT writings (400–500).

9. Council of Nicea (325).

10. Emergence of most canon lists (fourth and fifth centuries).

11. Earliest local church councils *broadly* agree on the scope of the OT and the NT (Laodicea [360], Hippo [393], Carthage [397]).

12. Church manuscripts display considerable, but not *complete*, agreement on the scope of the "biblical" writings (350–500).

13. Athanasius in 367 lists the OT books and *for the first time* the writings that now make up the current Catholic, Orthodox, and Protestant New Testaments. Not all Christians unanimously agreed with this list at that time; it took several centuries for full agreement on the books in the NT.

14. Subsequent church councils meet and determine the scope of the biblical canon: the Orthodox (seventh to ninth centuries), the Roman Catholics (Trent; April, 1546), and Protestants (1550–1885). All agreed finally on the list of NT books, but not on the list of OT books.

15. *Earliest English Bibles welcomed the Apocrypha: Wycliffe (1380), Tyndale (1525), Coverdale (1535), Matthew's Bible (1537), the Great Bible (1539), Geneva Bible (1560), Bishops Bible (1568), Douai Catholic Bible (1609), King James Version (1611).

16. *Modern Translations in English: Revised Version (1881), American Standard (1901), Revised Standard (1952), Berkeley Bible (1959), Amplified Bible (1965), Jerusalem Bible (1966), New English Bible (1970), Living Bible (1971), New American Standard Bible (1971), New International Version (1978), New Revised Standard Version (1990), Common English Bible (2010–2011), English Standard Version (2011), and New Living Translation (2021).

*These lists are selective, not exhaustive.

OLD TESTAMENT

Recognition of sacred writings	Early stages of Law written	Prophets written	Law recovered	Renewed commitment to Law (as Scripture)	Prophets recognized	Other OT writings recognized	Apocryphal and Pseudepigraphal writings
1400–1300 BC	1300–1200 BC	750–300 BC	619 BC	500 BC	500–200 BC	500–160 BC	300 BC–ca. AD 100

OLD TESTAMENT, cont'd.

OT finalized for most Jews	Some Christians accept OT & some Apocrypha writings	Pseudepigrapha writings rejected	Orthodox OT canon adopted	Catholic council of Trent reaffirms OT plus Apocrypha	Protestant rejection of OT Apocrypha
AD 100–400	AD 30–present	AD 230–900	7th–9th centuries	AD 1546	1525–1885

NEW TESTAMENT

Life and ministry of Jesus	Christian writings begin	Gospels written	Authoritative use of Gospels and Paul's letters in churches begins	Gospels read with OT in churches	Some Christian writings called Scripture	NT translations begin
6–4 BC – AD 30	AD 48–49	AD 62–95	AD 65–90	ca. AD 150	AD 130–200	AD 175–200

NEW TESTAMENT, cont'd.

Process of closing Bible canon begins	OT canon finalized for most Christians	Council of Laodicea Listing of OT & NT books	Athanasius gives first listing of all NT books	Council of Hippo affirms Athanasius's list	Council of Carthage reaffirms Council of Hippo on NT books	Second Council of Carthage reaffirms Council of Hippo on NT books
ca. 200–500	330–500	360	367	393	397	419

Chapter 1

What Is the Bible? An Overview

Three major religions in the world today, Judaism, Christianity, and Islam, each recognize a collection of sacred writings—that is, Scriptures—that identify their God, their belief system, and their religious activity.

Christians around the world welcome the Bible as an essential authority and reference point for their faith. In it they understand who God is, what God has done for them, who Jesus the Christ is and the work accomplished by him. As we have already observed, the Bible is also the source that clarifies for Christians who they are as a people of God and their mission in life. There is no close second-place book. Christians everywhere regularly read the Bible in their worship, and it is foundational for church school classes. They trust the message of the Bible and root their various beliefs in its teachings. Whatever the Bible teaches, for most Christians that is sacred and is a word from God, even *the* Word of God.

The importance of the Bible for Christians has never been in doubt, even though there has not been universal agreement on which books constitute the Bible. As noted in the introduction, Catholic, Orthodox, and Protestant Christians all agree on the books that comprise the New Testament and on most, but not all, of the books that comprise the Old Testament. The Protestants have opted for the most conservative list of books in their Old Testament. They accept the books that make up what is commonly referred to as the Hebrew Bible—that is, the Jewish Bible, but they normally list them in a different order. As noted earlier—the Roman Catholic and Orthodox Christians include several more books that Protestants refer to as the "Apocrypha." This term is the plural of a Greek noun and means "the hidden things." These are books found in the ancient Greek and Latin translations of the Bible, but not included in the Hebrew Bible. The labels "deuterocanon" and "deuterocanonical" (= "second canon" or "secondarily canonical") were given to this literature in the mid-1400s by a Catholic theologian, Sixtus of Siena, and both the Roman Catholic and Orthodox Christians accept this literature as the second part of their Old Testament canon. The Orthodox Christians include a few more books than the Catholics (see Table 3 on pp. 79–82). The Anglicans have a statement in their Thirty-Nine Articles (1562) that allows for the reading of the deuterocanonical or apocryphal writings (plus 3 and 4 Ezra), but they cannot be used to establish doctrine.

Throughout this book, I will be using the ancient term "canon," and I need to say something about its meaning here. The term initially referred to measurements, such as a ruler or guide, to measure distances or lengths. It came to refer to standards that were used in architecture and art, and even to standards in philosophy that determine what is true or worth pursuing. The following examples of architectural canons show how the Greeks developed three canonical orders (styles) of temples, columns, and capitals on the top of their columns. The Doric, Ionic, and Corinthian columns were common all over the Mediterranean world.

The Parthenon on the Acropolis in Athens, Greece. This famous temple is supported by Doric columns and capitals on each column.

Ruins of the Temple of Artemis at Sardis in modern Turkey. The temple was designed with Ionic capitals (see the image below). The standard columns and capitals of that day were Ionic, with volutes, circular shapes that resemble rolled-up scrolls, on each side of the capitals.

One of the Ionic capitals from a column at Sardis. Notice the distinctive and standard circles on each side of the column.

The Temple of Zeus in Athens, Greece. The temple has Corinthian columns and reflects the latest period of the Greek temples in antiquity.

Eventually "canon" was also used of literary collections that were recognized as standards for subsequent writers to follow in order to be welcomed by readers. By the fourth century AD, the term came to be used to identify a list of sacred books that comprised the church's Bible and were read in worship and viewed as sacred authorities for Christians. This list of sacred books became a standard for all Christians in terms of the books that gave them their identity, beliefs, and mission in the world.

Our focus in what follows will be on the various processes or stages of recognition of sacred books by the Jewish synagogues and the early churches that led to the formation or "canonization" of the Bibles that we use today.

The Origin of Scripture

It is not possible to know the origin of the Christian Old Testament without becoming aware of the origin of the Jewish Scriptures (Hebrew Bible) and the traditions that relate to what we call the Old Testament. The terms "Old Testament" and "New Testament," when used of collections of sacred books, are distinctly Christian terms. The term "new testament" or "new covenant" is used in Jeremiah 31:31–34 (see also Heb 8:8–11 where "new covenant" is contrasted with the "first covenant"), but not in reference to a collection of Scriptures. The terms were first mentioned in reference to collections of Scriptures by the Christians near the end of the second century AD. These terms were still unfamiliar designations to most of the Christian population even as late as the fourth century. By then, however, these designations were more familiar to larger numbers of Christians.

There are also other collections of ancient religious books that biblical scholars read regularly with considerable benefit, but they are not generally included in Protestant Bibles. The first of these collections is known as the Old Testament "Apocrypha," books that Roman Catholics regularly call deuterocanonical books. These books are included in the Roman Catholic and Eastern Orthodox Bibles. The Orthodox Christians have a few more books in their Old Testament than the Roman Catholics, and both include more books in their Old Testaments than do the Protestants.

The other collection is usually referred to as the Old Testament Pseudepigrapha; that is, "writings produced under a false name." Many of these pseudonymous writings emerged largely between the third century BC and the first century AD.

The titles of these collections, Apocrypha and Pseudepigrapha, are anachronistic terms; that is, they were later imposed on the writings by the church. The terms "Bible," "nonbiblical," "canon," "noncanonical," "Apocrypha," and "Pseudepigrapha" are all *later* designations for writings that were initially welcomed as sacred Scripture, even if some were later rejected from inclusion in the church's Scriptures. The term "deuterocanonical," what the Protestants usually call the "Apocrypha" or "apocryphal writings," literally means "second canon" and distinguishes the writings in it from the "protocanonical" books—those books found in the Jewish Bible and the Protestant Old Testament, though Christians placed these books in a different sequence.

As a matter of full disclosure, let me say at this point that I view the Bible, both Old and New Testaments in all of its teachings, as the church's sacred and authoritative Scripture. Christian faith is bound to this book in all that we believe and practice as Christians. While we recognize that the Bible is an authoritative and sacred book, we also recognize that this authority is a *derived* authority and that the final authority for all Christians is Jesus Christ (Matt 28:19). He is the Lord of the church (Rom 10:9), and the Scriptures accurately reflect his teachings, his life, his fate, and his significance for the church today. We do not worship the Bible but the God to whom the Bible directs our obedience, worship, and praise.

Because of the importance of the Bible for the church, however, we who are part of the church cannot ignore the significance of its origin and development. We do not deny the activity of God in the process of the Bible's development, but we also know that human institutions and human beings helped shape the Bible, and that is where we will direct much of our attention below.

While it is highly unlikely that recent attempts to expand the Bible by adding some books and any attempts to reject other books in the Bible will succeed, it is ever more obvious that those who want to understand the Bible in its original historical context are significantly rewarded if they also carefully examine the literature that was written close to biblical times but later excluded from the Bible. Biblical scholars whether conservative, moderate, or liberal have long recognized that these ancient nonbiblical books contain a considerable amount of useful information that often instructs us in our understanding of the greater context of early Christianity. They have also found that this literature often enlightens us on the meaning of difficult expressions or symbols, particularly some of those used in the New Testament. Many of the so-called apocryphal and pseudepigraphic books that were not included in the Bible are helpful in allowing us to piece together many otherwise untold stories of and about the Bible, including information about the origin and development of the biblical books.

I do not advocate abandoning the Bible or any portion of it, nor do I advocate its expansion by including new books, but I do think that it is important for Christians to be informed by the same literature that informed many early Christians. This literature includes books that many Christians now identify as apocryphal and pseudepigraphic writings.

In terms of the actual writing of books contained in the Bible, we can say simply that many persons wrote what they believed was the will of God and those who followed them and their writings agreed with them in that belief. It is for this reason that they preserved the writings that we now recognize as sacred Scripture. The Bible, then, is a collection of ancient religious writings produced by Israelites (the term for the subjects of the nation prior to about 586 BC) and Jews (the term for the people descended from the subjects of that nation after 586 BC) and in the second part of the Bible by followers of Jesus (most of whom were also Jews, though some non-Jewish [Gentile] writers were also among his followers). Those who brought these books together in the form that we now have them believed that these writings had their origin in God; that is, they believed that God inspired them. Jews and Christians believe that God prompted or inspired the biblical writers to produce their respective collections of writings. Virtually all of the *essential* Jewish and Christian beliefs and practices are rooted in their sacred Scriptures. Because of this, one can more easily understand the familiar reference to Jews, and subsequently to Christians, as the "people of the Book." As we will see, in a practical sense we can also speak of the "Book of the people" since the Bible was written by human beings and translated, interpreted, and preserved by faithful persons used by God throughout the centuries.

The term "Bible" comes from the Greek *ta biblia*, and it translates the Hebrew expression *ha-sefarim* ("the books"). The Jews regularly call their Bible or sacred Scriptures the *Tanak*, a term that is essentially an acronym comprised of the initial Hebrew letters in the Law (*Torah*), Prophets (*Nevi'im*), and Writings (*Ketuvim*), the three parts of the Jewish Scriptures. The sacred Jewish Scriptures are also referred to as *Miqra* (or *Mikra*), a Hebrew term that refers to "that which is read [aloud]"), which emphasizes not only that the books were written down, but also that they were also read orally in the synagogues and Jewish study houses. The equivalent terms "Holy Scriptures" and "Holy Bible" are derived from the Hebrew expression *kitvei ha-qodesh* ("holy writings").

There are twenty-four books in the Jewish collection of Scriptures, but they are the same as the thirty-nine books that comprise the Old Testament in Protestant churches (though presented in a different sequence). This difference comes from the Jewish practice of combining several books together that the Christians have counted separately. For example, the Jewish Bible counts 1 and 2 Samuel as one book, but in the Christian Bible they are counted as two books. The same is true of the Kings and the Chronicles. Likewise, the books that we number individually and call the Minor Prophets—the collection of twelve smaller prophetic books—are counted by the Jews as one larger collection of smaller books that are regularly called the "Twelve" or "Book of the Twelve."

Most Christians accept the thirty-nine books of the Old Testament, while some (many, in fact) accept more than these thirty-nine in their Old Testament, as we have noted above. All Christians also accept twenty-seven other books that we call the New Testament Scriptures: four Gospels, the book of Acts, thirteen letters attributed to Paul, the Book of Hebrews, seven General (or Catholic) Letters (James, 1 and 2 Peter, 1, 2, and 3 John, and Jude), and the book of Revelation.

It is worth noting that because the books that make up the Old and New Testaments were handwritten (long before the printing press), they initially circulated individually in single manuscripts or scrolls. Only subsequently were they combined and placed into larger scrolls (or rolls) and later in book form (a form originally called a "codex," plural "codices") while still handwritten. The early manuscripts containing these books seldom include all of the books of either the Old or New Testaments. The process of combining the books and putting them in a consistent sequence and ultimately into one volume took many centuries. Early codices combining more than a few biblical books were rare, enormous, and exceedingly expensive. The combining of the whole of the Christian Scriptures into one volume was very rare and only made practical by the invention of the printing press during the late Middle Ages.

As we noted earlier, many Christians also accept as a part of their Scripture collections other ancient religious books that are sometimes referred to as the "Apocrypha" by Protestant Christians or "deuterocanonical" books by some Roman Catholics. This larger collection of books includes Tobit, Judith,

Additions to Esther, 1 and 2 Maccabees, Wisdom of Solomon, Sirach (or Ecclesiasticus), Baruch (Baruch 6 = Letter of Jeremiah). The Latin Vulgate translation also contains 3 Esdras, 4 Esdras, and the Prayer of Manasseh in an appendix. The Greek Orthodox Bible includes these books along with 1 Esdras and 2 Esdras (which also contains Nehemiah), 1, 2, and 3 Maccabees and (in an appendix) 4 Maccabees, the Prayer of Manasseh, and Psalm 151; Slavonic Bibles also include 3 Esdras.

The Anglican or Episcopal Churches accept not only the thirty-nine books that Protestants accept, but according to Article VI of the Book of Common Prayer, it also encourages the apocryphal books to be "read for example of life and instruction of manners; but not to establish any doctrine." Their list of apocryphal books includes 3 and 4 Esdras, Tobit, Judith, Additions to Esther, Wisdom of Solomon, Sirach, Baruch, the Prayer of Azariah and the Song of the Three Youths, Susanna, Bel and the Dragon, the Prayer of Manasseh, and 1 and 2 Maccabees.

The majority of Christians in our world welcome most of these books in their Scripture collections, as we will see below, but Jews and Protestant Christians do not accept this additional literature in their Hebrew Bible or Old Testament Scriptures. The differences in the Old Testament collections for Protestant, Catholic, and Orthodox Christians highlight the fact that there were other ancient contenders for inclusion in the Bible; complete agreement among Christians over the scope of their Old Testament has never been achieved. We should note that only in the Reformation era did Protestant Christians begin to reject the apocryphal books, while some continued to read them in worship as late as 1831. Most Protestant Bibles included the Apocrypha before 1599, and many, including the King James Bible of 1611, continued to do so after that. Around 1650, Protestant Bibles began to eliminate the apocryphal books, and by 1831 almost all of the Protestant Bibles had eliminated the apocryphal books. Today some Bible translations, produced largely by Protestant translators, include the apocryphal books as an appendix to the Old Testament and place these books between the Old and New Testaments. All Jews and Christians, however, agree on the sacredness of the books that are in the Jewish Scriptures and the Protestant Old Testament.

It is worth remembering, then, that almost all Christians acknowledge the same New Testament books (although the Ethiopian Christians have a larger collection of New Testament Scriptures), and that the selections of the scope of the Christian Old Testament took many centuries—as did the composition of the books that comprise the Old Testament. Some may date from as early as 1000 BC, while the apocryphal books are generally recognized as having been written from around the early second century BC to the end of the first century AD. By contrast, the New Testament writings were largely written over a comparatively short period, from the middle to the end of the first century AD.

For the most part, the biblical writings were not initially accepted as sacred literature; that is, at the time when they were first written and circulated among the Jewish and Christian communities. That recognition of these writings as sacred often took a long time during which various communities of faith, both Jews and Christians, welcomed and made use of various portions of this literature in their worship and *catechesis*, or oral religious instruction. The practice of accepting writings as sacred literature took place before there was any agreement on what to call them and before any decisions were made about the scope or parameters of the Old or New Testaments. Only by around 130 BC did the biblical books begin to be identified by the term "Scripture." Many other terms were used for these writings before then, as we see in the twenty-two sections of Psalm 119, where examples such as "law of the Lord," "your precepts," "your statutes," "your commandments," and "your ordinances" are particularly prominent. Sacred writings were recognized and called Scripture long before (often centuries before) they were placed in *fixed* collections of Scriptures that we now call the Bible.

Some Basic Axioms about the Bible

In what follows, we will focus on the origin, stabilization, and transmission of the Bible and try to answer a number of questions that are regularly raised about its formation and authority. Years ago, E. P. Blair wrote a useful book titled *The Bible and You: A Guide for Reading and Understanding the Bible* that introduces Christians to the Bible. Fundamental to his approach is an opening collection of axioms that students of the Bible will still find helpful today in understanding their sacred Scriptures. I will summarize these here in a progressive and slightly different order, and I will also add another axiom to his list.

1. **The Bible Is a Library of Books.** As noted above, there are at least sixty-six books in all Christian Bibles (and some twelve to fifteen more in Anglican, Catholic, and Orthodox Bibles). Many persons were involved in writing these books over a period of a thousand years or longer. The message of the Bible comes in a variety of forms and with considerable diversity; for example, there are songs, parables, poetry, figurative language, preaching, letters, history, apocalyptic oracles, short stories, and other kinds of writing as well, and each form (or genre) of writing presents distinctive challenges for interpretation. The Bible is also a *collection of collections* of books. These various collections include books of law (the Pentateuch, which includes legal and ethical prescriptions and proscriptions), historical narratives (the Samuels, Kings, Chronicles, Ezra-Nehemiah, Acts), psalms, proverbs, prophets, gospels, epistles, and visionary language books (Daniel, Revelation). This library is quite diverse; but as we will see, there are some things that tie it together.

Site of the famous Pergamum library, second largest library in the Greco-Roman world. The city was also a large producer of parchment, the eventual favorite material for producing books in antiquity.

2. The Bible Is a Library of *Related* Books. Most of the books of the Bible were written independently, but they have much in common. Every author assumes God's presence and activity in the world and in the lives of men and women. They all have a focus on bringing persons into a right relationship with God or describing the actions that God does and expects in response from the people who follow God. There is considerable overlap in the call of the biblical writers for their readers and hearers to obey the will of God, and there is a large amount of attention given in several of the books to the consequences of disobeying the will of God.

3. The Bible Is a Library of *Ancient* Books. This library of diverse and related books was written to ancient communities. The biblical writers were not conscious of writing for all times, but rather they specifically addressed specific issues and problems present in their own day. They knew nothing of the high-tech world we live in, nor of many of the issues that we are familiar with today, such as genetic engineering, space travel, the internet, and so on; but they were well aware of the stresses and challenges that come to all who live in a world with many joys, challenges, and disappointments. While all of life's issues are not addressed in the Bible, many principles are regularly found in the Bible that relate to life's current situations. As a vital part of biblical interpretation, readers of the

Bible need to be aware of the ancient context of each of its books. The biblical message regularly displays an ancient setting and context. Twenty-first century standards of precision, modern scientific understandings, and current cultural norms should not be expected in contemporary biblical study, but the biblical principles and precepts are nonetheless valid today.

4. **The Bible Is a Library of *Ancient Near Eastern* Books.** The books of the Bible share a special culture influenced by a particular climate, geography, topography, language, and a society that is termed patriarchal. To what extent are these culturally related issues a part of the important and lasting message of the Bible? In other words, are all biblical issues and commands true for all time, or were some of the prescriptions, proscriptions, and admonitions only temporary and intended to deal with circumstances that no longer exist? For example, should women be allowed to wear jewelry, have braided hair (1 Tim 2:9), or come into worship with their heads uncovered (1 Cor 11:2–16)? Should wives be subject in all things to their husbands (Eph 5:22–24)? Should slavery be allowed and relations between slave and master be maintained when such relationships no longer exist (Eph 6:5–9)? Are these culturally conditioned and temporary commands or are they important for all circumstances and for all time? Much of the literature of the Bible focuses on the importance of blood relationships that is seen in the tribal heritages, genealogies, and even in the nomadic understanding of faith that is manifest in a faithful following of Jesus (see, for example, John 10:3–7; and Rom 1:5; Heb 3:17–4:6; 10:39).

Biblical faith is not only interested in *what we acknowledge as true about God*, but also in *faithfully following the call of God* that comes to us in proclamation of the biblical message (Rom 1:5; 1 Thess 1:2–3). Along this line, the Semitic language and Middle Eastern context of the origin of the Bible tends to be highly reflective, picturesque, and concrete. There are very few abstract teachings in the Bible, and the writers typically use concrete pictures or events that were familiar to the Jewish population in the land of Israel or in their exilic or post-exilic communities abroad. For instance, the biblical writers describe the abstract concepts of love, time, and wisdom in symbolic language in specific and concrete actions. In one of the most famous verses in the New Testament, Jesus says, "God so loved the world *that he gave his only begotten Son . . .*" Loving is frequently seen in the Bible as a giving of self rather than as an abstract thought (see John 3:16 and 13:34–35; 15:13; Luke 10:25–37).

5. **The Bible is a Library of *Redemptive* Books.** The biblical books are not objective and unbiased historical books unattached to the circumstances they describe. These books were never intended by their authors to serve as textbooks on zoology, history, astronomy, psychology, or any of the modern sciences. The Gospel writers would no doubt be offended if someone accused them of being

objective and only wanting to report the facts about Jesus. Instead, their books were intended to be calls to faith in him with the result of forgiveness of sins and a right relationship with God that issues forth in hope. Biblical literature typically focuses on how humanity can come into a right relationship with God (John 20:30–31) and on the activity of God in human history, especially in God's involvement in the Israelites' exodus from Egypt and in the resurrection of Jesus from the dead. These are called *redemptive events*.

6. **The Bible is a Library of *Translated* Books.** From ancient times, the Bible has been translated in many languages. Bible scholars generally recognize that Jesus regularly spoke the ancient Aramaic language and possibly also Hebrew, but the New Testament books were written exclusively in Greek. The Old Testament books were written in Hebrew and Aramaic and were translated into Greek between 281–280 BC and roughly 100 BC. In time, the biblical books were translated into many other languages. Christians were anxious to get their message out not only to Jews but also to the Gentiles who largely spoke Greek, Latin, and Syriac in the Mediterranean world. The earliest copies and translations of the Christian Scriptures were in these languages. The primary meaning of biblical literature can best be understood when the teachings of the Bible are explained in their original languages and in their original contexts. Words that mean one thing in one context or language often have somewhat different meanings in another context or language as that given language and context changes. There are many translations of the Bible. Indeed, today there are translations in some 370 languages of the whole Bible and translations of portions of the Bible in some 1,865 languages, with more that are in preparation.

7. **The Bible is a Library of *Selected* Books.** Many Jewish and Christian religious books were produced in antiquity that were initially recognized as sacred literature or Scripture but later were rejected by the majority of churches. There are some eighty known Jewish religious books that were not included in the Jewish or Christian Bibles. As I noted above, these books are often called "pseudepigraphic" books, and by the fourth century AD, most had been rejected by both Jews and Christians for inclusion in their respective canons. Similarly, there are some eighty known Christian "apocryphal" books that were largely, though not initially or universally, rejected by the ancient churches for inclusion in their collective canon. After several centuries, both Jews and Christians made determinations about the scope of their sacred literature. Many religious books were left behind, but others continued to be welcomed by the churches as their sacred Scripture. Those books were "canonized" and continue to comprise the Bible today. Some writers of the other "noncanonical books" made claims to being inspired by God when they wrote, and many Christians accepted those claims and welcomed their literature as sacred Scripture for a

time. For example, both Clement of Rome and Ignatius of Antioch, the authors of 1 Clement (47.3) and the Letters of Ignatius (*To the Philadelphians* 7.1b–2), claim inspiration for their writings. My point here is that the books that make up our Bible were selected from a broader collection of religious books. The logical questions that emerge from this fact, of course, include (1) who made the final decisions about which books would be included in the Bible, and (2) what criteria were used in those decisions? We will focus on these matters in subsequent chapters.

Those who read the Bible with a basic knowledge of these axioms are rewarded with a better understanding of biblical teaching in its ancient context, as well as a better understanding of the relevance of the Bible for the present generation. Generally speaking, the better we grasp these basic axioms, the more likely we will correctly interpret the Bible.

Four Faulty Assumptions

As we tell the story of the origin of the Bible, it is important to identify common but false assumptions about the origin and development of the Bible, which account for several mistakes made by those seeking to understand its formation. Among these false assumptions, the following four are perhaps the most prominent.

First, it is often assumed that if one ancient writer in a given location claimed that a particular writing was sacred Scripture, then all writers of the same era, location, and elsewhere throughout the Roman Empire drew the same conclusion. The evidence, of course, supports neither this notion nor that the early Christians held uniform thinking on most other matters. On the contrary, the early churches had a variety of beliefs and practices, and the variety of their perspectives is well known among biblical and early church scholars. For example, Christians seldom agreed on questions related to the organization of the church, the practice of baptism, the Eucharist (or Lord's Supper), the details regarding the return of Jesus Christ, the future of the church, and the books that informed their faith. More importantly, the earliest Christians did not fully agree on the identity of Jesus (Christology) or the nature of his saving work (soteriology). Who was he? For several centuries, they debated whether he was God, a god, an angel, a spirit, a human empowered by God, or some combination thereof. The majority of churches decided this issue in the fourth century, even though many Christians continued the debate for centuries after that. Given this diversity, it would be strange indeed if all Christians were nevertheless uniform in their thinking about the scope and authority of their sacred writings.

It took several centuries for the early churches to settle the major issues of their theological beliefs, and it would have been scarcely possible to make a determination of the scope of the churches' biblical literature before they were settled on the beliefs that identified them. That began to take place at the Council of Nicaea (325) that focused on the identity of Jesus. While the core beliefs of the churches are widespread in most ancient Christian writings, there are plenty of exceptions. Until the key elements of the church's theological identity were settled, it is difficult to imagine much interest in the notion of a fixed biblical collection or canon.

In some ways, this argument is circular, since the faith of the church was informed by the same literature that was eventually collected and placed in the collection of sacred writings that the church calls its Bible. On the other hand, that literature had to comply with the earliest teachings about Jesus that were circulating in the churches before those writings were produced. Many Christians concluded that some of the early Christian literature did not sufficiently or accurately inform Christian faith, and so it eventually was rejected. When church leaders at *local* (never ecumenical) church councils in the fourth and fifth centuries discussed the scope of the Christian Bible and which writings could or could not be read in the churches, there was hardly a full agreement on this matter then or for a considerable period of time thereafter. Debates over the sacredness of several books took place over many centuries, though generally not on the core books that informed their faith. In the Old Testament, the core books included the Pentateuch, the Prophets, and the Psalms. In the New Testament the core books that were seldom debated included the Gospels and the letters attributed to Paul. There does not seem to have been any doubt either about the inclusion of the Samuels, Kings, and Chronicles in the Old Testament, though there are fewer references to this literature in the surviving ancient Jewish and Christian writings. Something similar holds true in the New Testament. For example, there does not appear to have been a time when the book of Acts was in doubt, but neither is it widely cited in early Christian literature.

Second, it is often assumed that the early Christians responded to the second-century heresies by producing a fixed or set collection of sacred Scriptures; that is, a biblical canon. However, there is nothing in the history of the second- and third-century churches that supports this view. What we see in those writings is that the early Christians answered theological challenges (often termed "heresy") by setting forth a *canon* of faith (i.e., commonly affirmed truths), often called in Latin the *regula fidei* ("rule of faith") that had been passed on in the oral traditions of the churches from the beginning of the church in the first century. Several writings of the New Testament supported that canon of faith, but until the fourth century, there was no official gathering or council that welcomed or approved those writings. The Christians in the second century and immediately following welcomed those writings or books that agreed with the church's earliest teachings. The teachings that emerged in the second century and did not agree with the earliest core teachings of the church were eventually rejected. In other words, the early churches answered theological challenges with theological statements that most Christians believed to be true and were believed to have come to them through apostolic succession; that is, passing on the "apostolic deposit" of Christian teaching from one generation to the next through its bishops and also through the earliest Christian writings. I will address this issue more in the chapters that follow.

That canon or "rule of faith" is what Christians of the second century and later used to answer strange or doubtful teachings circulating in the churches. The New Testament writings, especially the Gospels and some of the letters of Paul, informed and supported the faith of the early Christians and cohered with the teachings handed on in the churches. No discussions of which books belong in a fixed sacred collection emerged during the second and third centuries, but the teachings that were most cherished in the churches were passed on and the writings from the first century that supported and affirmed those writings were widely welcomed. It is true that the church father Irenaeus did argue for only the four Gospels that now make up the Gospels in the New Testament, but he did not make similar arguments for the rest of the books of the New Testament.

Third, it is often assumed that whenever an ancient writer cited or quoted a particular text it must be regarded by that writer as sacred Scripture. Again, nothing justifies this conclusion. Some quotations were simply used as illustrations and were not cited in a scriptural manner, as when Paul cites ancient philosophers or poets in his speeches (e.g., Acts 17:28; Titus 1:12). Rather, each quotation or citation must be considered in its own right to determine how the writer viewed or made use of the source. In some cases, ancient writers cite both biblical and nonbiblical religious texts or sources to illustrate and support their points. One must determine if a cited text is used in an authoritative manner to establish Christian belief or to order behavior, or whether it is simply used to illustrate a point. This is not unlike how many ministers today make use of nonbiblical texts to support or illustrate a point they are making in a sermon.

The important question here is whether a text or source is cited as a sacred writing that calls for obedience to God and is a source for Christian belief. For example, the call to Christian faith such as we see in Rom 10:9, which is one of the oldest confessions in the church, can readily be cited as an appeal to faith as the means of achieving a right relationship with God. John 3:16 is also a frequently cited text from Jesus that claims that God gave his only Son so that those who put their faith in him would find the life that God has for them. Many such texts were cited in the early churches as authoritative religious texts that supported the church's call to obedience to the call of God. Again, each ancient source must be viewed separately to determine how it was cited, whether in an authoritative manner or simply as an illustration.

Fourth, and similarly, some Bible scholars assume that the total number of writings cited or alluded to by the early church fathers constitute the books that they believed were sacred Scripture. In other words, the cited books constituted their biblical canon or collection of sacred Scriptures. Apart from asking whether the writer in question also cites noncanonical sources, what is often forgotten is that the listed citations or allusions were frequently produced to address *specific problems in specific contexts*. The authors in such cases appealed only to those writings that would necessarily advance their arguments or perspectives *in those situations*, but this cannot be used to argue that the ancient writers, whose writings may have only partially survived, cited *all* of the literature that they considered sacred and inspired. If the ancient writers had addressed other situations, it is likely that they would have employed other sacred texts to argue their case. Since many of the ancient writings are ad hoc in nature—that is, written to address specific situations or circumstances as we see especially in the letters of the New Testament—it is unlikely that anyone compiling the sources those writers used will be able to produce the complete collection of writings that a given author considered sacred, even if we were to assume that we have access to everything that author ever produced. If the earliest church fathers actually listed the writings that they believed were sacred Scripture, as in the later cases of Augustine or Jerome, then that is a different matter and we would then have evidence of the specific books that the ancient writers considered Scripture. Before the fourth century, however, that is very rare.

These common assumptions often skew the results of some otherwise important studies on the formation of the Bible. The ancient citations must be examined in their own contexts, however, and care should be taken before concluding that everyone drew the same conclusions at the same time. The evidence that we find in the primary (earliest) ancient artifacts (the biblical and nonbiblical texts, early church history, and the surviving biblical manuscripts) often presents a different view of the acknowledged authorities in antiquity.

Some Important Preliminary Observations

As we begin our story of how the Bible came to be, we should be aware that even though the church inherited from the synagogue and their Jewish siblings the notion of sacred Scripture, *it did not inherit the notion of a fixed collection of sacred Scriptures*. Also, its notion of Scripture was heavily influenced by its Christology; that is, much of early Christian use of the Jewish Scriptures (Old Testament) focused on their christological fulfillment in Jesus. How Jesus, the Christ, fulfilled the Scriptures is at the heart of the early Christian use and interpretation of Scripture. The actual fixing of the biblical canon—that is, the selection of books that would eventually be included in the Christian Bible and the exclusion of all others—emerged centuries after the church began, and the final product, especially where the New Testament is concerned, has a Christ-centered focus.

The church was born as a sect of Judaism in the first century, and that context included the recognition and acceptance of a large collection of Jewish sacred Scriptures that the early Christians used and often cited in their preaching and teaching. The books that the early Christians most often appealed to included many, though not all, of the books that now comprise the Old Testament. Some of the books they cited most frequently were Deuteronomy, the Psalms, and Isaiah. These were the same books most cited by their fellow contemporary Jews, but some Christians also cited other books that were not eventually placed in the Hebrew Bible or the Old Testament Scriptures of the church, as in the citation of 1 Enoch 1:9 in Jude 14, as Scripture.

When the church began, the early Christians not only believed that they had inherited the Jewish scriptural traditions, they also saw themselves as living in the age of the Holy Spirit in which the living Word of God regularly addressed the people of God through a new generation of prophets. The earliest Christians believed that the prophetic voice was very much alive through the power of the Holy Spirit in their midst (see Acts 2:17–21; 1 Cor 12:10, 28; 13:2, 8; 14:6, 29–33). Centuries later, especially during the time of the Reformation but also before then, many teachers in the church assumed in practice (not in theory) that the Holy Spirit no longer spoke a new word to the people of God. For them, the Holy Spirit now spoke only through the churches' closed or fixed collection of sacred Scriptures. Given the criteria that were used to establish the current Bible, it is difficult to imagine how any new writings could be accepted—but again, that would depend greatly on the value and wisdom that one places on the decisions of ancient Christianity. I will address that issue in more detail below.

A special concern has emerged that focuses on the view that the Bible is closed and no more books can be added to it. This view has prevailed especially in Protestant theology since the Reformation and earlier in Catholic and Orthodox Christian theology, but on what grounds were Christians able to argue that inspired prophecy had ceased? How did some Christians come to believe that the Spirit of God somehow stopped speaking in the churches with inspired utterances when the last apostle died? The early church did not teach that view, of course, but by the fourth century it was commonly assumed that inspired scriptural writings were no longer being produced. The original apostles had all died along with those who were the eyewitnesses to the life and ministry of Jesus. With the emergence of the view that inspired scriptural writings had ceased, Christians continued to develop a variety of *hermeneutics*, or interpretive steps—many of which were "inspired" by interpretive examples found in the New Testament Scriptures—intended to aid their churches in applying the biblical message to the ever-new situations that they faced. While the church honored subsequent writings that were important to the advancement of the Christian cause, these were not placed in the church's Bible.

Scripture and Canon

Another important matter that is essential to our whole discussion is the meaning of the terms "scripture" and "canon." Surprising as it may seem, biblical scholars have not yet agreed on the meaning of these terms, and this has led to considerable confusion in the ongoing investigation of the formation of the Bible. There are several contemporary and significantly different meanings of these terms. Because of their lack of agreement on definition, biblical scholars regularly talk past one another when they discuss both Scripture and the formation of the Bible; that is, the formation of the biblical *canon*. The following are some well-known and workable definitions, even though there is no consensus among scholars about them.

Essentially, "scripture" refers to sacred writings that Christians believe had their origin in God; that is, individuals (prophetic figures) were "inspired" by God to write down what they believed God had communicated to them. These writings were called by the Jews "holy writings" and came to be expressed as simply Writings (Hebrew, *Ketuvim*). The Greek equivalent for this is *Hagiographa* ("holy writings"); the Greek term *graphē* ("writing," pl., *graphai*, "writings" or "scriptures") translated the idea behind the Hebrew word. The Latin term for writings is *scriptura*, and eventually the collection of sacred books that informed the Christian faith became known by the designation "Scripture." The Latin-derived term has continued in use in churches, and so the sacred books that we now have are called "Scripture" or "the Scriptures." Occasionally, as is often the case in this book, this word is capitalized: thus "Scripture" refers to the sacred books of the church, while "scripture" signifies the notion of sacred texts in a broader sense, whether those of Jews, Christians, or others.

So the understanding that God has spoken through the writings of individuals and that a number of religious texts comprise their sacred Scriptures is foundational to the beliefs of both Jews and Christians. These sacred texts function as their religiously authoritative writings, determining their identity and clarifying their mission.

What about the specific manner in which the Scriptures were cited? Frequently, the ancient Jews and Christians introduced their sacred writings with special designations such as "it is written," "as Isaiah [or another prophet] says," "as the Scriptures say," "the writings say," "the Scripture says," and "according to the Scripture." Whenever such designations were used, we can say with assurance that they were used to identify sacred Scripture. Occasionally, however, the writers of the New Testament books and the early church writings simply wrote without those familiar designations; we might say that they wrote "*with* scripture" even when they did not cite it as such. This means some early Christian writers simply included in their writings various sacred texts without the above scriptural designations. For example, Jesus cites Daniel 7:13 in Mark 14:62 with no introductory designations ("as it is written"), and yet Mark surely wanted his audience to recognize that the Daniel passage is cited authoritatively as Scripture. Similarly, the author of Hebrews writes "with scripture," citing more Old Testament texts proportionately than any other writer of the New Testament, but seldom uses the usual citations or designations for Scripture. The only place where "it is written" (Greek, *gegraptai*) or anything similar is employed is in Heb 10:7. More frequently, the author of Hebrews cites Scripture without the scriptural citation formulae: for instance, among the sources the writer cites in Heb 1:5–13 are Ps 2:7; 2 Sam 7:14; 1 Chr 17:13; Deut 32:43; Ps 104:4; Ps 45:6–7; Ps 102:25–27; Ps 110:1; and Ps 8:6–8, all without the typical scriptural designations noted above. In similar fashion, the same author also cites (or writes with) words from the apocryphal or deuterocanonical book, the Wisdom of Solomon (7:22 and 7:25, 26 and 8:1) in Heb 1:2–3. In the Gospel of Mark and the book of Hebrews, the authors rooted their arguments in their sacred writings. They believed that what they were saying was synonymous with divine authority, even if they did not employ the usual scriptural designations for the sacred texts they cited.

Because these Christians believed that their sacred writings originally came from God, those writings could not be changed but only believed and obeyed. This notion was originally applied to the law of Moses (see Deut 4:2), but was eventually applied to all sacred writings. The author of Revelation concludes his book with a similar admonition for his own prophecy and not of all others (22:18–19). Those sacred writings were eventually placed alongside other sacred writings and included in a collection of sacred Scriptures that in time became fixed: nothing could be added to or taken away from any sacred writing, and these writings together formed a Christian biblical canon.

The story of the recognition of the sacred status of religious literature in antiquity, then, while of special interest to contemporary Christians, was not a sufficiently important issue to the early churches. Consequently and remarkably, they left behind no clear discussion of how the Bible was formed. It may be that they assumed everyone knew it! The notion of a *fixed* collection of sacred writings is not discussed in any of the earliest surviving Christian writings.

In regard to the word "canon," there are two major competing understandings, but they are not mutually exclusive. As noted earlier, "canon," which originally referred to a measuring rod or stick, in time became a common term for models, guidelines, and examples or rules to follow whether in architecture, grammar, poetry, or rhetoric, and eventually was used in reference to the books that comprise the Bible; that is, the books by which Christians should order their faith and living. Those books alone were the canon or rule for Christians to follow in order to discern the will of God and their mission in the world. By the fourth century, the notion of "rule" or authority expanded to include the notion of a fixed *list* of sacred Scriptures. These meanings often overlap, and that is why some scholars place the formation of the "canon" much earlier than do others. For instance, when the Gospels were first cited to support the Christian witness and teachings, the word "scripture" was not used, but the citations were to be understood as authoritative nonetheless. I call this "canon 1." When in the fourth century various lists of sacred Scripture began to appear, we are speaking of "canon 2;" that is, inviolable and fixed collections of sacred Scriptures that functioned as a rule of faith for Christians that could be read in churches.

Some scholars contend that when the biblical books began to function in an authoritative manner (that is, as Scripture), then the notion of canon was present. They tend to place canon formation much earlier (some even think a biblical canon was present in the first century). Others think that it was largely a done deal by the end of the second century AD, and still others argue that the final *fixed* biblical canon emerged in the fourth century AD, even though the processes for canon formation began much earlier and variations in the books and texts in the church's Scriptures continued for centuries longer.

"Old" and "New Testament"

In the late second century AD, a few Christians began to identify their sacred Scriptures in terms of "Old" and "New Testaments." This was a Christian way of speaking about those writings that were produced by Jews under the "old covenant" or the law, as distinct from those that were produced in the time of the "new covenant" or the Christian era and by Christians. The terms "covenant" and "testament" are used interchangeably. In the New Testament, both terms are used, not in reference to a collection of books but rather in reference to a covenant relationship with God. The old covenant refers to God's dealings with his people on the basis of the law (see Heb 8:6–13). The term "new covenant," of course, goes back to Jeremiah 31:31–34; later, Jesus himself uses the term "covenant" as he introduces the Last Supper (Mark 14:22–24; Matt 26:27–28; Luke 22:18–19; compare with 1 Cor 11:25).

"Testament" and "covenant" are translated from the same Hebrew word (*berith*) or Greek word (*diathēkē*), but neither was used in antiquity for a collection of sacred Scriptures until the last quarter of the second century AD. Some scholars have suggested that the notion of identifying a collection of sacred writings by the term "testament" may have had its roots in the pseudepigraphic collection, Testaments of the Twelve Patriarchs, but this cannot be demonstrated. Nevertheless, it is instructive that the early churches valued their collections of sacred literature and eventually came to identify them as "testaments."

Writings that reflect what God has done for humanity in the death and resurrection of Jesus are called New Testament writings, but that designation was not used for Christian writings until the last third of the second century AD. The term "old" covenant is not found in the New Testament, but "first covenant" was used in Heb 8:7, 13, and 9:1 in reference to the old system of justification through the legal system that depended on the law.

So far as can presently be determined, the terms "Old" and "New" Testament first appear in the writings of Irenaeus (ca. AD 170–180) who writes:

> *In both Testaments* there is the same righteousness of God [displayed] when God takes vengeance, in the one case indeed typically, temporarily, and more moderately; but in the other, really, enduringly, and more rigidly... *in the New Testament*, that faith of men [to be placed] in God has been increased, receiving in addition [to what was already revealed] the Son of God, that man too might be a partaker of God. (*Against Heresies* 4.28.1–2, *ANF*; emphasis added).

Another tradition dating from the second century is reported later by Eusebius (ca. AD 325) who cites Melito (bishop of Sardis, ca. AD 170–180) as saying: "When I came to the east and reached the place where these things were preached and done [i.e., the Land of Israel], and learned accurately the *books of the Old Testament* [Greek = *palaias diathēkēs biblia*], I set down the facts and sent them to you" (*Ecclesiastical History* 4.26.13, adapted). After Melito, Tertullian wrote: "If I fail in resolving this article (of our faith) by passages which may admit of dispute out of the Old Testament, I will take out of the New Testament a confirmation of our view, that you may not straightway attribute to the Father every possible [relation and condition] which I ascribe to the Son" (*Against Praxeas* 15, *ANF*, ca. AD 200). And at about AD 220 in Alexandria, Egypt, Origen commented:

> It appears to me, therefore, to be necessary that one who is able to represent in a genuine manner the doctrine of the Church, and to refute those dealers [the gnostics] in knowledge, falsely so-called, should take his stand against historical fictions, and oppose to them the true and lofty evangelical message in which the agreement of the doctrines, found both in the *so-called Old Testament and in the so-called New*, appears so plainly and fully. (*Commentary on John* 5.4, *ANF*; emphasis added).

While describing the Hellenistic Jewish historian Josephus's canon of Scripture, Eusebius writes in the fourth century: "In the first of these he gives the number of the canonical Scriptures of the *so-called Old Testament*, and showed as follows which are undisputed among the Hebrews as belonging to ancient tradition" (*Ecclesiastical History* 3.9.5, LCL; emphasis added). Later, while speaking of the New Testament he says, "At this point it seems reasonable to summarize *the writings of the New Testament* which have been quoted" (3.25.1; LCL; emphasis added).

Again, these terms emerged in the second century AD, but were not *regularly* used or generally known in the churches for the two Testaments of sacred Scriptures until the middle to late fourth century, when they began to be used without qualification for the two parts of the Christian Scriptures. We see this in canon 59 of the Synod of Laodicea (ca. AD 360–363), where we read, "[*It is decreed*] *that private psalms should not be read in the church, neither uncanonized books, but only the canonical* [*books*] *of the New and Old Testament*" (translation Theron, 1957).

Even by the end of the second century, it was not altogether clear which writings were included in those two "testaments." Because the term "Old Testament" was not used in the Christian community for its earliest Scriptures until the end of the second century AD, it is premature to identify that collection of Scriptures thusly before, or even during, the New Testament era. The books that made up the "Old Testament" Scriptures were not widely identified in the Christian churches until long after the first century AD—namely, in the middle to late fourth century AD.

Some scholars have argued that if these two bodies of Scriptures were identified by these designations at the end of the second century, then it follows that the scope of those collections must also have been clear to some Christians at least. This, however, does not appear to have been the case. Collections of *Christian* writings were only beginning to be identified first as Scripture and then as Old and New Testament writings around AD 170. Only one reference by Eusebius from the fourth century AD identifies that an Old Testament collection from Bishop Melito of Sardis in the late second century AD exists, but that list is not the same as the Old Testament in Protestant Bibles today. We will say more about that list in the next chapter; for now, we can simply conclude that there were no *closed* collections of sacred Scriptures for the Christians before or at that time. Irenaeus alone argued for a fixed collection of the four Gospels, but he said nothing about a limited number of other sacred books in the church; and like others of his generation, he even welcomed the book of 1 Enoch as Scripture. The *Christian* Scriptures cited in the second- and third-century churches were primarily the Gospels and some of the letters of Paul. Only subsequently were the rest of the New Testament writings added to that collection.

With this brief introduction to the Bible and canon formation, we will now offer a more detailed picture of how the church got its Bible, starting with a deeper exploration of the process of recognition of the Old Testament Scriptures.

Chapter 2

The Origin of the Old Testament Scriptures

The Beginning of Scripture and Scripture Collections

After the creation and flood stories, the primary story of the Jewish Scriptures, what Christians call the Old Testament, begins with the story of God's call to Abraham to leave his homeland in Ur of the Chaldeans (near the delta of the Tigris and the Euphrates, in southeastern Iraq today). He was to go to the land of Canaan where God would make of him a great nation in the land that he would show him (Gen 12:1–3). This was the beginning of the Hebrew people and the Israelite nation. Abraham prospered and his family eventually grew in considerable numbers, but there was no sacred Scripture to which Abraham could turn for direction. The family of Abraham grew into a large nation of Israelites from the line of Abraham's son and grandson, Isaac and Jacob.

During a long sojourn of some four hundred years in the land of Egypt, during which time God preserved the family of Jacob (Gen 46–50), the Jews grew still greater in numbers and were subsequently oppressed by their Egyptian hosts. At that time, as the biblical story goes, God called Moses to lead his people out of Egypt and back to the land of Canaan, to the land that he had promised them. Following this "exodus" from Egypt, and while on the way back through the wilderness to Canaan, God called Moses to go to Mount Sinai, where he gave to him the divine commandments for the nation of Israel. Moses wrote down the commandments of God and told the story of God's deliverance from bondage in Egypt and the giving of the law (Exod 20). These narratives about Abraham, Moses, and the giving of the law are told in a collection of five books that make up what we now call the Pentateuch (Greek, *pentateuchos* = "consisting of five books"), or as Jews call it, the Law or *Torah*. The fifth book in this collection, Deuteronomy, retells much of the story in Exodus, Leviticus, and Numbers, and it admonishes the people to abide by the laws that God gave to them. It is the first biblical book to see itself as "scripture" in the sense of a written message from God to the people (see Deut 17:19–20; 28:58; 29:19; 31:11), although it does not use that term to describe its contents. There is, however, a strict command that its message cannot be changed (4:2–5), and it contains references to specific blessings for keeping all of the commandments in the book and judgments for failure to do so (11:8–21; 13:17–18).

The development of the concept of Scripture in ancient Israel appears to have come from a common belief at that time in the notion of a "heavenly book" that contained both divine knowledge and decrees from God. The form and substance of this heavenly book generally contained wisdom, destinies (or laws), a book of works, and a book of life. This notion goes back to ancient Mesopotamia and Egypt, where the heavenly book not only contained the future plans of God, but also the destinies of human beings. Traces of this notion of a heavenly book can be found in Psalm 139:15–16:

> My frame was not hidden from you, when I was being made in secret, intricately woven in the depths of the earth. Your eyes beheld my unformed substance. In your book were written all the days that were formed for me, when none of them as yet existed. (NRSVue)

This notion is also found in Revelation 5:1, 3 and in the description of the opening of a heavenly book in 6:1–17, containing the story of the future (see also 8:1–10:11). In 20:12–15, there are books opened before the great white throne of God in heaven ("the book of life") in which judgment is announced for those not found in the "book of life." This is similar to Exodus 32:33 where the Lord says that those who have sinned will be blotted out of his book. In the New Testament, Paul speaks of Clement and his colleagues in ministry "whose names are in the book of life" (Phil 4:3).

Moses received, delivered, and wrote down the words and ordinances of God (Exod 24:3; 34:4, 27), who was the divine author of the commandments (Exod 34:1 and Deut 4:13; 10:4). This activity likely led to the notion that the law of God had been delivered in written form through his prophet Moses, and this played a significant role in the development of the idea of a revealed and authoritative Scripture that was normative for all of Israel.

The basic properties of "scripture" both for ancient Judaism and Christianity appear to have included at least four essential ingredients. Generally speaking, Scripture is (1) a written document, (2) believed to have a divine origin that (3) communicates the will and truth of God for a believing community and (4) provides regulations for the corporate and individual life and conduct of a community of people. When Jews and subsequently Christians acknowledged that a particular writing was a divinely inspired and authoritative text from God, it was elevated to the status of Scripture, even before the writing was called "scripture." Occasionally, some writings were so acknowledged even though their recognition as Scripture was only temporary; for example, Eldad and Modad, the Epistle of Barnabas, the Shepherd of Hermas, 1 Clement, and the Letters of Ignatius. Some Christians at one time welcomed these and other writings as sacred Scripture; but for most, they eventually no longer held that distinction. There was limited discussion and less agreement in the early church on such matters, and in the first two centuries there was only selective agreement on the books acknowledged as Scripture. As we have already seen, before the third century AD, there was very little Christian discussion about the scope of the Old Testament Scriptures.

One might easily imagine that sacred commands, such as we see in Deuteronomy, would carry considerable weight in ancient Israel and that the Israelites would have been diligent in keeping the law of God given through Moses. However, very little of the Old Testament writings speak to the Israelites keeping the commandments we find in their Scriptures, and, as one reads the writings of their own prophets, they often seem unfamiliar with the commandments. While there are some references to sacred writings in the later Old Testament books, as in Psalm 119, there is very little reference to the law or sacred Scriptures in the Old Testament books themselves.

It sometimes seems strange to us that when Nathan the prophet confronted David about his sin against Uriah and with Bathsheba (2 Sam 12:1–15) that he did not strengthen his case against David by referencing the commandments he had broken or what the Ten Commandments had to say about murder and adultery (Exod 20:13–14). Although he did say that David had "despised the word of the Lord," there is no specificity there. At some point, and likely because of neglect, the divine law that Moses had received and given to the people was somehow lost or displaced in Israel. The nation was repeatedly warned by the later prophets to keep the commands of God, but without positive response (2 Kgs 17:34b–40).

Not much is said about the Scriptures before the late reforms during the reign of Josiah (2 Kgs 22–23). Readers will remember that when Hilkiah the high Priest in Jerusalem discovered a copy of the law (probably the book of Deuteronomy) in the temple, he brought it to King Josiah (2 Kgs 22:3–13; 2 Chr 34:8–21). Embracing the Scriptures led to reform throughout the land of Israel, even if only for a brief time.

How a sacred book or collection of sacred Scriptures could have been lost among the Jews remains a puzzle, though it is likely because of priestly neglect of reading the sacred texts to the people. Also, because the primary focus of the priests was on the sacrificial system related to the temple as well as the liturgies that surrounded it, and because most of the Jews did not read in those days and would not have had their own copy of the Scriptures, the reading of the law was ignored; in time, few knew of the law. With its rediscovery in the Temple ("house of the Lord"), a renewed focus began that called upon the people to obey the commands of the Lord found in the book of the law.

During the devastating destruction of the Jewish nation by the Babylonians in 587–586 BC, many of the leaders among the Jews were taken captive to Babylon. While in Babylon, some of the Jews began to reflect on the message of the prophets, who had earlier warned them about the consequences of forsaking the will of God, and they turned again to the laws of Moses and subsequently also to the messages of the prophets who had offered them hope if they kept (or returned to) the statutes of God (2 Kgs 17:13, 35–40). What the prophets had warned would happen if they failed to keep the commands of God did in fact happen, and the Jews remembered from their painful past that it was essential for them to keep the laws of God and to listen to the words of his prophets.

After some fifty years of captivity in Babylon, a decree from Cyrus, the Persian king who had defeated the Babylonians, allowed the Jews to return to their homeland and rebuild it. Not all of the Jews left Babylon, and not all who did returned to their homeland, but those who returned to the land of Israel followed the leadership of Ezra and Nehemiah who brought reform and renewal to the surviving remnant by renewing the nation's obedience to the laws of Moses (Neh 8:1–8). This was the beginning of a new epoch in the nation, and from that time on they regularly read and obeyed the laws of God. It appears that they also remembered the words of the prophets, but the law of Moses was still central to their renewal as a nation. After this time, there is a large gap in our knowledge of what took place during the Persian domination of the land of Israel, but it appears that the Jewish faithfulness to the law continued without interruption during this time.

In review, there is little evidence that the Law (Pentateuch) or the Prophets had much of an impact or influence on the Jewish people in the early stages of the Old Testament times. Prior to the Babylonian destruction of the Jewish nation and deportation of many of its people in 587 BC, only a brief reform led by Josiah came to the Land of Israel as a result of the discovery of the Law (probably Deuteronomy) in the Temple in Jerusalem.

It also appears that the priority given to the law was in part based on its time of origin as well as its purported authorship by Israel's greatest prophet (Deut 18:15). When the Jews returned from Babylon, there was renewal of their commitment to the "law of Moses" or "law" (they are the same) as we see stressed in the books of Ezra (3:2; 6:18; 7:6, 10, 12, 21, 25, 26; 10:2–3) and Nehemiah (8:1–9, 13–14, 18; 9:3, 13, 14, 29; 10:28, 29, 34, 36; 12:44; 13:3). Ezra twice gives specific names of *writing* prophets (5:1–2 and 6:14 mention by name Haggai and Zechariah) and notes as well the broader group of prophets who delivered the commandments of God (9:11). Nehemiah mentions *false* prophets in 6:7, 14 and the prophets of God are mentioned in 9:26, 30, and 32. As one can see, the "law of Moses" or "law" or commandment of God is given highest priority. Was there then a recognition of the authority of both Moses' laws *and* the work of the prophets? Undoubtedly, but still the priority went to the law of Moses. It is not clear if references to Moses were only in regard to Deuteronomy or the Ten Commandments, or perhaps the whole of the Pentateuch, but there is no question that Moses took priority, and the references to the prophets generally focus on reminding the people of the commandments or law of Moses.

By no later than the early second century (ca. 180 BC), a writer by the name of Jesus ben Sira (or Sirach) wrote a book now called Sirach (or Ecclesiasticus; again, not to be confused with Ecclesiastes) in which he presented what he believed was divine wisdom. In his book, he also reminded the Jewish nation of the great heroes of their past who were obedient to God and the consequences for those who were disobedient to the commands or statutes of God (Sirach 44:1–50:24). In his praise of earlier heroes, it is clear that Sirach was aware not only of many of the ancient heroes, but also of some of their sacred books. He mentions Ezekiel, Job, and the Book of the Twelve (Minor Prophets) by name (49:8–10), and even quotes Malachi 4:5–6 (48:10). While it is not clear what books he was familiar with, he certainly knew of the stories about the great leaders, prophets, and kings of Israel mentioned in Genesis, Exodus, the Samuels, Kings, and Judges.

Following Sirach, the citation or use of such prophetic works appears to have been common. Several Jewish writings reflect familiarity with the sacred Scripture collections that were circulating among the Jews in the middle to late second century BC. Among them is the *Prologue* to Sirach that was written by Sirach's grandson (ca. 130 BC) following his translation of that work into Greek. In it he speaks of the "Law and the Prophets, and the other books of our ancestors." It is not clear what books are classified as the Prophets or the "other books of our ancestors," but it is most likely that the grandson also included his grandfather's work among them. The later circulation of Sirach in the Greek Old Testament Scriptures confirms this.

There are references to collections of sacred Jewish Scriptures in later books. After Epiphanes III, the Greek leader of the Seleucid Dynasty headquartered in Damascus, took control of the land of Israel following a decisive battle against the Ptolemies of Egypt at Pan (or Caesarea Philippi, by the time of the New Testament) in 198 BC, there was peace for a season; but when Antiochus IV Epiphanes (= "[God] manifest") came to the throne in 175 BC (1 Macc 1:10–40), he burned the Jewish nation's cities, insisted that Jews make sacrificial offerings to Zeus, and offered a pig on the Jewish altar in the temple in Jerusalem. When the Jews rebelled, he was brutal against them and began an onslaught characterized by gruesome torture and the destruction of Jewish sacred Scriptures. This story is told in both 1 and 2 Maccabees, but in 2 Maccabees the author recounts the story after Judas Maccabeus defeats the Seleucids and then recaptures the Jewish temple: he collected "the books" that had been lost due to the war in their country and made them available to his fellow Jews as they had need of them. For our purposes, the relevant part of the story is as follows:

> The same things are reported in the records and in the memoirs of Nehemiah, and also that he founded a library and collected the books about the kings and prophets, and the writings of David, and letters of kings about votive offerings. In the same way *Judas* [Maccabeus] *also collected all the books that had been lost on account of*

the war that had come upon us, and they are in our possession. So if you have need of them, send people to get them for you. (2 Macc 2:13–15 NRSVue; emphasis added)

This text is not clear about what books its author has in mind here, though the mention of Nehemiah, books about the kings and prophets, Davidic writings, and letters of kings suggests a collection larger than simply the law of Moses. It is presumed that the books collected by Judas Maccabeus included especially the books of the Law since in 1 Maccabees 1:56 the author reports that the Greek soldiers "tore to pieces" the Jews' sacred Scriptures; that is, "the books of the law that they found."

The evidence that the Torah was recognized first among the Jews may be seen by the first translation of the Hebrew Scriptures (ca. 281–280 BC) that contained only the Pentateuch. Had other books been considered sacred Scripture *at that time*, it would seem that they too would have been included in the translation. Further evidence comes from the Letter of Aristeas (written around 100 BC), which tells the story of how some seventy scribal translators produced a Greek Pentateuch. Scholars have rejected the legendary elements in the document but acknowledge that there are some historical traditions in it; namely, that the translation took place in Alexandria, Egypt, perhaps at the instigation of the Pharaoh and the librarian who wanted to add the Jewish sacred books to the Alexandrian library, and that the Hebrew text used for the translation likely came from Jerusalem. The Jews in that region made use of this translation since by that time their mother tongue was no longer Hebrew but Greek. By around 130 to 100 BC, most of the rest of the Old Testament books had been translated into Greek along with many of the apocryphal or deuterocanonical books. The translation of the Old Testament Scriptures into Greek began, however, with the Pentateuch. If the other books in the Hebrew Bible had been widely recognized as sacred Scripture among the Jews when the Septuagint began, they likely would also have been included in the translation, but they were not.

We should not, however, neglect the likely significant influence of the Prophets among the Jews from the fourth century BC (possibly earlier) and thereafter. We see references to their work in 2 Kings 17:13, and we find other calls in later Old Testament writings to pay attention to the prophets—as we see in Jeremiah 26:4–6, 16–18 (citing the earlier Mic 3:12), 2 Chronicles 26:22 and 32:32 (referring to the prophet Isaiah), Ezra 9:10–12, and Zechariah 7:12. (For references to influential prophetic books now lost, see 1 Chr 29:29; 2 Chr 9:29; 12:15; 13:22; 33:19.) Nevertheless, there is no doubt that the Law was given priority among all of the writings, and it was believed to have been written before all other books in the Jewish biblical canon. Some scholars have suggested that there was a simultaneous recognition of the Law and the Prophets, but one does not get that impression from texts cited above. Likewise, the recognition of the Writings as a third part of the Jewish Scriptures is clearly late and does not show up in any list or collection of the Old Testament Scriptures until the middle to late second century AD. Were some additional collections emerging before then? That is likely, but they are not named nor can we tell what was in them except by anachronistically imposing later groupings on earlier references.

Ruins at Qumran of the Essene Jewish community, who copied and produced scrolls of their sacred texts from approximately 170 BC–AD 68. The larger room in the middle is called the scriptorium, where copies of their sacred texts were prepared.

The Dead Sea Scrolls

Many Jewish religious texts that were not included in any of the Scripture collections listed above were found among the Dead Sea Scrolls in 1947 and in the years following. Of the almost one thousand religious manuscripts discovered in the caves at or near Qumran, on the northwest shore of the Dead Sea, all of the Old Testament books except Esther were found, and some in multiple copies. The discovery was not only of the ancient biblical books, but many others also. About two hundred of the manuscripts contain biblical books, but some seven hundred manuscripts contain other Jewish religious books that informed the faith of the Essene sect of Jews from roughly 170 BC to AD 68. I should note here that it is difficult to be precise on the exact number of manuscripts since many are in broken parts and some of the parts thought to be from separate manuscripts may, in fact, be from the same manuscript. It is thus difficult to determine the precise number of manuscripts found there.

Replicas of jars that contained some of the Dead Sea Scrolls found in the vicinity of Qumran as displayed at the visitor's center there.

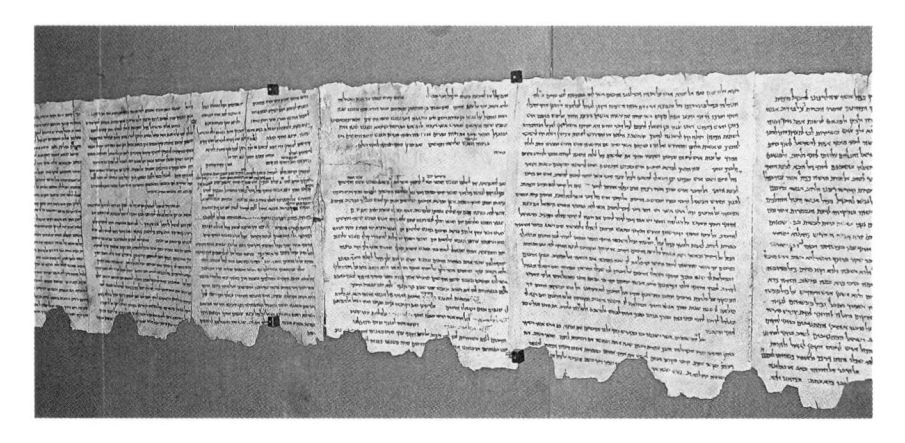

Replica of a Dead Sea Scroll displayed at the visitor's center at Qumran on the northwest shore of the Dead Sea

The presence of many nonbiblical books at Qumran, some of which may date from the late fourth century BC, suggests that the matter of the scope of the Jewish Scriptures was not settled in the time of Jesus. Since many other Jewish religious texts were written and welcomed by Jews during the second and first centuries BC and subsequently by Christians, it is difficult to believe that the Jewish biblical canon was settled before or during that time, as many scholars have alleged. Many of the writings that are now deemed nonbiblical were placed alongside the biblical books in the eleven known caves at or near Qumran and without any obvious or consistent distinctions. That suggests, of course, that the final shape of the Jewish Scriptures was still a work in progress during the first centuries BC and AD.

View toward the ruins of the Qumran Essene community on the northwest shore of the Dead Sea that can be seen in the background.

Most of the Dead Sea Scrolls discovered at Qumran were nonsectarian. That is, the small Jewish sect known as the Essenes who copied and preserved these manuscripts did not write all of these books, but they were brought into that community from elsewhere in the land of Israel and were in circulation during the time of Jesus. Some of the scrolls have parallels found in the language of the New Testament. For instance, there is a phrase in the *Parables of Enoch*, one of the five sections that comprise 1 Enoch, which speaks of the "Son of Man seated on the throne of his glory" (1 En. 62:5; for the Parables section, see 1 En. 37–71). This is only found elsewhere in the teachings of Jesus, who uses the same or similar phrasing in Matthew 19:28 and 25:31. Again, these words are not found anywhere else in Jewish literature. Likewise, as many know, Jude 14 cites 1 Enoch 1:9. Many such writings were circulating in the Land of Israel and elsewhere in the time of Jesus, and later many Christians included some of them in their early sacred collections. Some Christians continue to use and cite some of these books as sacred Scripture, especially in Ethiopia, but elsewhere also for several centuries.

The famous Cave 4 at Qumran, where the majority of the Dead Sea Scrolls were discovered. This cave is only a few hundred feet from the ruins at Qumran.

Also among the Dead Sea Scrolls is an important text that identifies different collections of sacred Scriptures among the Jews. That text is listed as 4QMMT (or, 4Q394–399, perhaps as early as ca. 150 BC) and also known as the *Halakic Letter* or *Miqsat Ma'aseh ha-Torah* (Hebrew, "some works of the law"). It refers to "the book of Moses and the words of the prophets and David . . . and generations." Some scholars have argued that this text refers to a three-part Jewish biblical canon; while it may be an early reference to the growth in the Jewish collection of recognized Scriptures, it is not entirely clear. "David" could refer to all of the Psalms of David, but also to other poetic writings, as some have suggested, or it may simply be a reference to the Psalms (as in the case of Luke 24:44).

Cave 11 of the Dead Sea Scroll caves at Qumran is best known for its large collection of psalms. Many of its psalms are the same as those in the biblical text, many are not; and in a few cases, the Qumran versions have helped scholars to fill in previous gaps or discrepancies among the canonical psalms.

It is clear that at Qumran the most common designations for the Jewish Scriptures are "Moses . . . and the Prophets" (1QS 1:23) or "the books of the law . . . and words of the prophets" (CD 7:15–17). The ellipses in these three texts show gaps in these fragmentary manuscripts.

Because the Dead Sea Scrolls are also fragmentary, often with gaps in the text due to worms and deterioration due to climate, they are often a special challenge to read. The following two examples from the Temple Scroll and the book of Joshua illustrate the difficulty of reading these texts. Fortunately, the availability of infrared cameras and technology makes it possible to discern the text more clearly in these manuscripts, though even these technologies cannot restore what is missing. That often takes scholarly guesswork to piece together the words of the original text.

Fragment (column 17) of the Temple Scroll found among the Dead Sea Scrolls in the vicinity of Qumran in standard photograph (left) and with enhanced photography (right). Note the greater clarity of the written text, especially the fourth of the five lines shown, in which the short line of text can hardly be seen in the standard photograph. (Courtesy of J. H. Charlesworth, Ken and Bruce Zuckerman, K. T. Knox, R. L. Easton, and R. H. Johnston)

Fragment of Dead Sea Scroll copy of Joshua 1:7–12; 2:2–3. Photo courtesy of The Schøyen Collection, MS 2713. View these and other manuscripts at collection@schoyen.net.

The presence of many nonbiblical books discovered among the Dead Sea Scrolls suggests that the matter of the scope of the Jewish Scriptures was not settled in or before the first century BC or AD. Since many other Jewish religious texts were written and welcomed by Jews during the second and first centuries BC and subsequently by Christians, it is difficult to believe that the Jewish biblical canon was settled before or during that time as many scholars contend. Many of the writings that are now classified as nonbiblical were placed alongside the biblical books in the eleven known caves and without any obvious or consistent distinctions. That suggests, of course, that the final shape of the Jewish Scriptures was still a work in progress during this time.

A view toward the mountains adjacent to Qumran, where some of the eleven caves containing Dead Sea Scrolls were discovered. The hand-made channel in the middle of the photo was a water canal going from the wadi (a frequently dry riverbed) to supply water to the cisterns at Qumran during times of heavy rain.

First-Century References to the Scriptures

The Hellenistic Jewish scholar Philo (ca. 20 BC–AD 40) of Alexandria wrote a treatise called *On the Contemplative Life* in which he speaks about a group of pious Jews who go by the name of Therapeutae and take with them into their special sanctuary places for prayer and study "laws and oracles delivered through the

Actual clay jar in which some Dead Sea Scrolls were found. This one is housed at the William Kando shop in Bethlehem. The current owner's father was the first to purchase some of the Dead Sea Scrolls from Bedouin shepherds who discovered them.

mouth of prophets, and psalms and anything else [or 'the others']" (*Contemplative Life* 3.25). Again, this passage seems to recognize not only the Law and the Prophets, but other writings as well. Unfortunately, Philo does not clarify what books are in any of those categories. The reference to "psalms" may be akin to the passage in Luke 24:44, noted above, which is likely only a general reference to an unspecified collection of psalms.

This example from Philo illustrates the slow process of recognition of the Old Testament Scriptures; namely, the recognition of the Law first and subsequently the Prophets. This can be seen in the priority always given to Torah over all other books as well as the priority always given to the practice of reading the Law in the synagogues. The Law was also stored separately in the synagogues and the Prophets or Writings could never be placed on top of it.

Similarly illustrative is the schism between the Jews and Samaritans that is well-known in the New Testament (Luke 9:52–53; 10:29–37; Matt 10:5–6). The schism took place during the Persian domination of the Land of Israel (ca. 500–330 BC) and is first referred to in Ezra 4. Subsequently (ca. 150–100 BC), the Samaritans produced their own edition of the Pentateuch that is at odds with the Jewish Pentateuch, especially in Exodus 20:17 and Deuteronomy 27:4, where Mount Gerizim is introduced as the place of sacrifice. In constructing their Pentateuch, it is likely that the Samaritans made use of the same or similar Hebrew text that lies behind the Greek Septuagint version of the Pentateuch, which likely dates from the early to middle of the third century BC. They also made use of an antecedent to the current Masoretic text of the Hebrew Bible. Only the Torah, or the Samaritan Pentateuch, is sacred Scripture among the Samaritans. They did not adopt the Prophets or Writings from the Hebrew Bible in their collection of sacred Scriptures, so it has been argued that when their separation from the Jews took place, there was no formal recognition of the Prophets as a part of the Jewish Scriptures. That argument may have some merit, though some biblical scholars have challenged it.

At the end of the first century AD, the Jewish historian and apologist Josephus wrote a defense of the Jews called *Against Apion* and presented it in Rome before Caligula, the Roman emperor. In that appeal, he spoke of a limited number of writings in the Jewish sacred Scriptures; namely, twenty-two. He categorized them by types of writings—that is, by *classification* or category—but did not identify them by name. Because the passage is so important for those who argue for an early date for the Jewish biblical canon, I include it here.

> It therefore naturally, or rather necessarily, follows (seeing that with us it is not open to everybody to write the records, and that there is no discrepancy in what is written; seeing that, on the contrary, the prophets alone had this privilege, obtaining their knowledge of the most remote and ancient history through the inspiration which they owed to God, and committing to writing a clear account of the events

of their time just as they occurred)—it follows, I say, that we do not possess myriads of inconsistent books, conflicting with each other. *Our books, those which are justly accredited, are but two and twenty, and contain the record of all time.*

Of these, *five are the books of Moses*, comprising the laws and the traditional history from the birth of man down to the death of the lawgiver. This period falls only a little short of three thousand years. *From the death of Moses until Artaxerxes,* who succeeded Xerxes as king of Persia, *the prophets subsequent to Moses wrote the history of the events of their own times in thirteen books. The remaining four books contain hymns to God and precepts for the conduct of human life.*

From Artaxerxes to our own time the complete history has been written, but has not been deemed worthy of equal credit with the earlier records, *because of the failure of the exact succession of the prophets.*

We have given practical proof of our reverence for our own Scriptures. For although such long ages have now passed, *no one has ventured either to add, or to remove, or to alter a syllable;* and it is an instinct with every Jew, from the day of his birth, to regard them as the decrees of God, to abide by them, and, if need be, cheerfully to die for them. Time and again ere now the sight has been witnessed of prisoners enduring tortures and death in every form in the theaters, rather than utter a single word against the laws and the allied documents. (*Against Apion* 1.37–43, LCL, trans. H. St. J. Thackeray; emphasis added.)

Not all Josephus scholars agree with Josephus's account that all Jews everywhere both know and would die for these twenty-two sacred books. We are unclear what those books are since he lists them only by category, but if "all Jews everywhere" knew them, it is remarkable that we do not find evidence of such a limited collection of Jewish Scriptures among the Jews in the Diaspora (those living outside of the land of Israel). Remember, for example, in Sardis—a large city with a substantial Jewish population at the end of the second century AD—Melito, the bishop of the church in that city (ca. AD 170–180), evidently did not know what Old Testament books were acknowledged as sacred Scripture and made a special trip to the land of Israel to find out. Why did he not go across the street and talk to the nearest Jew to find out, if the matter was well known long before his time? He returned to Sardis and published a list of the sacred Old Testament books, and his list contains almost all of the books of the Hebrew Bible, but is not exactly like the one listed by the rabbinic Jews in the second century, nor is their order or sequence the same. After Proverbs, Melito adds the apocryphal or deuterocanonical book Wisdom of Solomon, and he omits Esther. Below we will consider Melito's story, which was preserved in the fourth century by Eusebius (*Ecclesiastical History* 4.26.13–14).

At roughly the same time as Josephus, near the end of the first century AD, another important work was produced that sheds light on early signs of the stabilization of the Jewish biblical canon. 4 Ezra is a pseudonymous Jewish writing that was later interpolated by Christians, who likely added chapters 1–2 and 15–16 and included it in their Scriptures. The writer tells the story of how Ezra miraculously recovered the Scriptures of Israel following the return of the Jews from Babylon. According to the author of 4 Ezra, the process of the recovery involved God inspiring the scribes to write down the books that had been lost. The relevant part of the text reads as follows:

> Moreover, the Most High gave understanding to the five men, and by turns they wrote what was dictated, using characters that they did not know. They sat forty days; they wrote during the daytime, and ate their bread at night. But as for me, I spoke in the daytime and was not silent at night.
>
> So during the forty days, ninety-four books were written. And when the forty days were ended, the Most High spoke to me, saying, "*Make public the twenty-four books that you wrote first, and let the worthy and the unworthy read them; but keep the seventy that were written last, in order to give them to the wise among your people.* For in them is the spring of understanding, the fountain of wisdom, and the river of knowledge." And I did so. (4 Ezra 14:42–48 NRSVue; emphasis added)

The author of the text above welcomed not only the twenty-four books that could be read by "the worthy and unworthy," but also an additional collection of seventy books reserved for the "wise among your people." It is not clear what was in either collection, though perhaps the twenty-four books were the same as those in the later b. Bava Batra text (see below) and/or the collection mentioned by Josephus, though numbered and ordered differently (above).

It is important to reflect here on the numbers twenty-two and twenty-four and their significance. Neither number reflects the exact number of the books in the Hebrew Bible, and there are actually thirty-nine books in the Hebrew Bible and thirty-nine in the Protestant Old Testament, but arranged differently. Both of those numbers are the same as the letters in the Hebrew (twenty-two) and Greek (twenty-four) alphabets. Their significance dates back to the emphasis on the completeness and divineness of the letters of the Greek alphabet in Homer's writings, the *Iliad* and the *Odyssey*. Each book has twenty-four books or chapters, and each begins with a different letter of the Greek alphabet. The later Jewish rabbis (first century AD and thereafter) were well aware of Homer and his influence in the Greco-Roman world and opted for the Greek alphabet as the sacred number of their sacred Scriptures. Their collection of sacred books had to be combined to arrive at that number as was the case when those books (likely the same books) were identified as twenty-two in number, but later Jews opted for the twenty-four because of its popularity and spoke of the completeness of the divine Scriptures.

Well before the time of Jesus, portions of the Hebrew or Old Testament writings made use of the Hebrew alphabet to identify completeness and fulfillment of the divine will. There are several examples of this in the Psalms and the best-known example is in Psalm 119 that has twenty-two sections in it of eight verses each, all praising the word of God, and each beginning with a different letter of the Hebrew alphabet. The NIV includes a transliterated Hebrew letter before each section.

The deities mentioned in Homer's volumes noted above are the same ones that became normative in the Greek religion. Knowing this helps us understand the New Testament references to God and Jesus as the "Alpha and Omega"—namely, the first and last letters of the Greek alphabet (Rev 1:1:8; 21:6; 22:13)—in other words, the beginning and end of all things that reflects the presence and activity of God in Christ. This is also seen in the origin of the Jewish practice of dividing some chapters of the Psalter (Psalms) into the letters of the Hebrew alphabet (for example, Pss 25 and 34) with each line beginning with a sequential letter of the Hebrew alphabet. Each psalm has twenty-two verses. Psalm 119 has twenty-two sections of eight verses in each section, and each section begins with a different sequential letter of the Hebrew alphabet. Like those who revered Homer and used the alphabet to designate chapters in his works, some Jews identified the number of books in their sacred collection with the number of letters in the Hebrew alphabet (twenty-two); but later the rabbis adopted the number of the Greek alphabet (twenty-four) to number their sacred Scriptures, most likely because of its popularity throughout the Greco-Roman world.

Later rabbinic sages show their familiarity with Homer's works through comparing their sacred Scriptures with the writings of Homer. For example, in the Mishnah we read:

> The Sadducees say, "We cry out against you, O ye Pharisees," for ye say, "the Holy Scriptures render the hands unclean," [and] "the writings of Hamiram [Homer] do not render the hands unclean . . . Even so the Holy Scriptures: as is our love for them so is their uncleanness; [whereas] the writings of Hamiram [Homer] which are held in no account do not render the hands unclean." (m. Yadayim 4:6, Danby)

As noted, Rabbinic Jews showed a preference for a twenty-four-book canon over a twenty-two-book collection that likely included the same books as those in the twenty-four-book collection. The twenty-two-book sacred collection, as we saw earlier in Josephus, was the same as the number of letters in the Hebrew alphabet that was replaced by some Jews at the end of the first century with twenty-four, the number of letters in the Greek alphabet. For several centuries, church fathers continued to speak of the Jews' twenty-two book scriptural collection, and we see that as early as the end of the first century AD (90–95) in 4 Ezra 14:22–48 and later in b. Bava Batra 14b–15a (ca. AD 150–180), the later Amoraim Jewish interpreters of their oral traditions (third–sixth centuries AD) began to prefer the number twenty-four for counting their sacred scriptures (see b. Ta'anit 8a; Numbers Rabbah 13:16; 14:4, 18; 18:21; Song Rabbah 4:11; Ecclesiastes Rabbah 12:11–12).

However, at the same time, the number twenty-four was also quite common in the early Christian writings. See, for example, the author of the Gospel of Thomas (ca. AD 100–140) says that "Twenty-four prophets spoke in Israel, and they have all spoken of you [Jesus]" (Gos. Thom. 52). This passage obviously refers to the books of the first Scriptures among early Christians, and it is quite significant since it is the earliest known *Christian* document that points to a limited number of books in the Christian Old Testament (Hebrew Scriptures). The dating of the Gospel of Thomas draws mixed positions, but it is more likely that the Gospel of Thomas depends on Tatian's *Diatessaron* (ca. AD 170) and would, if correct, modify the usual earlier dating of this document and date it around 180, which is also the earliest listing of the Hebrew Scriptures in b. Bava Batra 14b. In his commentary on Revelation, Victorinus (ca. AD 280) refers to Rev 4:7–10 saying: "The twenty-four elders are the twenty-four books of the law and the Prophets, which give testimonies of the Judgment.... The books of the Old Testament that are received are twenty-four, which you will find in the epitomes of Theodore" (*Comm. Apocalypse* 4:7–10, *ANF* 7:348). Interestingly, Hilary of Poitiers (d. AD 367) mentions the twenty-two books of the Old Testament in accordance with the Hebrew alphabet, but then adds Judith and Tobit because the Greek alphabet has twenty-four letters (*Instructio Psalmorum* 15)!

In his prologue to Samuel and Kings, Jerome (ca. 390–400) compared the twenty-four books of the Hebrew Scriptures with the twenty-four elders of the book of Revelation (Rev 4:4, 10; 5:8; 11:16; and 19:4; *Prologus in Libro Regum* [= *Prologus Galeatus*]). Like other church fathers, he preferred to speak of the twenty-two-book Hebrew canon that follows the Hebrew alphabet, but acknowledges that the number can be twenty-four by the way that the books are counted and combined. By adding Ruth and Lamentations (*Kinoth*), there are "twenty-four" books. From this he concludes: "We should thus have twenty-four books of the old law. And these the Apocalypse of John represents by the twenty-four elders, who adore the lamb" (*Prologue to the Books of Samuel and Kings*).

Again, the books in the Hebrew Scriptures are more in number than twenty-two or twenty-four, but various combinations were devised to bring the number to the letters in either the Hebrew or Greek alphabets. The Scriptures in both collections are widely believed to be the same. At about the same time (ca. AD 90), the pseudonymous author of 4 Ezra from Palestine wrote 4 Ezra in Hebrew, and it was later translated into Greek. The author speaks of two collections of sacred texts that were both inspired by God. The first collection is the twenty-four books that are to be read to all persons publicly, but the other seventy books are reserved for the wise. "Make public the twenty-four books that you wrote first and let the worthy and unworthy read them; but keep the seventy that were written last, in order to give them to the wise among your people" (4 Ezra 14:45–46 NRSVue).

The number twenty-four prevailed in Judaism, though the same books were probably included in both numbers. Like the use of the Greek alphabet in Homer's writings, the use of the Greek alphabet in the Hebrew Bible represented the completion and perfection of the Scriptures and pointed readers to their divine origin. Rabbinic Judaism opted for the twenty-four-letter Greek alphabet as a symbol of the Hebrew Bible's completeness and included various combinations of books to achieve that number such as the combination of Ezra and Nehemiah. This number prevailed among the Amoraim leaders of rabbinic Judaism from the third to the sixth century AD (see b. Taanith 8a; Bemidbar Rabbah 13.16; 14.4, 18; 18.21; Shir Ha-Shirim Rabbah 4.11; Koheleth Rabbah 12.11–12), and clearly the number comes from the Greek alphabet. While the number of inspired books likely stayed the same with some debated for a time, the books that comprised those twenty-four books emerged through the combination of several books (e.g., Ruth with Judges, Ezra with Nehemiah). Some rabbis continued to contest the scriptural status of several biblical books including the Song of Songs long after the number (but not identity) of sacred books was settled. See also m. Eduyyot 5.3; m. Yadayim. 3.5; b. Megillah. 7a; t. Yadayim. 2.14 for questions about Ecclesiastes (b. Shabbat 100a; see also Jerome on Eccl 12:14), Ruth (b. Megillah 7a); Esther (b. Sanhedrin 100a; b. Megillah 7a. cf. t. Megillah 2.1a), Proverbs (b. Shabbat 30b), and Ezekiel (b. Shabbat 13b; b. Hagigah 13a; b. Menahot 45a).

The big question here, of course, is why would the Jews change from using the number of letters in their own alphabet and use instead the number in the Greek alphabet and still have the same books? We can only guess here, but it is likely that the influence of Homer and the widespread familiarity and significance of the Greek alphabet influenced the rabbinic Jews. The Christians did not number their NT sacred books in terms of either alphabet. It appears that the influence of the Greek perspective of sacred writings also influenced the Jewish tradition. Why else would there be a change from the obvious number of books in the Hebrew Bible (twenty-two) that included the same books to the number of the books in each of Homer's *Iliad* and *Odyssey* (twenty-four)?

Collections of Scriptures in the Second Century AD

The first listing of the books in the Jewish biblical canon is in a second century rabbinic text, likely from Babylon, called b. Bava Batra 14b (ca. AD 140–180). It not only identifies the number as twenty-four (as in 4 Ezra 14) but also groups them significantly as Law, Prophets, and Writings. This is the first clear (and still extant) reference to the three parts of the Jewish Scriptures and the specific books in them. The relevant part of that text is as follows:

Our Rabbis taught: the order of the Prophets is, Joshua, Judges, Samuel, Kings, Jeremiah, Ezekiel, Isaiah, and the Twelve Minor Prophets. Let us examine this. Hosea came first, as it is written (Hosea 1:2): *God spoke first to Hosea*. But did God speak first to Hosea? Were there not many prophets between Moses and Hosea? R. Johanan (250–290), however, has explained that [what it means is that] he was the first of the four prophets who prophesied at that period, namely, Hosea, Isaiah, Amos, and Micah. Should not then Hosea come first?—Since his prophecy is written along with those of Haggai, Zechariah and Malachi, and Haggai, Zechariah and Malachi came at the end of the prophets, he is reckoned with them. But why should he not be written separately and placed first?—Let us see again. Isaiah was prior to Jeremiah and Ezekiel. Then why should not Isaiah be placed first?—Because the book of Kings ends with a record of destruction and Jeremiah speaks throughout of destruction and Ezekiel commences with destruction and ends with consolation and Isaiah is full of consolation; therefore we put destruction next to destruction and consolation next to consolation. [Our Rabbis taught:] The order of the Hagiographa is Ruth, the book of Psalms, Job, Proverbs, Ecclesiastes, Song of Songs, Lamentations, Daniel and the Scroll of Esther, Ezra and Chronicles. Now on the view that Job lived in the days of Moses, should not the book of Job come first?—We do not begin with a record of suffering. But Ruth also is a record of suffering?—It is a suffering with a sequel [of happiness], as R. Johanan said: Why was her name called Ruth?—Because there issued from her David who replenished the Holy One, blessed be He, with hymns and praises.

Who wrote the Scriptures?—Moses wrote his own book and the portion of Balaam and Job. Joshua wrote the book which bears his name and [the last] eight verses of the Pentateuch. Samuel wrote the book which bears his name and the book of Judges and Ruth. David wrote the book of Psalms, including in it the work of the ten elders, namely Adam, Melchizedek, Abraham, Moses, Heman, Yeduthun, Asaph, and the three sons of Korah. Jeremiah wrote the book which bears his name, the book of Kings, and Lamentations. Hezekiah and his colleagues wrote . . . Isaiah, Proverbs, the Song of Songs and Ecclesiastes. The Men of the Great Assembly wrote . . . Ezekiel, the Twelve Minor Prophets, Daniel and the scroll of Esther. Ezra wrote the book that bears his name and the genealogies of the book of Chronicles up to his own time. . . . Who then finished it [the book of Chronicles]?—Nehemiah the son of Hachaliah. (Leiman 1974, 52–53)

What is clear in most of the above texts is that various influential collections of Jewish Scriptures were circulating among the Jews at least from the time of Josiah (ruler of Judah, 640–609 BC) to the first century AD and following. What comprised those collections is seldom clear in any but the last of the above references. The b. Bava Batra 14b text is thus the first clearly stated and still extant listing of the collection of books that comprise the Jewish Scriptures (Hebrew Bible). Prior to this text, it was not clear what the third part of the Jewish Scriptures was or what books were in the Prophets or the Writings. No doubt most (if not all) of the writings listed had long been accepted as Scripture among the Jews, but we know of no earlier confirmation than this. In the New Testament, for instance, the reference to "prophets" may simply have included all of the Scriptures that were not in the Law, including some or all of the Psalms. The "Law and the Prophets" appear to include all of the Jewish Scriptures (see, for example, Matt 5:17, 7:12; Luke 24:7; Luke 16:16; John 1:46; Rom 3:21; and Acts 28:23). Occasionally, the "law" seems to be a designation for all of the Jewish Scriptures, as we see in John 10:34, which cites Psalm 82:6 as the "law," and 1 Corinthians 14:21, where Paul introduces Isaiah 28:11–12 with "in the law it is written"—a typical formula for the citation of Scripture, like those we observed earlier.

It is important to point out that while the early Christians accepted the Jewish Scriptures that were finally identified in the second century, they did *not* accept the Jewish three-part Hebrew Bible structure. There is nothing inherently wrong with this threefold organization, but Christians for the most part did not follow it; even the Roman Catholic and Orthodox canons, which include all of the books in the Hebrew Bible plus several of the apocryphal or deuterocanonical books, do not follow the threefold structure of the Hebrew Bible. *By contrast, the Christian Old Testament books are generally grouped as Law, History, Poetry (or, alternatively, Wisdom), and Prophets.* What most likely accounts for this organizational divergence is that the three-part structure did not exist in the period when Christians began to separate from the Jewish community (AD 62–135). We might recall that Jewish literature through the first two centuries regularly referred to the sacred Scriptures as either "the Law" or "the Law and the Prophets"—and that even the divisions of "Law" and "Prophets" were not that clearly defined during the first century, as we saw above. The threefold division of the Hebrew Scriptures was late in coming and not especially popular among the rabbis until much later.

As we have seen, *some* of the second-century rabbis began to divide their Scriptures into three parts (Law, Prophets, and Writings) and numbered them as twenty-four books. Although the Christians number the same books as thirty-nine, the Jews combined several books, as in the case of 1 and 2 Samuel, into one book. The same is true of 1 and 2 Kings, 1 and 2 Chronicles, and the Book of the Twelve (Minor Prophets). Ezra and Nehemiah are sometimes also listed as one book; so also Judges is listed with Ruth and Jeremiah with Lamentations. When these books are counted separately, they are the same in number as the thirty-nine books of the Protestant Old Testament. Sometimes the Jewish Scriptures are listed as twenty-two books, but they are most likely the same books as the twenty-four, combined in a different way. Instead of adopting the three-part Hebrew Bible canon structure, Christians instead divided their Old Testament Scriptures into four (or five) major sections; namely, the Law (or Pentateuch), History (Joshua to Esther), Poetry and/or Wisdom (Job to Song of Songs), and Prophets (Isaiah to Malachi). The only known exceptions to these divisions are Codex Sinaiticus and Jerome's list of Old Testament Scriptures, both produced in the late fourth century and likely showing Jewish influence from their place of origin; i.e., the Land of Israel. (These two examples are listed in Table 4 at the end of chapter 4.) In neither instance, however, do the writers identify their classifications as Law, Prophets, and Writings. Both lists have books differing from the Jewish sequence, and they also include other books as well. The overwhelming evidence from the early church is that the divisions in their Old Testament Scriptures differ from those in the Jewish three-part canon. Also, the three-part division of the Jewish Scriptures originated *after* the separation of the Christians from the Jews.

In the first century AD, then, the books that comprised the Jewish Scriptures (Hebrew Bible) were not yet settled for the Jews or for the early followers of Jesus, though most if not all of the books that later comprised the Jewish biblical canon were widely acknowledged as sacred Scripture by that time. However, for at least a century after the Christian era began, rabbinic Jews were still discussing the viability and sacredness of some of their scriptural books, as in the case of Song of Songs, which is essentially a love poem between a man and a woman; Esther, which does not mention the name of God; and Ezekiel, whose plans for the reconstructed temple were at odds with earlier Pentateuchal descriptions of it. They also discussed whether Ecclesiastes was a sacred book since it is so negative, even pessimistic, about life. (See, for example, the discussion in the Mishnah, m. Yadayim 3.5.) Many rabbis of the second and third centuries AD also continued to approve the sacredness of Sirach (Ecclesiasticus), though later rabbis dropped it from their sacred collections. Eventually the number and names of the sacred books in the Jewish Scriptures became more stabilized, but there is no evidence that the rabbinic Jews or those that followed them ever made a formal announcement on the scope of their sacred Scriptures.

The majority of Jews in the Greco-Roman world, however, did not know Hebrew or Aramaic (a few portions of the Old Testament were written in Aramaic, as in the case of about half of Daniel; moreover, the language of the Jews in Israel was Aramaic in the time of Jesus, as is attested by several of the expressions found in the Gospel accounts). Consequently, they made use of the Greek translation of their Scriptures; that is, they read the Septuagint (LXX) as did the early Christians, who cited the Septuagint when they quoted the Old Testament Scriptures. The Septuagint also included many of the apocryphal (deuterocanonical) books that are now a part of the Catholic and Orthodox Bibles. Those additional books were commonly known and used in the Jewish communities in the diaspora in the Mediterranean world.

The Law clearly was the *first* recognized Scriptures of the Jews, though the Prophets (both the proclaiming and writing prophets) began to exert an increasing influence, especially at the end of the Old Testament era. There is no known tradition that clarifies when the Prophets were specifically recognized as sacred Scripture, nor which books were so recognized; but the recognition of their divine authority was obviously known by fifth century BC and possibly earlier, since it was later acknowledged that they played a more significant role in Jewish life from then on. They begin to be more acknowledged by name and inference by no later than 180 BC (Sirach). From the second century BC, the Jewish Scriptures were commonly identified as the Law and the Prophets, but as we saw above, the distinctions between these groups were not always clearly drawn. The Writings became a separate collection of sacred books among some Jews in the second century AD, but this action may have been anticipated by earlier references to "David" in the texts cited above.

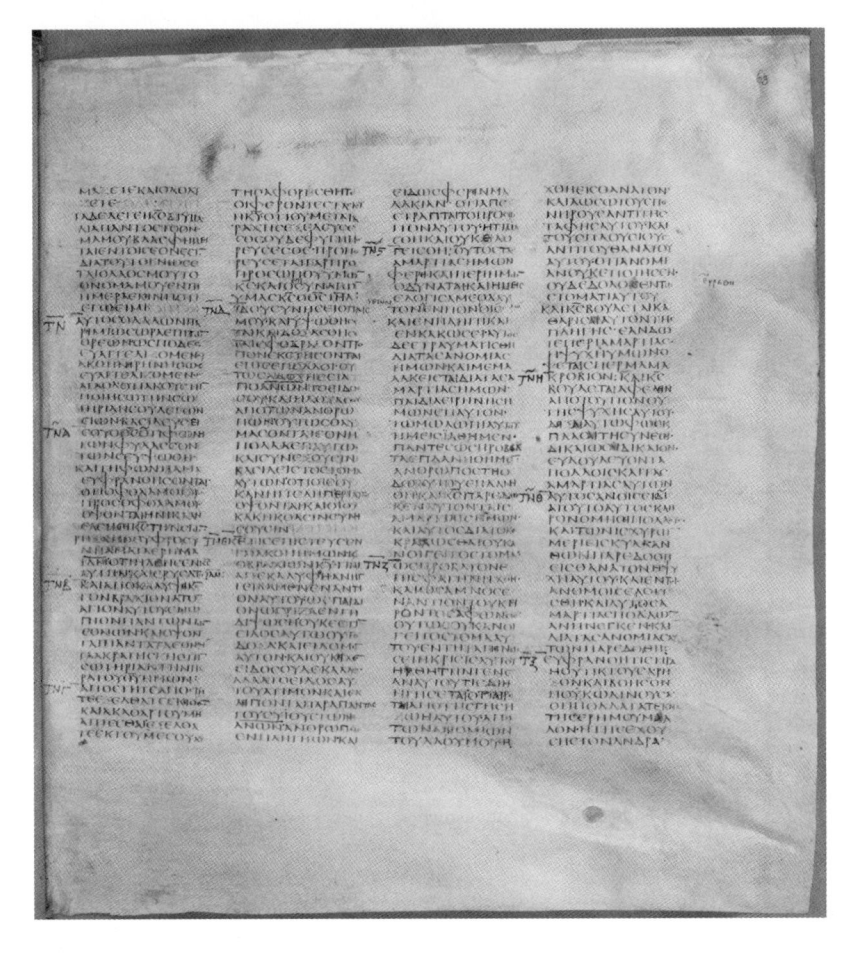

Isaiah 53 in Codex Sinaiticus (ca. 375), one of the two oldest Christian copies of the Greek Old Testament, the Septuagint. Q45-f.6r [BL-f.63] for Isa 52:5–54:1. (Reproduced by permission of the British Library)

The Scriptures of Jesus and the Early Christians

What Scriptures did Jesus recognize? The initial answer is that we do not know for sure, since we have no evidence that he ever provided his disciples with a list of the Scriptures that he approved or accepted. We can say for sure that he favored Deuteronomy (cited fifteen times in the four canonical Gospels), Isaiah (forty times), and the Psalms (thirteen times) since he cited them more frequently than the rest of the books in the Old Testament Scriptures. He apparently did *not* cite about a third of the Old Testament books: of the thirty-nine books in the Protestant Old Testament, Jesus quoted or cited twenty-three of them. He does not cite or quote Song of Songs, Ruth, Lamentations, Ecclesiastes, Esther, Ezra, or Nehemiah. Some of Jesus' teachings have parallels in certain nonbiblical books. To return to an example noted earlier, his reference to "the Son of Man *sitting on his throne of glory*" in Matthew 19:29 and 25:31 has parallels only in 1 Enoch 62:2–3: "*The Lord of the Spirits has sat down on the throne of his glory, and the spirit of righteousness has been poured out upon him*" (emphasis added). There are several other such parallels to apocryphal or nonbiblical writings in the New Testament.

Several biblical scholars have argued that Jesus passed on to his disciples a fixed collection of Old Testament Scriptures and that it contained the books in the Protestant Old Testament Scriptures or the Hebrew Bible. If that were so, however, the early disciples apparently lost it, since they never refer to such a collection and often cite other religious texts not in the Hebrew Bible. When such fixed collections do begin to emerge (in the fourth century AD), they are almost never identical. The point to remember here, once again, is that there were no fixed biblical canons in the churches for several centuries, though the core books of the Old Testament (Law and the Prophets and the Psalms, even if sometimes classified differently) were widely accepted and frequently cited by the early church fathers.

The processes that led to the current Old Testament for the early Christians were slow and complex, but also inextricably bound to the *cultural* and *linguistic* developments reflected in the Jewish Scriptures that the early Christians adopted from their Jewish siblings. The majority of Christians read their Old Testament Scriptures in the Greek language (the LXX), and this also gave them considerable access to the Hellenized, Greek-speaking Jewish audiences in their early missionary activities around the Mediterranean world. (As we have seen with other divergences among early canons, the Septuagint included the books that later formed the Hebrew Bible but also included many books that are now considered nonbiblical by many Christians.) The New Testament writers overwhelmingly made use of Greek translations—among which there were at least slight variations, as we might expect of hand-copied documents—of their Old Testament Scriptures (over 94 percent of the time) rather than the Hebrew text.

Consequently, when Christians today read their New Testament's citations of the Old Testament, they are often confused when they refer to those passages in their Old Testament, as they are likely to notice that the wording, and even the overall meaning, varies considerably in many cases (for example, see the ways in which Paul's combined citation of Isa 25:8 and Hos 13:14 in 1 Cor 15:54 differs from the wording of the texts as they appear in the Hebrew Old Testament). There is often a considerable difference between the Greek and Hebrew text of the Old Testament Scriptures. Until recently, many professors in seminaries all but ignored the Septuagint in their studies and appeared unaware that this was the Scriptures of the early churches! Happily, there is now much more frequent and in-depth study of the parallels and differences between the Hebrew and Greek Scriptures, as well as their implications for the interpretation of Scripture. Some Jewish and Christian scholars also recognize that in some cases the Greek translation of some Old Testament texts is based on an earlier Hebrew antecedent than the current Hebrew Old Testament text.

The inclusion and exclusion of apocryphal or deuterocanonical books also serves to illustrate vital issues about the Scriptures the early Christians knew and read. Several of the ancient Christian Greek Old Testament manuscripts contain the so-called apocryphal books along with the twenty-four (or thirty-nine, when counted differently as we saw above) books in the Hebrew Bible. Including a few of the apocryphal books was common enough in the early churches, but so was their exclusion until the late fourth century, when Augustine included them in his list of the church's Scriptures. Although Jerome was opposed to including them in his Latin translation, the Vulgate, he nevertheless conceded to pressure from Augustine who argued that they must remain. Most of the apocryphal books were included in the council decisions at Laodicea (AD 360) and Carthage (AD 397 and 419, article 26).

In the sixteenth century, Protestant Christians began eliminating the Apocrypha from their Bibles, although many continued to include it, often following Martin Luther's practice of placing them as appendices between the Old and New Testaments. This continued until 1827–1831, when they were removed from subsequently printed Protestant Bibles. (In the mid-twentieth century, Protestant Bibles once again began to appear with the Apocrypha as an appendix to the Old Testament.) In Roman Catholic and Orthodox Bibles, the apocryphal or deuterocanonical books are interspersed throughout their Old Testaments, as we see in many ancient lists of the church's Scriptures as well as in several ancient manuscripts (again, see the examples in Table 4 at the end of chapter 4).

I noted earlier that all Christians accept the twenty-four books in the Jewish Scriptures (= the thirty-nine books in the Protestant Old Testament). Roman Catholic and Orthodox Christians also include 1 and 2 Esdras, Tobit, Judith, Additions to Esther, 1–2 Maccabees, Wisdom of Solomon, Ecclesiasticus (Sirach),

Baruch, and the Additions to Daniel; namely, the Prayer of Azariah and the Song of the Three Young Men, Susanna, and Bel and the Dragon. In addition to these books, the Orthodox Christians add 3 Maccabees, Psalm 151, and the Epistle of Jeremiah. In their appendices, they tend to include 4 Maccabees, the Prayer of Manasseh, and 3 Esdras. These books are cited as Scripture by various early and later church fathers. Orthodox Christians include these additional books in their Bibles, but they do not treat them as Scripture like Catholics do, but more as inspirational reading. Some Orthodox churches have them between the Old and New Testaments, and some place them variously throughout their Old Testaments.

Thus Christians received their understanding of sacred Scripture and their Old Testament Scriptures from the Jews before they separated from them. And the separating Christians accepted a not-so-well-defined collection of Scriptures. Initially, some of their Scriptures included both apocryphal books and several of the books that we now call "pseudepigraphic" books (see the list of books in this collection in Table 4 in chapter 4 below). The majority of Christians had, however, rejected the Pseudepigrapha by the fourth and fifth centuries, often because those books were believed to have been written in someone else's name, but it is not altogether clear why some of them were rejected.

Protestant Bibles began to exclude the apocryphal or books by the mid-1500s, but most of the translations still included the apocryphal books, including the first edition of the 1611 King James Version. As was noted earlier, Protestants finally dispensed with these books in their Bibles between 1827–1831. Earlier, Martin Luther had included them in his translation of the Bible and placed them between his Old and New Testaments, but he objected to 2 Maccabees especially because it commends prayer for the dead so that they may be atoned and delivered from their sin. This text was the basis for the Roman Catholic teaching about purgatory (2 Macc 12:41–45). He also objected to 2 Maccabees 15:12–14 because he thought it promoted the sale of indulgences in churches, another practice he despised. Apart from these texts, however, there is little in the apocryphal books that would cause alarm to Protestants or be considered heretical either in the past or today.

On the other hand, there is much in the apocryphal or deuterocanonical books that is not only interesting but also useful in understanding portions of the New Testament. For example, after the Jews led by Judas Maccabeus recaptured the Jerusalem Temple around 165 BC, they cleansed the temple because the Seleucids had committed sacrilege in it by sacrificing a pig on the temple altar and establishing an idol of Zeus there. After the Maccabees had cleansed the temple, they subsequently celebrated this event on 25 Kislev, beginning on the third anniversary of its desecration in 165 BC. In New Testament times, the celebration was called the "festival of dedication" (John 10:22; Hebrew, *Hanukkah* = "Dedication"). We can learn much about the context of the New Testament by becoming more familiar with the apocryphal books. While it is not necessary for Protestants to expand their Bibles by including the Apocrypha in them, that collection is helpful in understanding the historical context in the time of Jesus. They would also benefit by studying the same literature that informed the earliest Christians.

Summary: Formation of the Old Testament

The Old Testament was formed first by the recognition that the law of Moses was a divinely inspired and authoritative document for Jews. Biblical scholars usually agree that the Law (possibly only Deuteronomy) was recognized as authoritative Scripture in the days of King Josiah (640–609 BC) at the latest. The whole Pentateuch was likely also recognized as sacred Scripture by ca. 500–450 BC, during the time of Ezra/Nehemiah (Neh 8:1–8). A number of the Prophets were also influential at that time, but there is no question that the Law held the highest priority. Later in the early third century BC, it was *only* the Law that was translated into Greek. This suggests that the Prophets, though influential, had not at that time reached a level of scriptural recognition. The Prophets were *beginning* to be recognized as authoritative Scriptures by around 400 BC (see 2 Kgs 17:13), but by ca. 200 BC, their recognition and acceptance were widespread.

The third part of the Jewish Scriptures, the "Writings" (or *Ketuvim* = Hebrew for "writings"; or *Hagiographa* = Greek for "holy writings"), were recognized for the first known time as a distinct collection of Jewish Scriptures in the middle to late second century AD by *some* rabbinic Jews, *but not all*. Many had long recognized the books in this collection as sacred Scripture, but the specific identification of this third category of Jewish Scriptures called "Writings" was new.

As we saw above, for several reasons it is highly unlikely that all Jews accepted this three-part biblical canon long before the time of Jesus since there are no known references to it before the second century AD. First, in all but one instance in the New Testament, Jesus referred to the Jewish Scriptures as either the "Law," the "law of Moses," or the "Law and the Prophets"; in that one exception, Luke 24:44, he describes the Scriptures of Judaism as the "law of Moses, the prophets, and the psalms." While some biblical scholars claim that this signified the third part of the Jewish Scriptures, equivalent to the later Writings identified in the middle to late second century AD, there is no convincing evidence for that, or any reason to think that this referred to anything other than "psalms," either in general or as a book. More specifically, besides the poetic and wisdom writings in that third part later identified as "Writings," the rabbis included the Chronicles, Ezra-Nehemiah, Daniel, Ruth, and Esther, which are never attributed to David nor are they a part of the wisdom or poetic literature. That Jesus clearly welcomed Daniel as a sacred scriptural book is clear from the Gospels where he quotes from it (see, for example, Mark 14:62, citing Dan 7:13). Jesus—and likely most Jews of that time—viewed Daniel as a prophetic writing, but most probably as a part of the Prophets. As we stated earlier, all sacred books that were not a part of the Law (Torah) were considered by Jews, Jesus, and his followers to be a part of the Prophets. Even the "psalms" mentioned in Luke 24:44, then, may reflect a growing Jewish tendency to isolate the Psalms as Scripture among the rest of the Jewish Scriptures. Their placement or location in the Scriptures was in question; their sacred status was not.

Secondly the Septuagint translation (begun ca. 281–280 BC) initially included only the writings of Moses. Had the Prophets and the Writings been either complete or recognized as sacred Scripture *on par with the Law at that time*, they would most likely have been included in this translation. They were not. Most of the books of the Hebrew Bible, however, had been translated into Greek by ca. 130–100 BC, and by that point there was likely widespread recognition of their sacred status.

Third, there were still discussions and debates taking place among the rabbis in the second to the sixth centuries AD about the sacredness of several books (Esther, Ezekiel, Song of Songs, Sirach, and others). It is difficult to argue that all Jews everywhere held to the same views when the rabbis themselves were not in full agreement over the status of some books, as we saw above. There never was a formal Jewish pronouncement about which books comprised the Hebrew Bible at these relatively early stages of canonical development. The issue was apparently settled for the Jews in the east on the basis of tradition, though not completely; but for those in the Mediterranean world to the west of the land of Israel, the question was still open until as late as the eighth or ninth centuries AD. They continued to use the Septuagint that included apocryphal books.

Finally, the Christian understanding of the scope of the Old Testament Scriptures reflects the status of books that were widely accepted as sacred Scripture among Jews in the first century AD. The Christians adopted those Scriptures before they separated finally from the Jews—at the latest by AD 135. Those books included not only the apocryphal books but also 1 Enoch (recalling the citation of 1 En. 1:9 in Jude 14), which the early church fathers continued to cite as Scripture until the third century AD.

Examples of the extensive Christian citations of 1 Enoch as Scripture or in an authoritative manner in the early centuries in Christian literature are as follows:

1. Epistle of Barnabas (ca. 70–100 or 130–150 and possible as late as 140, Alexandria) 4:3 cites 1 Enoch (use of *gegraptai*); 16:4–6 (= a summary of 1 En. 106:19–107, esp. 91:13; cf. also 1 En. 89:56–74).

2. Apocalypse of Peter (ca. 100–110, possibly Egypt) 2–8 (1 En. 108:7–9; 106:2, 10; 61:9–11; 53:3).

3. Justin Martyr (ca. 100–165), *First Apology* 2.5 (cf. 1 En. 7; 8:9; 15:8–9).

4. Athenagoras (fl. ca. 170–180, Athens), *Legatio pro Christianis* 24, 25 (cf. 1 En. 6–7, 13:5; 15:3, 8, 10; 60:15–21).

5. Minucius Felix (second or third century, North Africa), *Octavius* 26 (1 En. 8; 15:8–12; 16:1; 19:1).

6. Irenaeus (ca. 130–200, Bishop of Lyons), *Adversus haereses* 1.2.1 (1 En. 10:13–14); 1.8.17 (1 En. 7:1; 8:1); 4.16.2 (1 En. 12:4–6; 13; 14:3–7; 15; 16); 4.36.4 (1 En. 10:2); 4.58.4 (1 En. 7:1); 5.28.2 (1 En. 15:3; 99:7; 19:1); 5.5.1, plus 1.15.6 (1 En. 8:1; cf. 10:8); *Adversus haereses* 4.36.4 draws on 1 Enoch re: angelic rebellion. *Adversus haereses* 4.16.2 (cf. 1 En. 12:13, 6ff., 10). See also 4.36.4. where Irenaeus understood Gen 5:21–24 and 6:1–4 in light of 1 Enoch.

7. Clement of Alexandria (ca. 150–215), *Eclogae prophetarum* 2.1, 53; 3.456 (1 En. 19:3); 3.474 (1 En. 8:2–3); *Stromateis* 3.9 (1 En. 8; 16:3).

8. Tertullian (ca. 160–225, Carthage), *Apologeticus* 22 (cf. 1 En. 15:8, 9); *De cultu feminarum* 1.3.1 (1 En. 8:1, 3); 2.10 (1 En. 8:1); *De idolatria* 4, 15 (1 En. 19:1; 99:6–7); 9 (1 En. 6; 14:5), 15; *De virginibus velandis* 7 (1 En. 6; 14:5; see also *De anima* 50).

9. Hippolytus (ca. 170–236, Rome), *De antichristo* 43–47; *Or. adv. Graecos* (cf. 1 En. 22:3; 21:1).

10. Origen (ca. 185–254, Alexandria and Caesarea), cites 1 Enoch as "Scripture" (*De principiis* 1.3; 4.35). There are many more citations of 1 Enoch listed in my *Formation of the Biblical Canon* 1:360–65.

It is not certain when the Enochic writings were specifically excluded as scriptural documents *by name,* but after Origen there are few *positive* citations of the Enochic literature in church literature, but 1 Enoch has continued as Scripture in the Ethiopian biblical canon to this day. By the fourth century AD, 1 Enoch is largely rejected as a scriptural book, but not completely. Even where it is rejected as Scripture, the rejections suggest that some Christians were still reading the book. Beckwith's view of 1 Enoch does not appear reflective of the views of it in the early churches where many accepted it *as Scripture*, including Jude. If Jude used 1 Enoch only as illustrative material to make a point and not as sacred literature, it is remarkable that the early church fathers including Irenaeus, Tertullian, and initially Origen did not realize it. Again, his comments are confusing since Jude appeals to 1 Enoch 1:9 as a *prophetic* text to establish his argument in Jude 14.

There is no convincing argument that the "prophets" in the time of Jesus was restricted to the writings in the second part of the Hebrew Bible, the "Prophets." The contents of that term were still in flux in the first century. Even in the late second century, some rabbis were stilling calling Job a prophet (b. Bava Batra 15b). The three-part Hebrew Bible was a later development following the separation of the church from Judaism. Again, there is nothing inherently wrong with the three-part Hebrew Bible; and if it had been well known before the Jews and Christians parted, then it would have likely been a part of the Scriptures of early Christianity, but it was not. For further discussion of this, see the discussion of the order of the Scriptures in the next chapter that will focus on the criteria employed in the fixing or closing of the church's Old Testament, as well as a number of lists of Old Testament books and their order in early Christianity.

Chapter 3

The Closing of the Old Testament Scriptures

The Jewish Bible

After the destruction of Jerusalem and the Jewish temple in AD 70, a group of religious Jews met at Jamnia (also known as Yavna/Javneh, located north of Gaza and south of Joppa, just inland from the Mediterranean) to address the question of how Judaism would survive without its temple and the sacrificial and religious activities that formed the geographical and theological center of Jewish communal identity. For more than a hundred years, one of the more popular views regarding the completion of the Hebrew Bible Scriptures has been that the third part of the Hebrew Scriptures was defined, recognized, and closed at this special "council" of rabbis that took place at Jamnia at or near the end of the first century AD. That view is still held by a few scholars today, but more recent examinations of the ancient texts that this view depends on have undermined its credibility.

This has led some scholars to conclude that the most reasonable alternate time for finalizing the third part of the Hebrew Bible was earlier than Jamnia, perhaps even as early as the time of Judas Maccabeus (ca. 165 BC). He is reported to have collected the Hebrew Scriptures after Antiochus IV Epiphanes tried to destroy them. It is argued that Judas's collection of the scattered and surviving Scriptures provides the most obvious time of termination for the Hebrew Bible (see the citation of 2 Macc 2:13–15 in the previous chapter), in this view. The passage cited in support of this position (1 Macc 1:56–57) only refers to the "law" being destroyed, though it is possible that more was intended (see 2 Macc 2:13). Even though "law" likely applied to all of the sacred Scriptures of the Hebrew Bible at that time, it is not clear from this passage that the Bible was fixed in its current shape as a result of Judas's activity. In fact, the evidence against that position was shown in the previous chapter.

At the end of the first century, the Jewish historian Josephus claimed that other books could not be included after the time of Artaxerxes (possibly Artaxerxes I, ca. 458 BC; see Ezra 7:7). But it is interesting that the only criterion that Josephus mentions is a date (*Against Apion* 1.40, cited in chapter 2 on pp. 51–52); namely, from the death of Moses until Artaxerxes (ca. 465 BC).

According to the rabbis of the third century AD and later, only those books that were written in Hebrew or Aramaic were acceptable as sacred Scripture, and they believed that prophecy (divine revelation to prophets) had ceased following the time of Artaxerxes. While some Jews believed that all prophecy had ceased (1 Macc 14:41), clearly many disagreed. In fact, outside of the rabbinic circle, there is very little evidence that others held that view, as we see in the case of Philo, the Alexandrian Jewish teacher whose life and career overlap with Jesus (see his *Moses* 2.187), and Josephus (*Jewish Antiquities* 3.311–313; *Jewish War* 6.286, 300–309), but also in the early Christian teaching (1 Cor 12:4–11, 28; Rom 12:6; Eph 4:11). Likewise, the later rabbis maintained that those writings that survived only in Greek were rejected and only those in Hebrew were acceptable. Even translations of Hebrew books into another language were considered undesirable. The late rabbinic conclusion was that the day that the Torah was translated into Greek "was as intolerable for Israel as the day the golden calf was made [Exod 34], for the Torah cannot be translated adequately" (see *Masekhet Soferim* 1).

As stated in the previous chapter, the third part of the Hebrew Bible, the Writings (*Ketuvim* or *Hagiographa*), and the full scope the Christian Old Testament had not come to finalization before or during the time of Jesus, nor even in the early second century AD. A much larger collection of Jewish sacred writings (the Apocrypha and Pseudepigrapha) continued to circulate in the Septuagint, the Greek translation of the Hebrew Scriptures. These were the Scriptures of the Jews in the *Diaspora* (those living outside of the land of Israel and especially those to the west, south, and north) and many of the early Christians in the first century and later. The rabbinic Jews near the end of the second or early third century AD chose a more restricted collection of Scriptures than did the diaspora communities and the Christians. Some have suggested that the origin of this restricted collection was Babylon and may have been brought from there to the land of Israel by Hillel, an influential Jewish teacher from the late first century BC and early first century AD.

It is also possible that famed Greek writer, Homer, had some influence on the number of books that were admitted into the Jewish biblical canon. No one was quoted more frequently in the ancient world and no author more highly prized than Homer. Alexander the Great was so moved by Homer that he started a Homeric cult in Alexandria. Many believed that Homer knew everything and was the source of all wisdom. Virtually, all Greek education began with knowledge of Homer and his works. Homer's impact on the shape of the biblical canon is difficult to prove decisively, but biblical scholars are beginning to make note of several Homeric parallels in the New Testament, as well as Jewish familiarity with Homer, both in Josephus and the second- through sixth-century rabbis. Those familiar with Homer's *Iliad* and *Odyssey* know that each chapter, or book, of both of those writings begins with a different letter of the Greek alphabet. Only Homer's writings have such introductions. There are twenty-four letters in the Greek alphabet and twenty-four chapters or books in the *Iliad* and the

Odyssey. Also, only the gods identified in Homer's writings were acknowledged and worshiped by the Greeks. The Jews initially chose twenty-two books for their sacred collection of Scriptures, evidently following the twenty-two letters of the Hebrew alphabet. Subsequently, and permanently, the Jews chose a twenty-four book canon of Scriptures. Most biblical scholars believe that they selected the same books, but combined them in different ways to come to the acceptable number. Such recombinations and renumerations were not unknown at the time: at roughly the same time as Josephus, the author of 4 Ezra (ca. AD 90) spoke of twenty-four books that were made public and seventy others that were reserved for the wise (4 Ezra 14:45–47).

So the rabbis settled on the number twenty-four for their sacred books instead of twenty-two, following the more popular Greek alphabet instead of their own Hebrew alphabet. The books were most likely the same in each account, but by combining Judges with Ruth and Jeremiah with Lamentations, the number came out the same. There is admittedly no ancient text that makes this case, but the coincidence is worth considering. In the New Testament, the reference in Revelation 1:8 and 22:13 to the "Alpha and Omega," the first and last letters in the Greek alphabet, also reflects the influence of the Greek alphabet used in Homer's writings. Is it a further coincidence that there are twenty-four elders in Revelation (Rev 4:4; 5:8)? There is hardly an educated person in antiquity that would not have been familiar with the writings of Homer, the poetic use of the Greek alphabet, and the significance of the number twenty-four. Such parallels in the use of both alphabets reflect an intriguing mix of traditional and classical influences on the formation of the Jewish and Christian biblical canons.

Closing the Christian Old Testament Canon

For the Christians, the *final* process of determining the scope of their Old Testament definition and delimitation appears to have taken place in the fourth and fifth centuries, though as we saw earlier, the whole Christian church has never fully agreed on the scope of its Old Testament. They accepted as Scripture those sacred writings that were circulating among their Jewish siblings prior to their separation from them (no later than AD 135). That included many noncanonical writings. To be sure, the vast majority of the early church fathers' quotations and citations were from the Old Testament books, but other books were also cited as sacred Scriptures. This, of course, suggests that the Old Testament canon was not fixed or finalized until long after the time of Jesus.

Had the Old Testament Scriptures already been fixed before Jesus' time, it would be difficult to understand why the early Christians continued to cite other books as Scripture after other books had been officially rejected. Similarly, the many variations in the Old Testament Scripture catalogues (see Table 4 at the end of chapter 4 for a listing of the most important of these catalogues) would hardly be understandable if there was some well-known and formally accepted Old Testament canon among them. If the earliest Christians had a well-defined canon of Old Testament Scriptures in the first century AD, we must conclude that subsequent generations of Christians either lost it or they were indifferent to it. In the last chapter, we discussed these options, finding them both incredible and without foundation. If Jesus had given to his disciples a fixed biblical canon, it makes sense that they would have at least once shared it with other Jesus-followers. It is better to conclude that a fixed collection of the Jewish or Old Testament Scriptures did not exist in the time of Jesus or before.

Since we have no *complete* record of all that Jesus said and only *selected* passages of his teachings that advanced the Gospel writers' mission (observe John 20:30), we cannot say that we know everything that Jesus said or approved in regard to the Old Testament Scriptures. We can say, as we did above, which books he cited, including which ones he cited the most; but since he made no list of the ones that he considered sacred Scripture, we cannot reconstruct Jesus' "biblical canon." Jesus' primary mission was to proclaim the kingdom of God and to tell persons how to have a right relationship with God and their fellow human beings. Had he spoken on all of the subjects known among the Jews in his day, he might well have cited many other sacred texts; but based on available sources, we simply cannot know all of the books that Jesus accepted as sacred Scripture.

Both the Old and New Testament Scriptures were regularly used by the early church fathers to advance their mission, but only one known catalogue of Old Testament Scriptures existed before the fourth century (Melito's list, cited earlier), and seldom were any of the church fathers' lists exactly the same. There was considerable overlap in the lists, however, as we will see in Table 4 at the end of chapter 4. The core books were always the Law (or Pentateuch) and the Prophets and the Psalms, even though there were variations in some of the other books.

So we can say that the biblical canon was *largely* fixed for most Christians by no later than the fourth to the sixth centuries AD, but there was never complete agreement on the matter, and unanimity does not exist in churches today. Based on what we have observed up to this point in this study, our conclusions about the available evidence are: (1) the status of the Old Testament Scriptures in the time of Jesus *and* in the early church was still fluid; (2) the order of the Christian Old Testament differs considerably from the Jewish Hebrew Bible, suggesting that the latter had not yet been formed in its current groupings of texts (or even in the texts themselves) when Jews and Christians parted ways; and (3) the Old Testament canon lists in the early church (from the fourth through the fifth centuries AD) vary, but the Law and the Prophets, as well as most of the books identified as Writings in the Hebrew Bible, were fairly stable. Many of the so-called apocryphal books, however, were also included.

The Order of the Scriptures—and More

As we have already begun to discover, the differences in the order and sequence of the biblical books in the Hebrew Bible and the Christian Old Testament tell an important message about what those who determined the sequence were trying to say about their Scriptures. These differences are often overlooked, but their significance is considerable. The same books in the Jewish biblical canon are also in the Christian Old Testament along with a few others in the Catholic and Orthodox Bibles, but they differ considerably in their order or sequence. Although in both biblical canons the Law or Pentateuch has the place of priority, the order in the rest of the books varies considerably. As we noted earlier, the Hebrew Bible (*Tanak*) begins with the books of the Law (Torah = Genesis, Exodus, Leviticus, Numbers, and Deuteronomy), then comes the Prophets (*Nevi'im*) beginning with the Former Prophets (Joshua, Judges, Samuels, and Kings) and then the Latter Prophets (Isaiah, Jeremiah, Ezekiel, and the Book of the Twelve Minor Prophets); the *Nevi'im* thus occupy the middle of the collection. Finally, the Hebrew Bible concludes with the Writings (*Ketuvim*)—that is, the wisdom and poetic books (Psalms, Proverbs, Job, Song of Songs, Ruth, Lamentations, Ecclesiastes), one further prophetic book (Daniel), as well as the rest of the historical books (Esther, Daniel, Ezra, Nehemiah, and 1–2 Chronicles). The collection concludes with the story of how Israel's history declined from its former glorious days that peaked during the reign of Solomon (1 Kgs 10) to the point of captivity, deportation, and finally restoration to the land.

Following such destruction and captivity, the final part of this collection calls the remnant of Israel to personal faithfulness to the Lord (Yahweh), but there is no significant, unifying focus in this final section on the coming kingdom, the blessings of God for his people, or any other great promise for the nation of Israel—a striking contrast to the history of God's redemptive acts that precedes this stage of the story. The call is to be faithful to Yahweh, the Lord. This order is easier to understand when we recall that the context that gave rise to it was another, later period of imperial occupation of Israel, a period that played a grave role in shaping Israel's reflections on earlier times of destruction and exile. The Roman Empire devastated the Jewish nation, first at the end of the war, AD 70 and again in crushing the brief messianic fervor of the Bar Kokhba rebellion (AD 132–35). There was very little in these circumstances that offered hope, joy, or excitement for the Jewish people. These are the tragic historical circumstances in which the Jews decided the sequence of the books in the third part of their Hebrew Bible.

On the other hand, the Christian Old Testament canons for the Protestants and Roman Catholics are sequenced so that they end on a message of hope from the Prophets (Isaiah to Malachi), concluding with Malachi's claim that before the coming of the Day of the Lord, "the prophet Elijah will come and turn the hearts of the parents to the children and the children to their parents" (Mal 4:5–6). In the next book of the Christian Bible, Jesus says that John the Baptist is Elijah (Matt 11:7–15), and in the three transfiguration stories in the Gospels (Matt 17:1–13; Mark 9:2–13; Luke 9:28–36), Elijah again plays an important role. The Orthodox Church's Old Testament takes still another path, concluding with the Additions to Daniel—namely, the Prayer of Azariah (one of those recorded as having been thrown into the fiery pit in Daniel)—who prays, significantly, for deliverance; then comes the song of the three Jews thrown into the fiery pit, who begin to sing hope and blessing, concluding with "all who worship the Lord, bless the God of gods, sing praise to him and give thanks to him, for his mercy endures forever" (Pr Azar 67 NRSVue). The Chronicles are placed immediately after the Kings; and Ezra, Nehemiah and Esther are also included in this timeline. The Prophets' role in the sequence of the Christian Bible, then, was intended not so much to explain the adversity that had befallen Israel as it was to point to the good news and hope that is found in Jesus Christ.

By concluding the First (or Old) Testament with the Prophets, the church claimed that the prophetic literature pointed forward to a new day of hope and joy for those who are faithful to God. They will be blessed and judgment will come to those who are disobedient. As the first part of the Christian Scriptures (the Old Testament) ends, that "ending" anticipates a future that is described in the second part of the Christian Scriptures, the New Testament.

Eventually, however, the Jewish and Christian communities of faith both decided that *more* writings were necessary to complete their sacred collections and to clarify their faith and mission. For the Jews, that included the codification of the oral traditions surrounding the keeping of the law (the Mishnah) that focused on how the law applied to daily living and religious conduct. By the mid-third century AD, additional materials were placed alongside the Mishnah (symbol = m.), which were referred to as the "Tosefta" (Aramaic = "supplement," symbol = t.). The rabbinic teachers of the third to the sixth centuries interpreted the mishnaic teachings, adding biblical support for them, and these interpretations were called *gemara* (Aramaic = "completion"). Those interpretations later became known as the Talmud (Hebrew = "learning"). There were two major Talmuds (pl. *Talmudim*), following the order of the Tractates of the Mishnah. The two Talmudim have separate origins: one in Palestine called the *Yerushalmi* (symbol = y.), and the other from Babylon called the *Bavli* (symbol = b.). The rabbis distinguished these writings from the Scriptures of the Hebrew Bible, but they were also treated as sacred *interpretations* of those Scriptures that presented implications for religious conduct. They formed something like a second canon for the rabbinic Jews and eventually for most Jews.

Similarly, the early Christians acknowledged the Jewish Scriptures that they began to call the Old Testament by the end of the second century, but soon after the death and resurrection of Jesus, they also began to recognize the value and usefulness of many Christian writings in their worship, teaching, and mission. By the middle of the second century AD, some of those additional writings were being read alongside the Old Testament Scriptures, and by the end of the second century, several of the Christian writings began to be called "scripture" as they were increasingly viewed as the church's "New Testament" writings. Along with their Old Testament Scriptures, these additional books formed the rest of the Christians' Bible. We will focus on the fixing of those Scriptures in chapter 7, but first we will need to deepen our understanding of the specifically Christian understanding of the Old Testament (and, early on, other significant texts) as Scripture (chapter 4), and of the origin and shaping of the New Testament (chapters 5–6).

Table 1: Lost Ancient Books Mentioned in the Bible

The Bible mentions several books that for whatever reasons did not survive the challenges of ancient history. The following list of these books is likely incomplete, but those included are the ones that are known from their mention in the Bible itself (as indicated in parentheses below). Some of them may be overlapping references to the same book or books, identified differently, but even allowing for such duplicate references, the list is still impressively large.

A. In the Law or Torah: Book of the Wars of the Lord (Num 21:14)

B. In Joshua, Judges, 1–2 Samuel, 1–2 Kings:

1. Book of Jashar (Josh 10:12–13; 2 Sam 1:18–27 [see also 10:25]; 1 Kgs 8:12–13 in LXX)
2. Book of the Annals of the Kings of Judah (1 Kgs 14:29; 15:7, 23; 22:45; 2 Kgs 8:23; 12:18; 14:18; 15:6, 36; 16:19; 20:20; 21:17, 25; 23:28; 24:5)
3. Book of the Annals of the Kings of Israel (1 Kgs 14:19; 15:31; 16:5, 14, 20, 27; 22:39; 2 Kgs 1:18; 10:34; 13:8, 12; 14:15, 28; 15:11, 15, 21, 26, 31)
4. Book of Acts of Solomon (1 Kgs 11:41)

C. In Chronicles, Ezra, and Nehemiah:

1. Book of the Kings of Israel (1 Chr 9:1)
2. Book of the Kings of Judah and Israel (2 Chr 16:11)
3. Book of Kings of Israel and Judah (2 Chr 27:7)

4. Annals of the Kings of Israel (2 Chr 33:18)

5. Records of the Seer Samuel (1 Chr 29:29)

6. Records of the Seer Gad (1 Chr 29:29)

7. Records of the Seer Nathan (1 Chr 29:29)

8. History of the Prophet Nathan (2 Chr 9:29)

9. Prophecy of Ahijah the Shilonite (2 Chr 9:29)

10. Visions of the Seer Iddo (2 Chr 9:29)

11. Records of the Prophet Shemaiah and the Seer Iddo (2 Chr 12:15)

12. Annals of Jehu the son of Hanani ("which are recorded in the Book of the Kings of Israel"; 2 Chr 20:34)

13. Records of the Seers (2 Chr 33:19)

14. Story of the Prophet Iddo (2 Chr 13:22)

15. Commentary on the Book of the Kings (2 Chr 24:27)

16. A book written by the prophet Isaiah son of Amoz containing the history of Uzziah (2 Chr 26:22)

17. A vision of the prophet Isaiah son of Amoz in the Book of Kings of Judah and Israel (2 Chr 32:32; cf. Isa 1:1)

18. Annals of King David (1 Chr 27:24)

19. Annals of "your ancestors" (Ezra 4:15)

20. Book of the Annals (Neh 12:23)

21. "Laments" (2 Chr 35:25; not a reference to Lamentations, but rather to a book evidently produced by or for Josiah that is now lost)

22. See also Esther 2:23; 6:1; and 10:2 (perhaps more annals cited, but not Jewish annals)

Table 2: Jewish Religious Books Not in the Christian Scriptures

The so-called Old Testament Pseudepigrapha initially enjoyed some acceptance in Judaism as well as in early Christianity, but both communities eventually rejected these books. Most of this literature is preserved in Ethiopic, Syriac,

Armenian, Slavonic, and/or Greek translations. This literature is often grouped in the following five *loosely defined* categories:

A. Apocalyptic and Related Works:

1 (Ethiopic Apocalypse of) Enoch (Jewish, ca. 200 BC–AD 50)

2 (Slavonic Apocalypse of) Enoch (Jewish, ca. AD 75–100)

3 (Hebrew Apocalypse of) Enoch (Jewish, in present form ca. fifth to sixth century AD)

Sibylline Oracles (both Jewish and Christian, ca. second century BC to seventh century AD)

Treatise of Shem (ca. end of first century BC)

Apocryphon of Ezekiel (mostly lost, original form ca. late first century BC)

Apocalypse of Zephaniah (mostly lost, original form ca. late first century BC)

4 Ezra (original Jewish form after AD 90, with later Christian additions and included in many Christian Bibles)

Greek Apocalypse of Ezra (present form is Christian, ca. ninth century AD, with both Jewish and Christian sources)

Vision of Ezra (Christian, from fourth to seventh century AD)

Questions of Ezra (Christian, but date is imprecise)

Revelation of Ezra (Christian, sometime before ninth century AD)

Apocalypse of Sedrach (present form is Christian, from ca. fifth century AD with earlier sources)

2 (Syriac Apocalypse of) Baruch (Jewish, from ca. AD 100)

3 (Greek Apocalypse of) Baruch (Christian, utilizing Jewish sources, ca. first to second century AD)

Apocalypse of Abraham (Jewish primarily, ca. AD 70–150)

Apocalypse of Adam (gnostic derived from Jewish sources from ca. the first century AD)

Apocalypse of Elijah (both Jewish and Christian, ca. AD 150–275)

Apocalypse of Daniel (present form ca. ninth century AD, but contains Jewish sources from ca. fourth century AD)

B. Testaments:

Testaments of the Twelve Patriarchs (current form is Christian, ca. AD 150–200, but Levi, Judah, and Naphtali are Jewish and date before AD 70 and probably second to first century BC)

Testament of Job (Jewish, ca. late first century BC)

Testaments of the Three Patriarchs (Jewish Testaments of Abraham, Isaac, and Jacob from ca. AD 100, linked with the Christian testaments of Isaac and Jacob)

Testament of Moses (Jewish, from ca. early first century AD)

Testament of Solomon (Jewish, current form ca. third century AD, but earliest form ca. AD 100)

Testament of Adam (Christian in current form ca. late third century AD, but used Jewish sources from ca. AD 150–200)

C. Expansions of OT and Legends:

Letter of Aristeas (Jewish, ca. 200–100 BC)

Jubilees (Jewish, ca. 130–100 BC)

Martyrdom and Ascension of Isaiah (has three sections: the first is Jewish from ca. 100 BC; the second and third sections are Christian, with the second from ca. second century AD and the third—the "Testament of Hezekiah"—ca. AD 90–100)

Joseph and Aseneth (Jewish, ca. AD 100)

Life of Adam and Eve (Jewish, ca. early to middle first century AD)

Pseudo-Philo, also known as *Liber antiquitatum biblicarum* (Jewish, ca. AD 66–135)

Lives of the Prophets (Jewish, ca. early first century AD with later Christian additions)

Ladder of Jacob (earliest form is Jewish, dating from late first century AD; one chapter is Christian)

4 Baruch (Jewish original but edited by a Christian, ca. AD 100–110)

Jannes and Jambres (Christian in present form, but dependent on earlier Jewish sources from ca. first century BC)

History of the Rechabites (Christian in present form, dating from ca. sixth century AD, but contains some pre-AD 100 Jewish sources)

Eldad and Modad (before the first century AD, now lost, but quoted as Scripture in Shepherd of Hermas, ca. AD 140)

History of Joseph (Jewish, date imprecise)

D. Wisdom and Philosophical Literature:

Ahiqar (Jewish, dating from late seventh or sixth century BC and cited in apocryphal Tobit)

3 Maccabees (Jewish, ca. first century BC)

4 Maccabees (Jewish, ca. before AD 70)

Pseudo-Phocylides (Jewish maxims attributed to sixth-century Ionian poet, ca. 50 BC–AD 100)

The Sentences of the Syriac Menander (Jewish, ca. third century AD)

E. Prayers, Psalms, and Odes:

More Psalms of David (Jewish psalms from ca. third century BC to AD 100)

Prayer of Manasseh (sometimes in Apocrypha, Jewish from ca. early first century AD)

Psalms of Solomon (Jewish, ca. 55–50 BC)

Hellenistic Synagogal Prayers (Jewish, ca. second to third century AD)

Prayer of Joseph (Jewish, ca. AD 70–135)

Prayer of Jacob (mostly lost Jewish document from ca. fourth century AD)

Odes of Solomon (Jewish-Christian songs, ca. AD 100–125)

Table 3: The Names and Sequence of Books in the Hebrew Bible & Christian Old Testament

HEBREW BIBLE (TANAK)	PROTESTANT OT
Torah	**Pentateuch**
Genesis	Genesis
Exodus	Exodus
Leviticus	Leviticus
Numbers	Numbers
Deuteronomy	Deuteronomy
Prophets	**Historical Books**
Joshua	Joshua
Judges	Judges
1 & 2 Samuel	Ruth
1 & 2 Kings	1 & 2 Samuel
Isaiah	1 & 2 Kings
Jeremiah	1 & 2 Chronicles
Ezekiel	Ezra and Nehemiah
Hosea	Esther
Joel	**Poetic Books**
Amos	Job
Obadiah	Psalms
Jonah	Proverbs
Micah	Ecclesiastes
Nahum	Song of Solomon
Habakkuk	**Major Prophets**
Zephaniah	Isaiah
Haggai	Jeremiah
Zechariah	Lamentations
Malachi	Ezekiel
	Daniel
	Twelve Minor Prophets
	Hosea
	Joel

Table 3: The Names and Sequence of Books in the Hebrew Bible & Christian Old Testament

ROMAN CATHOLIC OT	EASTERN ORTHODOX OT
Pentateuch	**Historical Books**
Genesis	Genesis
Exodus	Exodus
Leviticus	Leviticus
Numbers	Numbers
Deuteronomy	Deuteronomy
Historical Books	Joshua
Joshua	Judges
Judges	Ruth
Ruth	1 Kingdoms (= 1 Samuel)
1 Samuel	2 Kingdoms (=2 Samuel)
2 Samuel	3 Kingdoms (=1 Kings)
1 Kings	4 Kingdoms (=2 Kings)
2 Kings	1 Chronicles
1 Chronicles	2 Chronicles
2 Chronicles	1 Esdras
Ezra (1 Esdras)	2 Esdras
Nehemiah (2 Esdras)	Nehemiah
Tobit	Tobit
Judith	Judith
Esther (with six additions)	Esther (with six additions)
1 Maccabees	1 Maccabees
2 Maccabees	2 Maccabees
Wisdom Books	3 Maccabees
Job	**Poetic and Didactic Books**
Psalms	Psalms (with Ps 151)
Proverbs	Job
Ecclesiastes	Proverbs
Song of Songs	Ecclesiastes
Wisdom of Solomon	Song of Songs
Ecclesiasticus (Sirach)	Wisdom of Solomon
	Wisdom of Sirach

Table 3: The Names and Sequence of Books in the Hebrew Bible & Christian Old Testament

HEBREW BIBLE (TANAK)	PROTESTANT OT
Writings (*Ketuvim*)	Amos
Psalms	Obadiah
Proverbs	Jonah
Job	Micah
Song of Songs	Nahum
Ruth	Habakkuk
Lamentations	Zephaniah
Ecclesiastes	Haggai
Esther	Zechariah
Daniel	Malachi
Ezra & Nehemiah	
1 & 2 Chronicles	

Table 3: The Names and Sequence of Books in the Hebrew Bible & Christian Old Testament[1]

ROMAN CATHOLIC OT	EASTERN ORTHODOX OT
Prophetic Books	**Prophetic Books**
Isaiah	Hosea
Jeremiah	Amos
Lamentations	Micah
Baruch (Ch. 6 = Epistle of Jeremiah)	Joel
Ezekiel	Obadiah
Daniel (with three additions: The Prayer of Azariah and the Song of the Three Young Men, Susanna, and Bel and the Dragon)	Jonah
Hosea	Nahum
Joel	Habakkuk
Amos	Zephaniah
Obadiah	Malachi
Jonah	Isaiah
Micah	Jeremiah
Nahum	Baruch
Habakkuk	Lamentations of Jeremiah
Zephaniah	Epistle of Jeremiah
Haggai	Ezekiel
Zechariah	Daniel (with Prayer of Azariah and the Song of the Three Young Men, Susanna, and Bel and the Dragon)
Malachi	

---

1. The canon lists of the Russian and Oriental Orthodox Churches include mostly the same books, but not always, and they often vary on their order and how they are used in Orthodox churches. The Ethiopian Orthodox Church has the largest Old Testament canon.

Chapter 4

The First Scriptures of the Earliest Christians

There is little doubt that what was at the center of the sacred writings—what would later come to be known as the Old Testament—of the earliest Christian community was the Law and the Prophets and most, if not all, of what the second-century rabbis called the Writings. The number of citations of the majority of the Old Testament books in the New Testament is considerable, even though several of those books—such as Judges, Ruth, Esther, and others—are not quoted or cited and they do not appear to have played much of a role in the formation and ministry of the early churches. The New Testament writers make numerous references to the Law and the Prophets, or Moses and the Prophets (as we see in Matt 7:12; John 1:45; Acts 13:27; 28:23 and Rom 3:21). According to Acts, both the Law and the Prophets were read regularly in the synagogue: "After the reading of the law and the prophets, the officials of the synagogue sent them [Paul and Barnabas] a message, saying, 'Brothers, if you have any word of exhortation for the people, give it'" (13:15 NRSVue). In Luke 4:17, Jesus read "scripture" in the synagogue from the "scroll of the prophet Isaiah" (Isa 61:1–2; compare 58:6).

As we have already seen, there is only one clear reference to a third part of the Jewish Scriptures mentioned in the New Testament: namely, Luke 24:44. The reference to "psalms" is without any qualifications or definite article, suggesting that a collection is in view, though we cannot say definitively that more than "psalms" in general were intended. But we might add that the numerous references in the New Testament to a two-part collection of sacred writings (Law and Prophets) and only one text that refers to a third part made up of psalms suggest that when Luke wrote his Gospel (ca. the middle to late 60s AD) there was no widespread recognition of a three-part biblical canon—though it is likely that many of the books that make up that later third part of the Jewish Scriptures were already in use, incorporated under the heading of the "Law and the Prophets." Those who think that a three-part biblical canon existed before and during the time of Jesus have difficulty explaining why a third part is mentioned in only one text written in the middle to late sixties of the first century.

The popularity and welcome of the Jewish Scriptures in the early churches is undeniable, since all known Christian biblical canons today accept all of the books in them, but the fact that all of the lists of Old Testament Scriptures from churches of the fourth to the sixth centuries *differ* from the Jewish biblical canon also suggests that the Christians' positive attitude toward the books in the Jewish Scriptures was not the only factor in the selection of the Christian Old Testament Scriptures. Even where there was an attempt to reproduce the Jewish Scriptures, sometimes Esther is absent (as in the list offered by Melito, immediately below) or such books as the Epistle of Jeremiah or Baruch are added, as in several of the lists below. At any rate, none of the early church lists are exactly the same as the Jewish Scriptures.

The church father Melito of Sardis (d. 180) was the earliest Christian writer to produce a list of the books that made up the Old Testament Scriptures. He refers to the whole collection of Old Testament Scriptures (omitting Esther and adding the Wisdom of Solomon) as the "Law and the Prophets." Again, this shows that at the end of the second century, a three-part Old Testament canon had not yet been developed either for the Jews or the Christians.

> "Melito to Onesimus his brother, greeting. Since you often desired, in your zeal for the true word, to have extracts from the *Law and the Prophets* concerning the Saviour, and concerning all our faith, and moreover, since you wished to know the accurate facts about the ancient writings, how many they are in number, and what is their order, I have taken pains to do thus, for I know your zeal for the faith and interest in the word, and that in your struggle for eternal salvation you esteem these things more highly than all else in your love towards God. Accordingly when I came to the east and reached the place where these things were preached and done, and learnt accurately the books of the Old Testament, I set down the facts and sent them to you. These are their names: five books of Moses, Genesis, Exodus, Leviticus, Numbers, Deuteronomy, Joshua the son of Nun, Judges, Ruth, four books of Kingdoms, two books of Chronicles, the Psalms of David, the Proverbs of Solomon *and his Wisdom*, Ecclesiastes, the Songs of Songs, Job, the prophets Isaiah, Jeremiah, the Twelve in a single book, Daniel, Ezekiel, Ezra. From these I have made extracts and compiled them in six books." Such are the facts about Melito. (Eusebius, *Ecclesiastical History* 4.26.13, 14, LCL; emphasis added)

The three Jewish sources cited earlier (*Against Apion* 1.37–43, 4 Ezra 14:44–47, and Bava Batra 14b–15a) represent the most important late first- and second-century Jewish traditions about the composition of the Jewish Scriptures. However, Jewish interest in a fixed collection of Scriptures apparently had *no* impact on the writers of the New Testament or the early church fathers. The New Testament itself shows no special interest in limiting the books of the Bible. The New Testament writings and early church fathers do, however, contain many references to noncanonical literature, and they often refer to it explicitly as "Scripture." For instance, Mark 10:19 appears to make use of Sirach 4:1 along with Exodus 20:12–16 and Deuteronomy 5:16–20. Second Timothy 2:19 appears to cite Sirach 17:26 in conjunction with Numbers 16:5. It is also likely that

Paul, in Romans 1:24–32, makes use of Wisdom of Solomon 14:22–31 and in Romans 5:12–21 he apparently employs ideas present in Wisdom of Solomon 2:23–24. The question of Wisdom's canonicity does not appear to concern Paul, but only the theological arguments in it. In 1 Corinthians 2:9, Paul cites as "scripture" either the Ascension of Isaiah 11.34 or a lost Elijah Apocalypse derived from Isaiah 64:3. Jude 14 expressly cites the pseudepigraphic book 1 Enoch (1:9), as previously noted. Second Peter also has parallels with 1 Enoch in 2:4 and 3:6. The author of Hebrews 1:3 makes obvious use of the Wisdom of Solomon 7:25–26, and James 4:5 appears to cite an unknown Scripture.

Yet these uses of (or references to) non-canonical literature in the New Testament did not raise the issue of a biblical canon either for Paul or for others in the New Testament era. The core of the biblical literature for Jews in the first century and later was always the Law of Moses. Although the Gospel writers regularly cited the Psalms in telling the story of Jesus, the Law of Moses still formed the backbone of any "canonical" collection embraced in the first century AD and following—insofar as we can even speak of such a collection at the time—just as it had done among Jews since well before the time of Jesus.

In the Apostolic Fathers, the successors of the earliest Christian community (the label also applies to the collective body of writings they produced), there are a number of even more striking uses of such non-canonical literature. There is no question that the vast majority of the references and quotations in the late-first-century 1 Clement refer to the canonical literature of the Old Testament (along with a few references to some New Testament literature and also to apocryphal books). Notice, for example, that Clement quoted Sirach 2:11 in 1 Clement 60.1, the Wisdom of Solomon 12:10 in 1 Clement 7.5, and Wisdom of Solomon 12:12 in 1 Clement 27.5, with related allusions in 3:4 and 7:5. In 1 Clement 55.4–6, both Judith 8 and Esther 7 and 4:16 are cited in the same way—that is, *as Scripture*. Second Clement also has a number of quotations from otherwise unknown, non-canonical writings (see 11.2–4, 11.7, and 13.2) as well as a quote from Tobit 16:4. The Epistle of Barnabas includes quotations from Wisdom of Solomon (in 20:2), 1 Enoch (4:3; 16:5), 4 Ezra (12:1) and other quotations from unknown "scripture" as in 7.3, 8 and 10.7. The Didache (ca. AD 70–90), which was itself added to some canonical lists but finally excluded by Athanasius in the fourth century, makes use of Wisdom of Solomon in 5.2 and 10.3 as well as an unknown quotation in 1.6. Polycarp cites Tobit in his Martyrdom 1.6.

Further examples continue to demonstrate the blurred distinctions between canonical and noncanonical writings—and, ironically, the ways in which some of the sources now considered noncanonical helped to shape the canons themselves. Justin Martyr, in his *Dialogue with Trypho* (ca. 160), appears to refer to the Ascension of Isaiah (see 120.5), but ultimately makes his argument on the basis of the books accepted as canonical by the Jews. Like Melito, he refers to

Genesis, Exodus, Leviticus, the Kingdoms (1–2 Kings), the Psalms, Proverbs, and also quotes Job. He names the prophets Isaiah, Jeremiah, Ezekiel, and Daniel, as well as the Twelve Minor Prophets and Esdras (see *Dialogue with Trypho* 72.1). He also quotes, without referring to them by name, Numbers, Deuteronomy, and 2 Chronicles. This does not necessarily imply a fixed biblical canon, since in the *Dialogue* he is speaking to specific situations, but it is instructive on the question of the commonly accepted literature among Christians in the middle of the second century. Justin is nevertheless silent about Ecclesiastes, Song of Songs, and Esther, which may reflect the continuing doubts that existed about these books in the Jewish community and possibly also the Christian community. Later Christians may have avoided using these writings because they did not address the special concerns of their Christian community (Christ and his salvation) unless they allegorized or spiritualized the texts. Some Bible scholars have suggested that the mere citation of noncanonical texts does not necessarily mean that they were received as Scripture. That, of course, is correct, but the manner and function of the quotations reveals the significant place that those extra writings had in the minds of those who used them. All of this does not necessarily suggest that the apocryphal and pseudepigraphic books were used as much in early Christianity as most of the Old Testament books, but that literature nevertheless impacted the early church's theology and development.

Several of the themes of the New Testament have their roots in the apocryphal and pseudepigraphic literature. This is further confirmed by the use of the additions to biblical books that appear in the Septuagint (LXX) but were not accepted by the Jews in the second century. For example, Clement of Alexandria (ca. AD 180) and Origen (early third century) cited two of the Additions to Daniel: Susanna and Bel and the Dragon. Irenaeus, Tertullian, and Origen also cited and accepted the apocryphal portions of the LXX. The Additions to Esther, mentioned in Josephus, are regarded as Scripture by Clement of Rome, Clement of Alexandria, and Origen. The Prayer of Manasseh is cited in the Syriac Didascalia from the third century AD and in the Apostolic Constitutions and Canons (2.22.12–14). Psalm 151 as well as 1–4 Maccabees are included in the fifth century Codex Alexandrinus (see the list below). Interestingly, the only explicit quotation in the Shepherd of Hermas (ca. 140–150), the visions of which rival the book of Revelation, is of the lost Eldad and Modad (Shepherd of Hermas, Vision 2, 3, 4; for a background of these names, see Num 11:26). An examination of the Apostolic Fathers (ca. AD 90–140) shows conclusively that the writers often appealed to the apocryphal and pseudepigraphic literature in much the same way that they appealed to the Scriptures of the Hebrew Bible. There are four very important codices from the fourth and fifth centuries that also support this conclusion. They include: (1) Codex Sinaiticus (designated codex "aleph" [א]; ca. middle to late fourth century), which includes, along with the New Testament collection of Scriptures, an Old Testament collection that incorporates Tobit, Judith, Wisdom of Solomon, Sirach (Ecclesiasticus) and 1 and 4 Maccabees; (2) Codex Vaticanus (designated codex B; mid-fourth century), which includes Baruch, the Epistle of Jeremiah, Wisdom of Solomon, Ecclesiasticus (Sirach), Judith, and Tobit, but not the Maccabees; (3) Codex Alexandrinus (designated codex A; fifth century), which includes the Apocrypha, Psalms of Solomon, and 3 and 4 Maccabees (these additional books are included along with the other books of the Old Testament and without any distinction being made); and (4) Codex Ephraemi Syri Rescriptus (designated codex C; a fifth-century manuscript, containing some 209 leaves, of which 64 are fragments of portions of the OT). Among the portions found here are Sirach, the Prologue to Sirach, and Wisdom. Not all of the Old Testament books are in it, but due to its fragmentary nature, it is difficult to be dogmatic about the full contents of the manuscript.

The evidence above assures us that a *fixed* biblical canon in the early churches *began* to develop during the fourth century. Of the ancient codex (or book) manuscripts containing Old Testament books (there are twenty-four of these that survive antiquity), the majority contain the Psalter (the book of Psalms). Several later codex manuscripts combine books in sequences that we would find strange today. For example, Matthew is joined with Acts, which appears reasonable in a Christian manuscript, but some manuscripts of canonical books also circulated with noncanonical books. The Song of Songs is bound together with the Apology of Aristides and the Acta Pauli (Acts of Paul) in Greek. The Song of Songs and Lamentations in Coptic are combined with Sirach (Ecclesiasticus) in Greek and Coptic. Such examples illustrate that the Old Testament canon was not fixed before or even during the fourth century.

Below are some of the best known ancient lists of the church's Old Testament Scriptures. I invite readers to look at them carefully, before turning to consider the development of the New Testament in the next chapter, to see which books and sequences of books they reflect. You will see many parallels in what I call the "core" books, as well as some variation in terms of what other apocryphal or deuterocanonical books are also included, but also the absence of Esther in various lists. The actual footnotes for each of the tables will appear at the end of the chapter.

Table 4: Old Testament Catalogues of Scriptures

Table 4A. Old Testament Lists from the Eastern Churches[1]

Melito[2]	Origen[4]	Laodicea Council, Canon 60[6]	Athanasius[7]	Cyril[8]
Gen	Gen	Gen	Gen	Gen
Exod	Exod	Exod	Exod	Exod
Lev	Lev	Num	Lev	Lev
Num	Num	Lev	Num	Num
Deut	Deut	Deut	Deut	Deut
Josh	Josh	Josh	Josh	Josh
Judg	Judg/Ruth	Judg	Judg	Judg/Ruth
Ruth	1–2 Kgdms	Ruth	Ruth	1–2 Kgdms
1–4 Kgdms	3–4 Kgdms	Esther	1–2 Kgdms	3–4 Kgdms
1–2 Chr	1–2 Chr	1–4 Kgdms	3–4 Kgdms	1–2 Chr
Pss	1–2 Esdras	1–2 Chr	1–2 Chr	1–2 Esdras
Prov	Pss	1–2 Esdras	1–2 Esdras	Esther
Eccl	Prov	Pss	Pss	Job
Song	Eccl	Prov	Prov	Pss
Job	Song	Eccl	Eccl	Prov
Isa	Isa	Song	Song	Eccl
Jer	Jer/Lam/Ep Jer	Job	Job	Song
Dan	(Twelve omitted)[5]	Twelve	Twelve	Twelve
Esdras	Dan	Isa	Isa	Isa
(Esther omitted)[3]	Ezek	Jer	Jer/Bar/Lam/ Ep Jer	Jer/Lam/ Ep Jer/Bar
	Job	Baruch	Ezek	Ezek
	Esther	Lamentations	Dan	Dan
		Ep Jer		
		Ezekiel		
		Daniel		

Table 4B. Old Testament Lists from the Eastern Churches

Epiphanius[9]	Epiphanius[10]	Epiphanius[11]	Gregory[12]	Amphilochius[13]
Gen	Gen	Gen	Gen	Gen
Exod	Exod	Exod	Exod	Exod
Lev	Lev	Lev	Lev	Lev
Num	Num	Num	Num	Num
Deut	Deut	Deut	Deut	Deut
Josh	Job	Josh	Josh	Josh
Judg	Pss	Job	Judg/Ruth	Judg
Ruth	Prov	Judg	1–4 Kgs	Ruth
Job	Eccl	Ruth	1–2 Chr	1–4 Kgs
Pss	Song	Pss	1–2 Esd	1–2 Chr
Prov	Josh	1 Chr	Job	1–2 Esd
Eccl	Judg/Ruth	2 Chr	Pss	Job
1 Kgdms	1–2 Chr	1 Kgdms	Eccl	Pss
2 Kgdms	1–2 Kgdms	2 Kgdms	Song	Prov
3 Kgdms	3–4 Kgdms	3 Kgdms	Prov	Eccl
4 Kgdms	Twelve	4 Kgdms	Twelve	Song
1 Chr	Isa	Prov	Isa	Twelve
2 Chr	Jer	Eccl	Jer	Isa
Twelve	Ezek	Song	Ezek	Jer
Isa	Dan	Twelve	Dan	Ezek
Jer/Lam/ Ep Jer/Bar	1–2 Esd	Isa		Dan
Ezek	Esther	Jer		Esther
Dan		Ezek		
1 Esd		Dan		
2 Esd		1 Esd		
		2 Esd		
		Esther		

Table 4C. Old Testament Collections from the Western Churches

Hilary[14]	Jerome[15]	Jerome[16]	Rufinus[17]	Augustine[18]	Carthage[19]
5 Moses	Gen	Gen	Gen	Gen	Gen
	Exod	Exod	Exod	Exod	Exod
	Lev	Lev	Lev	Lev	Lev
	Num	Num	Num	Num	Num
	Deut	Deut	Deut	Deut	Deut
	Job	Josh	Josh	Josh	Josh
Josh	Josh	Judg/Ruth	Judg/Ruth	Judg	Judg
Judg/Ruth	Judg	1–2 Kgdms	1–2 Kgdms	Ruth	Ruth
1–2 Kgdms	Ruth	3–4 Kgdms	3–4 Kgdms	1–4 Kgdms	1–4 Kgdms
3–4 Kgdms	Sam	Isa	1–2 Chr	1–2 Chr	1–2 Chr
1–2 Chr	3–4 Kgdms	Jer	1–2 Esd	Job	Job
1–2 Esd	Twelve	Ezek	Esther	Tobit	Pss
Pss	Isa	Twelve	Isa	Esther	1–5 Sol
Prov	Jer	Job	Jer	Judith	Twelve
Eccl	Ezek	Pss	Ezek	1–2 Macc	Isa
Song	Dan	Prov	Twelve	1–2 Esd	Jer
Twelve	Pss	Eccl	Job	Pss	Ezek
Isa	Song	Song	Pss	Prov	Dan
Jer/Lam/ Ep Jer	Wis	Dan	Prov	Song	Tobit
Dan	Esther	1–2 Chr	Eccl	Eccl	Judith
Ezek	1–2 Chr	1–2 Esd	Song	Wisdom	Esther
Job	Ezra-Neh	Esther		Sirach	1–2 Esd
Esther				Twelve	1–2 Macc
(Tobit)				Isa	
(Judith)				Jer	
				Dan	
				Ezek	

Table 4D. Important Biblical Manuscripts with Old Testament Collections

Vaticanus (B) (4th cent.) ... [20]	Sinaiticus (ℵ) (4th cent.) ...	Alexandrinus (A) (5th cent.)
Genesis	Genesis ...	Genesis
Exodus	...	Exodus
Leviticus	...	Leviticus
	Numbers ...	Numbers
Deuteronomy		Deuteronomy
Joshua	...	Joshua
Judges	...	Judges
Ruth	...	Ruth
1–4 Kings	...	1–4 Kings
1–2 Chronicles	1 Chronicles ...	1–2 Chronicles
1–2 Esdras	... 2 Esdras	Hosea
Psalms ...	Esther	Amos
Proverbs	Tobit	Micah
Ecclesiastes	Judith ...	Joel
Song of Solomon	1–4 Maccabees	Obadiah
Job	Isaiah	Jonah
Wisdom	Jeremiah	Nahum
Sirach	Lamentations ...	Habakkuk
Esther	Joel	Zephaniah
Judith	Obadiah	Haggai
Tobit	Jonah	Zechariah
Hosea	Nahum	Malachi
Amos	Habakkuk	Isaiah
Micah	Zephaniah	Jeremiah
Joel	Haggai	Baruch
Obadiah	Zechariah	Lamentations
Jonah	Malachi	Epistle of Jeremiah
Nahum	Psalms	Ezekiel
Habakkuk	Proverbs	Daniel
Zephaniah	Ecclesiastes	Esther

Table 4D. Important Biblical Manuscripts with Old Testament Collections (cont'd)

Vaticanus (B) (4th cent.)...	Sinaiticus (ℵ) (4th cent.)...	Alexandrinus (A) (5th cent.)
Haggai	Song of Solomon	Tobit
Zechariah	Wisdom	Judith
Malachi	Sirach	1–2 Esdras
Isaiah	Job	1–4 Maccabees
Jeremiah		Psalms[21]
Baruch		Psalm 151[22]
Lamentations		Job
Epistle of Jeremiah		Proverbs
Ezekiel		Song of Solomon
Daniel		Wisdom
		Sirach

Table Notes

1. Note: Readers will observe considerable overlap in these canon lists and manuscript lists and also some differences. It is clear from them that there was considerable agreement on most of the books in the Old Testament from the fourth century on, but also differences over some of the deuterocanonical books.

2. Eusebius, *Ecclesiastical History* 4.26.14 (ca. 320–25, Caesarea, Palestine).

3. Books in parentheses are omitted from this source.

4. Eusebius, *Ecclesiastical History* 6.25.2 (ca. 320–25, Caesarea, Palestine).

5. Books in parentheses are omitted from this source.

6. This list (ca. 360) is preserved in Swete (1989, pp. 209).

7. Athanasius, *Festal Letter* 39.4 (ca. 367, Alexandria, Egypt).

8. Cyril of Jerusalem, *Catech.* 4.35 (ca. 394, Bethlehem, Palestine).

9. *Against Heresy* 1.1.8 (ca. 374–77, Salamis, Western Syria).

10. *On Weights and Measures* 4 (ca. 374–77, Salamis, Western Syria).

11. *On Weights and Measures* 23 (ca. 374–77, Salamis, Western Syria).

12. Gregory of Nazianzus, *Carm.* 1.12.5 (ca. 390, Cappadocia, Asia Minor).

13. Amphilochius, *Iambi ad Seleucum* 2.51–88 (ca. 396, Iconium, Asia Minor).

14. Hilary, *Prolog. in Lib. Ps.* 15 (ca. 350–65, Poitiers).

15. Jerome, *Ep.* 53.8 (ca. 394 Bethlehem, Palestine).

16. Jerome, *Praef. in Lib. Sam. et Mal.* (ca. 394 Bethlehem, Palestine).

17. Rufinus, *Comm. in Symb. Apost.* 35 (ca. 404, Rome Italy).

18. Augustine, *De Doct. Christ.* 2.13 (ca. 395, Hippo Regius, North Africa).

19. Council of Carthage (397 AD), canon 26; it is likely that its "five books of Solomon" (noted here as "1–5 Sol.") = Prov, Eccl, Song, Sir, and Wis, but this is uncertain.

20. The "…" marks indicate losses or omissions in the manuscript.

21. Inserted before the Psalms is a letter of Athanasius to Marcellinus about the Psalter and a summary of the contents of the Psalms by Eusebius.

22. After the Psalms, there are a number of canticles extracted from other parts of the Bible.

Chapter 5

How the New Testament Came to Be

The Status of Scripture in the Early Church

If it can be said that considerable complexity attended the origin and development of the Christian Old Testament, we can also say the same with regard to the New Testament. As in the case of the formation of the Old Testament, no ancient traditions exist that tell us about the formation of the New Testament Scriptures. We do have some hints at how it all developed, however, and our discussion of those hints will follow.

The early churches from their beginning were accustomed to the notion of sacred Scripture, the authority of which was indisputable, even if we are unsure of the full parameters of that collection of writings. As we have seen, there is no convincing evidence that the early church was born with a fixed biblical canon in its hands, but the precedent of a sacred Scripture was already well established in the Jewish community long before the birth of Jesus. Again, at that time, Scripture was generally acknowledged to be the "Law and the Prophets" or simply the "Law." While it is not clear what books comprised those Scriptures, as we have already shown, the early Christians assumed that the way and will of God were communicated through them. As the church grew, it also saw great value in having its own collection of sacred Scriptures along with those that it received from its Jewish heritage. Over time, the church came to believe that the word and will of God were communicated not only in its Old Testament Scriptures, but also in several comparatively new and distinctly Christian writings. The Christians added to their sacred collection such Christian literature that they believed was inspired by God and came from the apostolic community.

The early followers of Jesus did not make a conscious effort to produce their own written Scriptures, but rather they chose to preserve those Christian writings that were helpful to them in advancing their mission. Before long, these writings were being read in churches during their worship services and used in their catechetical instruction and proclamation. With only two possible exceptions, nothing in the New Testament writings suggests that the writers believed they were writing anything equivalent to Holy Scripture. Only the book of Revelation comes close to claiming divine inspiration, the essential ingredient of Scripture, by claiming that anyone who adds to or takes away from "the words of the prophecy of this book" will face divine judgment (22:18–19). The second and more distant possibility is found in 1 Corinthians 7:40, where Paul claims to have the Holy Spirit in the advice that he advances, but claiming scriptural, even canonical, authority *for himself* may not have been what he had in mind. He certainly does not always write like he was conscious of writing Scripture; rather, his priority is on giving advice and admonitions that he believes are appropriate for Christian belief and behavior. He consciously distinguishes what he has to say, however, from what Jesus had said (see 1 Cor 7:8–12). He even says that he does not have a word from the Lord on the issue he is dealing with in 1 Corinthians 7:25, but thinks he has the Spirit on the matter. After boasting about his achievements in 2 Corinthians 11:1, he calls what he is about to say "foolishness" and after his boasting in 11:2–15, he clarifies that what he is saying is not according to the Lord (*kata kyrion*), but rather it is "according to the flesh" (*kata sarka*) 2 Corinthians 11:16–17. When Paul is speaking in anger against the Judaizers who are turning his converts away, he says angrily that he wishes they would castrate themselves (Gal 5:12). In 1 Corinthians 1:10–13, after speaking angrily against the Corinthian Christians he says that he is glad that he baptized none of them except Crispus and Gaius, but then corrects himself saying that he did baptize the household of Stephanus. It does not appear that he is consciously writing sacred Scripture at that time. Later, the emerging churches saw the practical value of Paul's writings and read his writings in the churches, and they began to call it later began to those writings "Scripture." That was a later development in the churches.

While most biblical scholars believe that all or most of the books of the New Testament were written in the first century AD, many locate the origin and growth of the New Testament canon in the second century, allowing only for minor modifications and adjustments in its subsequent development. They claim that second-century heresies led the church to define its New Testament canon, but when we examine this position more closely, there is no evidence that discussions about the shape or scope of the New Testament ever took place at that time. I will examine that assumption below, but will begin with the logical starting point for the origins of the New Testament writings: Jesus himself.

The Earliest New Testament Canon

Almost immediately after the death and resurrection of Jesus, stories about his life, teachings, actions, death, and resurrection were being circulated in the oral traditions of the early churches. Some of those stories no doubt began during his ministry as his fame grew in Galilee and subsequently in Judea. Within thirty to sixty years, some of those traditions were put into writing along with letters and other texts that reflected on the significance of Jesus for Christian faith. By the middle of the second century, the writings that told the story of Jesus were called "Gospels"; they were read alongside the Scriptures that the church had inherited from their Jewish siblings, what they would later call the Old Testament books.

Other, more personal types of early Christian literature arose in other contexts to address different challenges. Beginning around AD 48–49, some early Christian teachers and missionaries reflected in letters or "epistles" on what God had done in the life, death, and resurrection of Jesus, and the implications of these acts for Christian conduct and mission. The apostle Paul wrote a number of these letters to churches that he had established on his missionary journeys, or in communities that he planned to visit (Romans, 1 and 2 Corinthians, Galatians, Ephesians, Philippians, Colossians, 1 and 2 Thessalonians) or to individuals, as noted earlier (1 and 2 Timothy, Titus, and Philemon). Other writers also produced letters for other Christian communities, and several of these writings too were later included in the New Testament. These letters eventually became known as the General or Catholic Epistles (James, 1–2 Peter, 1–3 John, and Jude). This new and personal way of communicating divine truth was so widely accepted in churches that many other such letters were later produced in similar fashion, including Clement's letter to the Corinthians (1 Clement), the Epistle of Barnabas, and the Letters of Ignatius.

Christian literature was not limited to Gospels and Epistles. The evangelist we know as Luke originally wrote his story of the origins of the Christian faith in two volumes, the first being the Gospel of Luke and the second, the book of Acts. Acts was added because it showed the origin and development of the early church, forming a bridge between the Gospels and the Epistles that were circulating among Christians. Acts was separated from the Gospel of Luke early on (perhaps in the late first century?) and later often circulated as an introduction to the General or Catholic Epistles; only later was Acts placed before the letters of Paul in the New Testament. An anonymous lengthy sermon (Hebrews) was written to encourage Jewish Christians who were facing opposition and considering a departure from their Christian faith and returning to their earlier roots in Judaism. Finally, a book of revelations or visionary messages, known as the Apocalypse of John or, more commonly, the book of Revelation, was added to the literature that was eventually received into what we now call the New Testament. These writings circulated individually at first, but by the end of the first century some of the letters of Paul were being circulated together as an epistolary canon in the making.

The origin of the New Testament, however, rightly begins with the story of Jesus, who was acknowledged as the Lord of the church and its message (Rom 10:9; Matt 28:19–20). What Jesus said and did was authoritative for the early Christians, and his authority was never transferred to any other. The literature that comprises the New Testament largely focuses on Jesus, his significance, and the implications in daily life and ministry for what it means to follow him. The literature of the New Testament points us not to itself, but to Jesus who is the final authority for Christian faith (Matt 28:19).

Initially, there was no great interest in developing a Christian set of Scriptures, since there was a strong and widespread belief that Jesus was going to return soon and establish his kingdom on earth (Acts 1:6–8; 1 Thess 1:9–10, 2:19–20; Rev 22:10–11, 20–21). For the early Christians, there was already an authoritative collection of Scriptures that testified to Jesus significance and activity; namely, their First Testament of Scriptures, later called their Old Testament (1 Cor 15:3–9), although they did not identify them by that title at first. The early church's most urgent priority was the proclamation of its risen Lord. The hope of his imminent return was so immediate that there was no perceived need for another collection of Scriptures for the church.

So why were the additional writings produced? First, as time went on and the church expanded outside of the land of Israel, those who shared the stories of Jesus could not be in all of the places where the gospel story was being shared. As a result, some considered it necessary to communicate the story of Jesus in writing for those who could not hear it orally by the earliest witnesses to the story. Likewise, many of the earliest followers of Jesus paid the ultimate sacrifice through martyrdom for their faithfulness in their witness to this same story, so it became especially and increasingly necessary to put the story in writing. Collections of the sayings and deeds of Jesus likely were circulating in the land of Israel even before the death of Jesus, and soon these were collected and variously assembled in manuscripts that were later welcomed and shared in the churches. By the middle of the second century at the latest, the Gospels were being read in churches alongside many of the Old Testament Scriptures. For example, around the middle of the second century, the early church teacher and apologist Justin Martyr writes: "On the day called Sunday there is a meeting in one place of those who live in cities or the country, and the memoirs of the apostles [Gospels] or the writings of the prophets [Old Testament writings] are read as long as time permits" (*First Apology* 67.3).

The apostle Paul was actively involved in founding churches in the Mediterranean world, and he often wrote letters in lieu of a visit. Again, when he wrote letters to churches, he was not consciously aware that he was writing Scripture, but because of their enduring theological and practical value for Christian faith and conduct, his letters were collected, copied, and circulated among many more churches and used in teaching the truth of the Christian proclamation there. Paul knew how important it was for those who received his letters to pass them along, and he may have been the first instigator for an early circulation of his letters; we have evidence of this practice in Colossians 4:16. Paul's letters likely became the model for the letters to seven churches that we see preserved in Revelation 2–3, as well as in the early second century church father, Ignatius of Antioch, who, like Paul, also wrote epistles to churches for whom he was concerned.

By the second century, the Gospels, and especially the Gospel of Matthew (the most popular Gospel at the time) and to a lesser extent the Gospel of John, were circulating in many churches in the Mediterranean world and by the middle of the second century they were being read alongside the Old Testament Scriptures in churches and sometimes in place of them (see Justin, *First Apology* 64–67). As they contained the sayings and deeds attributed to Jesus, the Gospels had been welcomed in the churches and read in worship and instruction, *with the goal of aiding in advancing the church's mission*. As Christian writings began to be used *like* Scripture (no later than the middle of the second century), it was not long before they were actually *called* "Scripture," and by the end of the second century this became commonplace. The Gospels and several letters of Paul were among the first Christian writings to be called "scripture"; over the next two centuries, other Christian writings also received such a scriptural recognition in various churches, though not all at the same time.

By the end of the second century AD, as we saw in Melito of Sardis, several of the assembled Christian writings were *beginning* to be called a "New Testament" and the first Scriptures that Christians inherited from the Jews were beginning to be called an "Old Testament." It took several centuries for these designations to find regular use by a majority of Christians; in the fourth century, these terms still had to be explained in many churches. But as the Christian writings were increasingly recognized as Scripture, they began to be placed in collections along with other texts already accepted as sacred—the Old Testament writings—and eventually *fixed* together, not only in collections of Christian Scriptures but also in large books (codices) that contained all of the Scriptures of the Christian Bible.

We should be careful not to confuse this process of assembly and recognition with the ease of access to the Scriptures that many Christians enjoy today. Copying of ancient manuscripts was all done by hand and very slowly. Because of the considerable expense of the materials as well as the cost of paying copiers, many of the early manuscripts were sometimes produced on used materials (the term is "palimpsests") that were washed and previous writing rubbed out. The scribes or copiers who reproduced the manuscripts were literate and well-intentioned, but not always skilled; in many cases the copiers were amateurs, doing the best they could for churches anxious to have their own copies of these new collections of Christian Scriptures. We should also note that because of the expense of producing such manuscripts, very few churches would have had all of the Old Testament or New Testament books. As we will say again later, because of the limited technology for producing codices in the first two centuries, it was not possible to put all of the books of the New Testament or the Old Testament in one volume. Of the 127 papyrus manuscripts that currently exist—these are the earliest manuscripts of the New Testament writings, only fourteen of them have more than one book! Some collections had more than others, but *none* of the earliest biblical manuscripts had all of the books of the New Testament and some had non-New Testament books in them. Combining multiple books in one collection only became possible in the fourth century, so that is when we begin to see larger collections of the church's Scriptures circulating in more complete units, but even then most churches did not have all of the biblical books.

Some of the writings that were earlier included in collections of Christian Scriptures were eventually deleted or dropped from circulation because they were either no longer considered relevant to the life and ministry of the emerging churches, or they were no longer considered to be reliable witnesses to the story of Jesus. Some of them were even considered heretical (e.g., the Gospel of Peter), that is, they departed from the faith that had been handed on in the churches from the very beginning. This process of adding and deleting books from the various collections took centuries and did not take place in all churches at the same time. When church councils began to list the books that could be trusted and read in the churches' worship and instruction classes (Laodicea in 360–363, Hippo in 393, and Carthage in 397), they were essentially reflecting the practice of churches in their regions, rather than making a "top-down" decision about them for all churches.

Unfortunately, there is no known *discussion* of a fixed collection (or canon) of Christian Scriptures before the fourth century AD. However, it is likely that Origen in the third century acknowledged a specific collection, but it was his own and not a widely acknowledged biblical canon in churches, and the next evidence comes from Eusebius in the fourth century. Before that, there was widespread agreement on the scriptural status of several of the New Testament books (especially the Gospels and some of the letters of Paul), but for several centuries there was no universal agreement on all of the books. Some popular books, such as the Gospel of Peter, the Shepherd of Hermas, and the Epistle of Barnabas, were initially given a scriptural status in some churches; but by the fourth and fifth centuries, many churches expressed doubts about them. Even writings that were finally included in the church's New Testament were initially disputed in some churches in the early part of the fourth century (namely, Hebrews, James, 2 Peter, 2–3 John, Jude, and Revelation), but eventually were more widely accepted.

In some instances, the process of canonical decision-making was closely linked to other questions about life and liturgy in the church. In the fourth century, for example, a controversy arose over when to celebrate Easter. The church father Athanasius of Alexandria was designated to send out an annual letter that informed churches of the time to celebrate this important date. Often these letters also included other matters deemed relevant and important for the churches that received them. In his *Thirty-Ninth Festal Letter* of 367, Athanasius listed for the first time all of the twenty-seven books in the New Testament, and these books were commended for reading in the churches. This same list was affirmed by the highly influential church father Augustine, and ratified again at the church councils of Rome (392), Hippo (393), and Carthage (397 and 419). This does not mean that all churches agreed at that time. As late as the fourth and fifth centuries, noncanonical Christian writings such as the Didache, the Epistle of Barnabas, 1 and 2 Clement, and the Shepherd of Hermas continued to be read in some churches and appeared in various collections of sacred books and catalogues (see the various lists of New Testament books in Table 5 in chapter 5). More copies of the Shepherd of Hermas have survived antiquity than any of those of the New Testament books except for the Gospels of Matthew and John, reflecting the early popularity of this book. Many other nonbiblical books remained similarly popular for centuries, but generally the books that were most popular among the early Christians were those we know as the New Testament writings, especially the Gospels and letters attributed to Paul.

The first step in the process of canon formation, then, began with the recognition of the *usefulness* of the Christian writings in worship, instruction, and advancing the mission of the church. The next step toward canon formation of Christian writings was their recognition *as Scripture*. The final step took place in the *selection* or *refinement* process in which some Christian writings were affirmed as worthy of being read in the churches, while others were eliminated from most collections of Christian Scriptures. An important and logical feature in this canon formation process has to do with the theological agreements in the majority of churches in the fourth century. As we have seen, it would be difficult for churches to agree on the formation of their biblical canon until there was at least some agreement on what it was that they believed about Jesus. It took centuries to form widespread agreement on the essence of the Christian faith and what in general could be called "Christian."

What Historical Factors Led to the Closing of the New Testament Canon?

What circumstances led the churches to make decisions about which books to include in the New Testament? There are several social and historical factors that likely contributed to the decisions the ancient churches made about the scope of their Bibles. We will examine a few of them here.

The Burning of Christian Scriptures

During the early fourth-century persecutions (303–313) under Emperor Diocletian, Christians were forced under penalty of torture and death to hand over their sacred texts to local governmental authorities to be burned. Often at their own peril, local churches had to choose which books to save and hide, and which they would hand over to the authorities. Those books that were of less value to the local churches are more likely those that were surrendered. The churches, as one would expect, did not all choose the same books to turn over—even this unpleasant situation reflects urgent decisions about canon formation—but they did make choices. No doubt many copies of the most favored books, both canonical and noncanonical, perished during this search-and-destroy campaign against the Christians.

The following example of Roman attempts to destroy Christian Scriptures occurred in Alexandria, Egypt, in May of AD 303 and illustrates what took place throughout the empire.

> In the eighth and seventh consulships of Diocletian and Maximian, 19th May, from the records of Munatius Felix, high priest of the province for life, mayor of the colony of Cirta, arrived at the house where the Christians used to meet. The mayor said to Paul the bishop: "Bring out the writings of the law and anything else you have here, according to the order, so that you may obey the command."
>
> The Bishop: "The readers have the scriptures, but we will give what we have here."
>
> The Mayor: "Point out the readers or send for them."
>
> The Bishop: "You all know them."
>
> The Mayor: "We do not know them."
>
> The Bishop: "The municipal office knows them, that is, the clerks Edusius and Junius."
>
> The Mayor: "Leaving over the matter of the readers, whom the office will point out, produce what you have."
>
> [After this comes an inventory of various items discovered in the church produced in the presence of church leaders and three clergy. The story then resumes.]
>
> The Mayor: "Bring out what you have."
>
> Silvanus and Carosus (two of the subdeacons): "We have thrown out everything that was here."
>
> The Mayor: "Your answer is entered on the record."
>
> After some empty cupboards have been found in the library, Silvanus then produced a silver box and a silver lamp, which he said he had found behind a barrel.
>
> Victor (the mayor's clerk): "You would have been a dead man if you hadn't found them."
>
> The Mayor: "Look more carefully, in case there is anything left here."

Silvanus: "There is nothing left. We have thrown everything out."

And when the dining-room was opened, there were found there four bins and six barrels.

The Mayor: "Bring out the scripture that you have so that we can obey the orders and command of the emperors."

Catullinus (another subdeacon) produced one very large volume.

The Mayor: "Why have you given one volume only? Produce the scriptures that you have."

Marcuclius and Catullinus (two subdeacons): "We haven't any more, because we are subdeacons; the readers have the books."

The Mayor: "If you don't know where they live, tell me their names."

Marcuclius and Catullinus: "We are not traitors: here we are, order us to be killed."

The Mayor: "Put them under arrest."

They apparently weakened so far as to reveal one reader, for the mayor now moved on to the house of Eugenius, who produced four books.

The mayor now turned on the other two subdeacons, Silvanus and Carosus.

The Mayor: "Show me the other readers."

Silvanus and Carosus: "The bishop has already said that Edusius and Junius the clerks know them all: they will show you the way to their houses."

Edusius and Junius: "We will show them, sir."

The mayor went on to visit the six remaining readers. Four produced their books without demur. One declared he had none, and the mayor was content with entering his statement of the record. The last was out, but his wife produced his books; the mayor had the house searched by the public slave to make sure that none had been overlooked. This task over, he addressed the subdeacons: "If there has been any omission, the responsibility is yours." (*Gesta apud Zenophilum* XXVI in Stevenson, pp. 287–89)

Eusebius also describes in detail the burning of Christian sacred books and notes especially the martyrs at Nicomedia who refused to turn over their books to the authorities. He writes:

All things in truth were fulfilled in our day, when we saw with our very eyes the houses of prayer cast down to their foundations from top to bottom, and the inspired and sacred Scriptures committed to the flames in the midst of the market-places, and the pastors of the churches, some shamefully hiding themselves here and there, while others were ignominiously captured and made a mockery by their enemies; when also, according to another prophetic word, He poureth contempt upon princes, and causeth them to wander in the waste, where there is no way. . . .

It was the nineteenth year of the reign of Diocletian, and the month Dystrus, or March, as the Romans would call it, in which, as the festival of the Savior's Passion was coming on, an imperial letter was everywhere promulgated, ordering the razing of the churches to the ground and the destruction by fire of the Scriptures, and proclaiming that those who held high positions would lose all civil rights, while those in households, if they persisted in their profession of Christianity, would be deprived of their liberty. Such was the first document against us. But not long afterwards we were further visited with other letters, and in them the order was given that the presidents of the churches should all, in every place, be first committed to prison, and then afterwards compelled by every kind of device to sacrifice. (*Ecclesiastical History* 8.2.1, 4–5, LCL)

Those who handed over their sacred books were often called *traditores* ("traitors") by other Christians, who despised them for their betrayal of the church's sacred Scriptures. A group of Christians called the Donatists condemned all *traditores* among the clergy as those who had committed a sacrilegious act worthy of damnation in an everlasting fire because they sought "to destroy the testaments and divine commands of Almighty God and our Lord Jesus Christ." Christians began to call those who gave their lives as martyrs to protect their sacred books *confessors*; their story is recorded in *Acta Saturnini* (XVIII, col. 701). With the decree of Constantine (313), the persecutions ceased and the church had to face a new challenge: how to deal with those clergy who, under threat of death, "lapsed" and/or surrendered their sacred Scriptures.

Again, however urgent and unpleasant these decisions were, it is vital to remember that even (or perhaps especially) these life-threatening choices about canon—which books to surrender and which ones to risk keeping—were thoroughly integrated with choices about faith. To protect texts that Rome deemed not sacred but illegal was to commit treason against the empire and its emperor; to give up the texts was to betray the church and one's faith in Christ as Lord. The problem of deciding which books could be handed over to the authorities *without* incurring the charge of being a traitor was evidently settled by many churches at least by the time the persecutions broke out in the year 303. But as we have already said, churches did not agree completely on these matters and the decisions about which books to hand over to the authorities were no doubt determined by *individual* churches, not by church councils.

Constantine's Request for Fifty Copies of the Church's Scriptures

After the conversion of Constantine and the cessation of the persecutions of the church, Constantine requested from Eusebius in Caesarea that he produce fifty copies of the church's Scriptures for the churches in the "New Rome," Constantinople. Once completed, these copies would doubtless have had an influence on the churches of that region, and possibly an even more widespread impact given Eusebius's influence as a teacher and church leader among the churches in the east as well as Constantine's influence as Roman emperor. Some scholars think that the fourth-century and later *uncial* manuscripts (a style of manuscript written completely in capital letters) that contain both the Old and New Testaments may reflect these very influences—in other words, that they represent the kind of manuscripts that Constantine requested that Eusebius produce. It is likely that two manuscripts—namely, Codices Vaticanus and Sinaiticus—reflect the tradition of Scripture collections that Eusebius produced in 334–336. Eusebius tells the story of the fifty copies as follows:

> Ever careful for the welfare of the churches of God, the emperor [Constantine] addressed me personally in a letter on the means of providing copies of the inspired oracles [sacred scriptures], and also on the subject of the most holy feast of Easter. For I had myself dedicated to him an exposition of the mystical import of that feast; and the manner of which he honored me with a reply may be understood by anyone who reads the following letter. (Ch. 34)

> "VICTOR CONSTANTINUS, MAXIMUS AUGUSTUS, to Eusebius:

> "It is indeed an arduous task, and beyond the power of language itself, worthily to treat of the mysteries of Christ, and to explain in a fitting manner the controversy respecting the feast of Easter, its origin as well as its precious and toilsome accomplishment. For it is not within the power even of those who are able to apprehend them, adequately to describe the things of God. I am, notwithstanding, filled with admiration of your learning and zeal, and have not only myself read your work with pleasure, but have given directions, according to your own desire, that it be communicated to many sincere followers of our holy religion. Seeing, then, with what pleasure we receive favors of this kind from your sagacity, be pleased to gladden us more frequently with those compositions, to the practice of which, indeed, you confess yourself to have been trained from an early period, so that I am urging a willing man, as they say, in exhorting you to your customary pursuits. And certainly the high and confident judgment we entertain is a proof that the person who has translated your writings into the Latin tongue is in no respect incompetent to the task, impossible though it be that such version should fully equal the excellence of the works themselves. God preserve you, beloved brother." Such was his letter on this subject: and that which related to the providing of copies of the Scriptures for reading in the churches was to the following purport. (Ch. 35)

> "VICTOR CONSTANTINUS, MAXIMUS AUGUSTUS, to Eusebius:

> "It happens, through the favoring providence of God our Savior, that great numbers have united themselves to the most holy church in the city which is called by my name. It seems, therefore, highly requisite, since that city is rapidly advancing in prosperity in all other respects, that the number of churches should also be increased. Do you, therefore, receive with all readiness my determination on this behalf. *I have*

thought it expedient to instruct your Prudence to order fifty copies of the sacred Scriptures, the provision and use of which you know to be most needful for the instruction of the Church, *to be written on prepared parchment in a legible manner, and in a convenient, portable form, by professional transcribers thoroughly practiced in their art*. The catholicus [a title used in the early church for the head of the churches and/or monasteries of a given city] of the diocese has also received instructions by letter from our Clemency to be careful to furnish all things necessary for the preparation of such copies; and it will be for you to take special care that they be completed with as little delay as possible. You have authority also, in virtue of this letter, to use two of the public carriages for their conveyance, by which arrangement the copies when fairly written will most easily be forwarded for my personal inspection; and one of the deacons of your church may be entrusted with this service, who, on his arrival here, shall experience my liberality. God preserve you, beloved brother!" (Ch. 36; emphasis added)

Such were the emperor's commands, which were followed by the immediate execution of the work itself, which we sent him in magnificent and *elaborately bound volumes of a threefold and fourfold form*. [Note: This likely refers to three and four columns of text per page.] This fact is attested by another letter, which the emperor wrote in acknowledgment, in which, having heard that the city Constantia in our country, the inhabitants of which had been more than commonly devoted to superstition, had been impelled by a sense of religion to abandon their past idolatry, he testified his joy, and approval of their conduct. (Ch. 37) (Eusebius, *The Life of Constantine*, Book 3, *NPNF*; italics added)

When Constantine made his request of Eusebius, there was likely some broad agreement in the churches on the core books that comprised its sacred Scriptures, but as yet there was no complete agreement on the books that comprised the New Testament, as the major codices of the fourth and fifth centuries demonstrate. For example, Codex Sinaiticus (middle to late fourth century) includes all of the books of the New Testament, but also the Epistle of Barnabas and the Shepherd of Hermas. Codex Vaticanus (middle fourth century) does not include the Pastoral Epistles (1–2 Timothy and Titus), Philemon, or Revelation. Codex Alexandrinus (fifth century) includes all of the New Testament books, but adds 1 and 2 Clement and the Psalms of Solomon. Finally, Codex Claramantanus (fifth century) has all of the New Testament books except Philippians, 1–2 Thessalonians, and Hebrews, but also includes Epistle of Barnabas, Shepherd of Hermas, Acts of Paul, and Apocalypse of Peter. As we can see, the order or sequence of the New Testament books in these manuscripts varies considerably.

Again, the copies of the sacred books ordered by Constantine may well have become the standard or model for the later, more expertly copied biblical books by professional scribes. We do not know the specific contents of the Bibles that Constantine ordered, but these uncial (or *majuscule*) parchment manuscripts no doubt corresponded with a significantly improved quality in the copies of the churches' Scripture collections in the fourth century and later. Manuscripts of the entire Bible from any time in antiquity are very rare—indeed, less than 1 percent of the surviving manuscripts contain all of the books of the Bible, and most of those date from periods after AD 1000. Constantine's fifty copies of the Scriptures likely had a significant influence on the acceptance of individual books that eventually formed the New Testament canon, *but the deliberate production of complete Bibles* may well have been the more important consequence of his request. Certainly Eusebius, as the recipient of that request, played a major role in shaping the Bibles in question, but Constantine's involvement signaled a profound change in the role of governmental authorities with respect to canon formation. For who could have withstood the request from the emperor, given what is known of his involvement in the churches?

Constantine's Call for Unity and Canon Formation

Like all of his predecessors, Constantine took steps to unify his empire. So it makes sense that after his public conversion to Christianity, he also moved to bring unity in the churches, not only on matters of simply getting along but also in matters of doctrine and agreement on the Scriptures that were used in churches.

Whether or not Constantine's call for unity in both the Roman Empire and the churches had any significant influence on the contents of the biblical canon is difficult to determine; no church tradition states this in so many words. However, the well-known fact of Constantine's involvement in most major church decisions in matters of doctrine, discipline, leadership, and ecclesiastical harmony strongly suggests that he may well have had some influence on the contours of the biblical canon, and not just in ordering the production of Bibles as we saw in the previous point.

Although Constantine was initially *invited* by the Christians to settle ecclesiastical controversies, almost from the beginning he evidently saw it as his duty to become more involved in the decisions of the church. This involved not only the calling (ordering?) together of the bishops and other church leaders at various councils (according to Eusebius, *Life of Constantine* 3.6; 4.41–43), but also the resolution of theological disputes: one between Alexander and Arius (2.61), for instance, as well as the question of whether Eusebius himself was to go to Antioch (3.59–61). He was even involved in settling the time for the celebration of Easter (3.6–18), whether and how to punish heretics (3.20, 64–65), as well as when, where, and how to build churches (3.29–43).

He not only arbitrated in such matters, but he also *reconvened* a council when its decision went contrary to his own wishes, as in the case of the Donatist controversy in North Africa. Constantine threatened bishops with the penalty of banishment if they did not obey his orders to convene at Tyre (*Life of Constantine* 4.41–42), and he even sent a representative of "consular rank," Dionysus, to insure order at the council as well as to remind the bishops of their duty (4.42). He even ordered the same church leaders to Jerusalem to help him celebrate the dedication of the new church building there! On one occasion, he wrote that while the bishops were overseers of the internal affairs of the church, he himself was a "bishop, ordained by God to overlook whatever is external to the church" (4.24), but one is hard-pressed to find the "internal" issues in which he did not also involve himself.

Constantine tolerated no threats or rivals to the rule of peace and harmony either in his empire or in its churches. Those whose doctrines were not in keeping with the "orthodoxy" of the day were banished into exile, their writings burned, and their meeting places confiscated (3.66). At times he was gracious, generous, and even humble, but he did not tolerate differences of opinion or challenges to his authority in church matters (4.42). His understanding of "harmony" was not so much peaceful co-existence as uniform thinking—that is, the creation, or if necessary the imposition, of consensus. He did not hesitate to intimidate dissident bishops into conformity to his wishes or with those of the majority of the bishops (3.13).

Whether coincidental or not, it was during Constantine's reign that Christians showed considerable interest in dealing with the scope of their Scriptures. Did his moves toward unity in the churches contribute to the church's decisions about the scope of their biblical canon? I will focus more specifically on the contents of the ancient New Testament manuscripts in the next chapter, but for now, we must ask: What criteria did the early churches use to select which Christian writings to include in their Bibles? That is our next focus.

The Criteria Question

What criteria were used to determine canonicity in this historical context? The early churches never left behind a clear statement on the processes or criteria that they used to select the books that best reflected their faith and mission in the world. The following list of criteria is not found in any one place, and no early church father mentions them all, but these are the most common criteria found in the surviving church traditions.

Apostolicity

Apostolicity means that if the book was written by an apostle, it was more likely to be welcomed in the churches. This was the most basic and widely accepted criterion for canonicity found in the early church fathers. It also shows the church's aim of anchoring its faith in the traditions about Jesus that were produced by those who were closest to him: namely, the apostles.

Demonstrating the importance of this apostolic criterion, Irenaeus wrote:

> The blessed apostles, then, having founded and built up the church committed into the hands the office of episcopate [he then lists twelve successive leaders of the church]. ... In this order, and by succession, the ecclesiastical tradition from the apostles and the preaching of the truth have come down to us. And this is the most abundant proof that there is one and the same vivifying faith, which has been preserved in the Church from the apostles until now, and handed down in truth. (*Against Heresies* 3.3.3, *ANF*, ca. AD 170–180)

Subsequently, he added: "How should it be if the apostles themselves had not left us writings? Would it not be necessary in that case to follow the course of the tradition which they handed down to those to whom they handed over the leadership of the churches?" (*Against Heresies* 3.4.1, adapted from *ANF*).

If the churches believed that an apostle wrote a particular book, then it was accepted as a part of their collection of sacred Scriptures. If so, it was eventually recognized as Scripture and as part of the New Testament. It is likely that this is the criterion used to convince the broader church to include the book of Hebrews in the biblical canon, even though few scholars today believe that Paul wrote it. (Perhaps surprisingly, many early Christians also questioned Paul's authorship of Hebrews.) This raises the question of whether a book could be rightly accepted but for the wrong reasons! While Origen, a third-century church father, did not believe that Paul wrote Hebrews, he was not willing to dismiss or reject it since he, like many others, recognized the value of this book in the life of the churches. This assessment of value brings us to our second criteria, that of orthodoxy.

Orthodoxy

Did the writing conform to the generally accepted understanding of the Christian faith that was passed on in the churches, beginning with the apostles? Irenaeus was the first church father who presented this criterion as a means of rejecting those writings of second-century "heretics" whose teaching did not conform to the teaching that he believed was passed on in the churches from the apostles to the bishops of the churches.

His argument about apostolic succession is compelling. He writes:

> The blessed apostles, then, having founded and built up the Church, committed into the hands of Linus the office of episcopate. Paul makes mention of this Linus in the Epistles to Timothy. Anacletus succeeded him, and Clement was allotted the bishopric. Clement, since he had seen the blessed apostles and had been conversant with them, might be said to have the preaching of the apostles still echoing in his ears, and their traditions before his eyes, ... Evaristus succeeded Clement, and he

was succeeded by Sixtus, the sixth from the apostles. After him came Telephorus, who was gloriously martyred, then Hyginus, after him Pius, and then after him Anicetus was appointed. Anicetus was succeeded by Soter and Eleutherius, who is the twelfth from the apostles and now holds the inheritance of the episcopate. *In this order, and by this succession, the ecclesiastical tradition from the apostles and the preaching of the truth have come down to us. And this is the most abundant proof that there is one and the same vivifying faith, which has been preserved in the Church from the apostles until now, and handed down in truth.* (Adapted from *Adv. Haer.* 3.3.3, *ANF*; italics added.)

Irenaeus's also well-known summary of the proto-orthodox Christian faith and the centrality of Jesus as the Christ and Lord of the church is as follows:

The Church, though dispersed throughout the whole world, even to the ends of the earth, has received from the apostles and their disciples this faith: It believes in one God, the Father Almighty, Maker of heaven, and earth and the sea and all things that are in them and in one Christ Jesus, the Son of God, who became incarnate for our salvation and in the Holy Spirit, who proclaimed through the prophets the dispensations of God, the advents, the birth from a virgin, the passion, the resurrection from the dead, and the ascension into heaven in the flesh of the beloved Christ Jesus, our Lord. He also proclaimed through the prophets his future manifestation from heaven in the glory of the Father "to gather all things in one," and to raise up anew all flesh of the whole human race. [This will take place] in order that to Christ Jesus, our Lord, God, Saviour, and King, according to the will of the invisible Father, "every knee should bow, of things in heaven, and things in earth, and things under the earth, and that every tongue should confess" him. And he will execute just judgment towards all sending into everlasting fire "spiritual wickednesses," and the angels who transgressed and became apostates, together with the ungodly, and unrighteous, and wicked, and profane among men. But he will, in the exercise of his grace, confer immortality on the righteous and holy, and those who have kept his commandments, and have persevered in his love, some from the beginning of their Christian course, and others from the time of their repentance. He will surround them with everlasting glory. (Adapted from *Adv. Haer.* 1:10.1, *ANF*; compare with 3.4.2.)

This latter quote emphasizes that Jesus as Lord of the church is the primary "canon" of the early church. He is the *regula fidei*; that is, the rule or canon of faith!

Antiquity

Was the writing produced by the earliest community of Christians? If so, it was still more likely to be included in the collection of writings that made up the New Testament. The Gospels of Mark and Luke, who were not apostles, were likely included in the New Testament because they were believed to have been written during apostolic times and showed apostolic influence. The author of the

Muratorian Fragment, a middle to late fourth-century document, rejected the Shepherd of Hermas because it was not written in the apostolic period. He writes:

> But Hermas wrote the Shepherd very recently, in our times, in the city of Rome, while Pius, his brother, was occupying the [episcopal] chair of the church of the city of Rome. And therefore it ought indeed to be read; but it cannot be read publicly to the people in church either among the prophets, whose number is complete, or among the apostles, for it is after [their] time. (*Muratorian Fragment*, lines 73–80, trans. Metzger 1987, p. 307)

Widespread Use (Catholicity)

This criterion asks whether a book was widely used or cited by Christians in the majority of major churches in the first three centuries. In the fourth century, Eusebius classified sacred texts in the churches in three categories; namely, those that were widely read and used in churches (recognized or *homolegoumena* = "those agreed to"), those disputed (*antilegomena*, or "those spoken against"), and those deemed "spurious" (*notha*). The first category he called "encovenanted" or "testamented" (*endiathēkē*) Scriptures, and he listed twenty of the twenty-seven books of the New Testament that had been quoted by other trusted sources (*Ecclesiastical History* 3.25.1–7). Illustrating this criterion for accepting those books that had been widely received in the churches, Eusebius writes:

> Of the writings of John in addition to the gospel the first of his epistles has been *accepted without controversy by ancients and moderns alike but the other two are disputed*, and as to the Revelation there have been many advocates of either opinion up to the present. This, too, shall be similarly illustrated by *quotations from the ancients* at the proper time. (Eusebius, *Ecclesiastical History* 3.24.17–18, LCL; emphasis added)

The second category, disputed writings, included Hebrews, James, 2 Peter, 2 and 3 John, Jude, and Revelation. As we saw in the quotation above, Eusebius was particularly hesitant about Hebrews and Revelation. These disputed books were all included by the end of the fourth century in the majority of churches, but Eusebius's doubts are consistent with earlier concerns about them. The third category (*notha*) included those writings that were rejected as spurious by most churches (see *Ecclesiastical History* 3.25.1–7). Because this criterion asks questions about the use of a document by a majority, it has also been termed the criterion of catholicity, a word that derives from "catholic," or universal: in other words, can this be said to be true of (or according to) the *whole* church or the majority of the churches?

Adaptability

Some books cited as sacred Scripture in the early churches were eventually excluded from collections of the churches' Scriptures and various Scripture catalogues. This raises the question of the ability of a book to be continually adapted to changing circumstances and needs. Among those that appear to have failed this test were some of those that were initially most popular, including the Shepherd of Hermas, Epistle of Barnabas, Didache, 1 and 2 Clement, the Letters of Ignatius, the Gospel of Peter, the Gospel of the Hebrews, the Apocalypse of Peter, and the Acts of Paul and Thecla.

Why this took place is not always clear, but it is clear that it did happen. The late fourth-century biblical manuscript, Codex Sinaiticus, included the Epistle of Barnabas and the Shepherd of Hermas in its New Testament collection of Scriptures, but eventually they were dropped. This is remarkable since there is nothing heretical in either document; indeed, recalling the criterion of use or catholicity, the Shepherd of Hermas had been copied more often than any other book of the New Testament except for Matthew and John. What happened is unknown, but it eventually was dropped from the church's collection of sacred Scriptures. Similarly, Codex Alexandrinus (fifth century) included 1 and 2 Clement, but again, they eventually were dropped from canonical consideration.

Some biblical scholars today want to open the question of the biblical canon once again and include such writings as the Gospel of Thomas, the Egerton Papyri, and the so-called *Lost Gospel of Mark*. Alternatively, some would like to remove all material related to the future coming kingdom of God, such as the book of Revelation, Mark 13, Matthew 24, 1 Thessalonians 4:13–5:11, etc. The picture of Jesus and the Christian faith will, of course, vary considerably depending on what literature one uses to construct his story. I am not convinced that we need to expand or reduce the size of the current biblical canon, but I do believe that this criterion of adaptability still holds true today: Is it important for us to be informed by the same writings that informed the faith of the early Christians, including many of the excluded writings (see the Appendix below for a list of many of these apocryphal New Testament writings)?

Conclusion

The origin and development of the New Testament canon of Scriptures began in the life and teachings as well as in the death and resurrection of Jesus. Without Jesus' significant impact on his followers, *there would have been no New Testament*. The collection of his sayings, deeds, death, and resurrection was passed along in the church's oral traditions for years; but from the time that the stories about Jesus were written down, these written materials found widespread use in the churches. The Gospels and the recognized theological and practical value of the letters of Paul formed the earliest core of the New Testament. While the apostles and those who were with them were still alive, there was very little need for written traditions—especially if, as was anticipated, Jesus would soon return. But with the death of the apostles and the other eyewitnesses to the church's primary tradition, the gospel story, and the delay in Jesus' anticipated return, it became vitally important to commit to writing the oral traditions about Jesus that formed the heart of the early Christian proclamation.

The reading and use of Christian writings (alongside the Old Testament Scriptures) in Christian worship, instruction, and mission, as well as in the apologetic or defense of the Christian mission, proved quite valuable in the early churches. By the middle of the second century AD, many followers of Jesus were making use of expressly *Christian* written resources in their churches along with the Old Testament Scriptures. By the end of the second century, many (though not all) Christians began calling some of the Christian writings (again, not all of them) "Scripture." This was true especially in regard to the Gospels and most of the letters of Paul to churches. From the time the Gospels were written and well into the middle of the fourth century, most of the Christian Scriptures that are now a part of the New Testament were included in fixed collections. While that varies a bit in some of the subsequent collections and catalogues, there was widespread acceptance of the twenty-seven books that make up the New Testament biblical canon today. When Christians began limiting the writings that they included in their sacred Scriptures, most of the New Testament Scriptures already enjoyed long-established approval by the churches and were circulating in their sacred collections. It took several more centuries before there was universal (or catholic) agreement on *all* of the books in the New Testament and *only* those books. As late as Reformation times, Martin Luther challenged the value of several New Testament books, especially Hebrews, James, Jude, and Revelation—not coincidentally, some of the same texts that had struggled to meet the criteria above. Today, while some questions still persist, all major Christian churches (Protestant, Catholic, and Orthodox) accept the twenty-seven books that comprise the New Testament canon of Scriptures.

It is appropriate to conclude this chapter with an acknowledgement of one of the most significant challenges presented by the study of canon formation: like any stream of historical research, it often leaves us with lingering questions that we cannot fully resolve. Why, for one, did Christians select the books that were eventually included in the Christian Bibles, and why were other, often equally popular books (e.g., 1 Clement) finally excluded? Since we do not have any ancient resources that give an accounting for why each book was welcomed and approved (or, conversely, rejected), we cannot say with complete confidence why some components of the collection of ancient Christian writings were ultimately excluded from the Bible, as in the case of the Didache, 1 Clement, and others. After all, some of the excluded books are not significantly different from books that were included in the Bible: for instance, the Shepherd of Hermas resembles Revelation in terms of its focus on visions. Some books (e.g., Didache, Letters of Ignatius, Epistle of Barnabas, Shepherd of Hermas) that were initially welcomed in various Christian communities as "inspired" and believed to be of divine origin and convey the will of God, were once a part of sacred Scripture. It is not at all inappropriate to draw insight and even a measure of instruction from them. I have listed the best known of these books in Table 5 below, and I encourage readers to familiarize themselves with them before turning to the next chapter, in which I will focus on how ancient artifacts help tell the story of the origin and development of the New Testament canon. I list below most of the Christian apocryphal writings that were excluded from the ancient churches' Scriptures.

Table 5: The New Testament Apocrypha

The best-known examples of Christian writings rejected by the ancient churches include the following:

A. Gospels:

The Protoevangelium of James

The Infancy Gospel of Thomas

The Gospel of Peter

The Gospel of Nicodemus

The Gospel of the Nazoreans

The Gospel of the Ebionites

The Gospel of the Hebrews

The Gospel of the Egyptians

The Gospel of Thomas

The Gospel of Philip

The Gospel of Mary

B. Acts (the first five of these are called the "Leucian Acts" and were often circulated together):

The Acts of John

The Acts of Peter

The Acts of Paul

The Acts of Andrew

The Acts of Thomas

The Acts of Andrew and Matthias

The Acts of Philip

The Acts of Thaddaeus

The Acts of Peter and Paul

The Acts of Peter and Andrew

The Martyrdom of Matthew

The Slavonic Acts of Peter

The Acts of Peter and the Twelve Apostles

C. Epistles (some add here the Pastoral Epistles and 1, 2 Peter):

Third Corinthians

The Epistle to the Laodiceans

The Letters of Paul and Seneca

The Letters of Jesus and Abgar

The Letter of Lentulus

The Epistle of Titus

D. Apocalypses (writings following the genre found in the book of Revelation and some add here the Shepherd of Hermas):

The Apocalypse of Peter

The Coptic Apocalypse of Paul

The First Apocalypse of James

The Second Apocalypse of James

The Apocryphon of John

The Sophia (Wisdom) of Jesus Christ

The Letter of Peter to Philip

The Apocalypse of Mary

E. Additional Apocryphal Writings:

Apocryphon of James (preserved in Nag Hammadi Codex I)

Dialogue of the Savior (preserved in Nag Hammadi Codex III)

Gospel of the Ebionites (preserved in quotations by Epiphanius)

Oxyrhynchus Papyrus 840

Oxyrhynchus Papyrus 1224

Papyrus Egerton (+ Papyrus Köln 255)

Fayyum Fragment (= Papyrus Vindobonensis Greek 2325)

Chapter 6

What the Ancient Manuscripts Tell Us

Long before the biblical books were prepared, the art of writing was common in several ancient societies. These writing systems employed various forms of alphabets to create treatises, shipping manifests, deeds, marriage licenses, and other types of documents. There were also several materials employed in writing, especially ink, ink wells, pens or stylus, and various kinds of writing materials (papyrus, parchment, copper, wood, stone, wax, clay). Our interest here concentrates on the texts that would become the Christian canon.

The biblical books were first placed on scrolls; that is, rolls of animal skins (parchment) that were sewn together and the biblical text written on them. As a "book," these scrolls bear little resemblance to today's professionally bound volumes of paper. We can catch a glimpse of the Bible's integral relationship to the traditions of Western civilization in its etymology: the root of the word "Bible" derives from the Greek term for "book," *biblos* (or *biblion*, pl. *ta biblia*, "the books"; also see the Latin *volumen*, or "volume"). In the following paragraphs, I will focus on the use and significance of the form of the materials used in copying and passing along the biblical books, noting the surprising ways in which small, technical details can have a sizeable impact on the formation of the New Testament and our understanding of that process.

Writing Materials and the Bible

Ancient Writing Materials and Formats

The first ancient writings were, as far as can be known, etched in stone or painted on walls. The most ancient writings that have survived were usually written in the protected confines of a cave, although some were carved at great expense into stone, much as is done to this day on monuments. Over time, the technology of writing developed significantly, from imprinting soft clay tablets with a knife or stylus pen (and then drying the tablets or even baking them to harden them), to imprinting wooden tablets laden with wax for more temporary use, to the use of ink on leather sheets crafted from animal skins (parchment), and on to the use of ink on papyrus sheets.

Inscriptions carved on a stone wall in ancient Delphi, Greece.

At an early stage in writing, scribes often used clay tablets to write out messages or to keep records. This clay tablet (ca. 1950–1835 BC) is on display in the Archaeological Museum in Istanbul and describes an agreement on a land purchase.

Stone tablet dating from approximately 2000 BC (Istanbul Archaeological Museum).

During the first century AD, some writings were even being copied on metal (hammered copper or silver). Sometimes shorter messages were written with ink on *ostraca* (broken pieces of discarded ceramic vessels, frequently called potsherds), but longer messages or treatises were written with ink either on scrolls of papyrus—made from an Egyptian plant that grows along the Nile—or on parchment (animal skins). Until the fourth century AD, most longer documents, what we might consider "books," were written on scrolls, just as in the case of the books of the Bible. Longer documents were also produced using papyrus sheets, likely because they were often less expensive than parchment. But as the church emerged as a newly legal and imperially endorsed institution, its needs and preferences would become important factors in shaping the direction and industry of writing and book-making.

The Scroll: Parchment and Papyrus

While some written communications were copied on potsherds and wooden tablets, the use of the scroll or roll was a far more common format for producing or copying ancient volumes. Jewish scribes, like those who produced other formal documents, made copies of their Scriptures on scrolls. Some of these were made of animal skins, or parchment, which was widely used (see 2 Tim 4:13) but more expensive to produce and so reserved for important writings. Parchment is made of specially prepared animal skins—flayed, soaked in lime, with the epidermis scraped off the outer side and the flesh from the inner side, then stretched, smoothed out, sewn together, and trimmed to form sheets of uniform size.

Early Greek ostracon. The message on this piece of pottery reads: "to his son many greetings and to his father/mother many greetings. You sent the curator's ostraca . . . temple/tomb of Pompey . . . the curator . . . you sent . . . centurion." (Photo and translation courtesy of Paul Wegner)

The use of parchment may have developed in ancient Pergamum, though that is difficult to confirm; certainly, the Pergamenes were the largest producers of animal skins for writing purposes. Even as late as the Middle Ages, parchment was the preferred material for writing. One important value of parchment was that it was easier to write on and also easier to erase when mistakes were made or when a writer wanted to reuse older writing material for a different purpose. The cost of the parchment was high, so it was often necessary to reuse it by washing and scrubbing off the original writing on a manuscript and then writing over it once again. Sometimes the ink could not be completely removed, so it is often possible to read the original writing on the parchment volume. These reused manuscripts are known as "palimpsests" (from Greek *palin* = "again" and *psestos* = "rubbed smooth"). We will uncover more about the use of parchment when we consider the codex, but first we must consider the other material that was used to make scrolls.

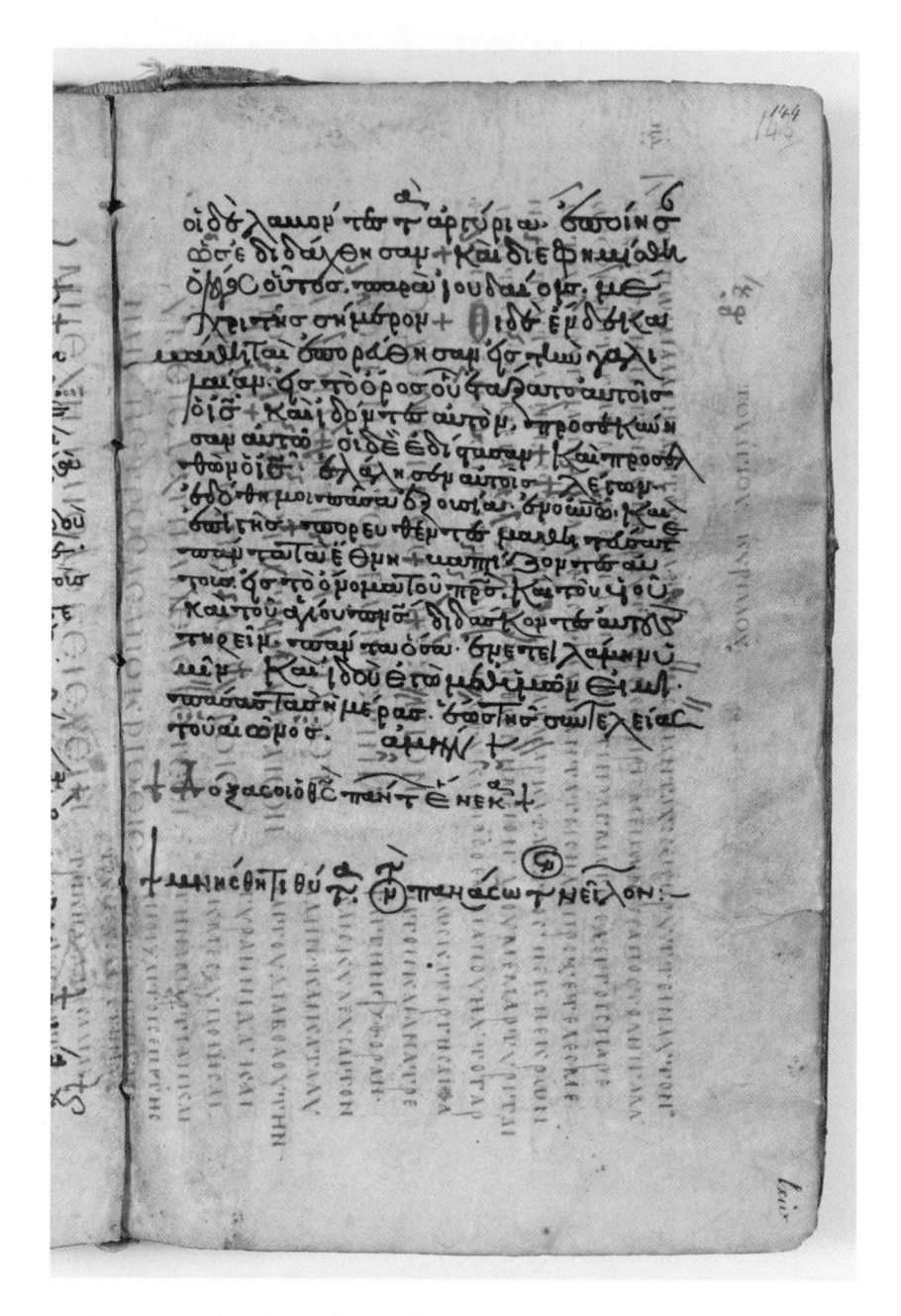

Codex Zacynthius (X 040), a twelfth-century palimpsest manuscript that was written over a seventh- or eighth-century copy of the Gospel of Luke. The common practice of washing and reusing parchment demonstrates how costly the material used for writing was in antiquity. (Courtesy of Cambridge University Library)

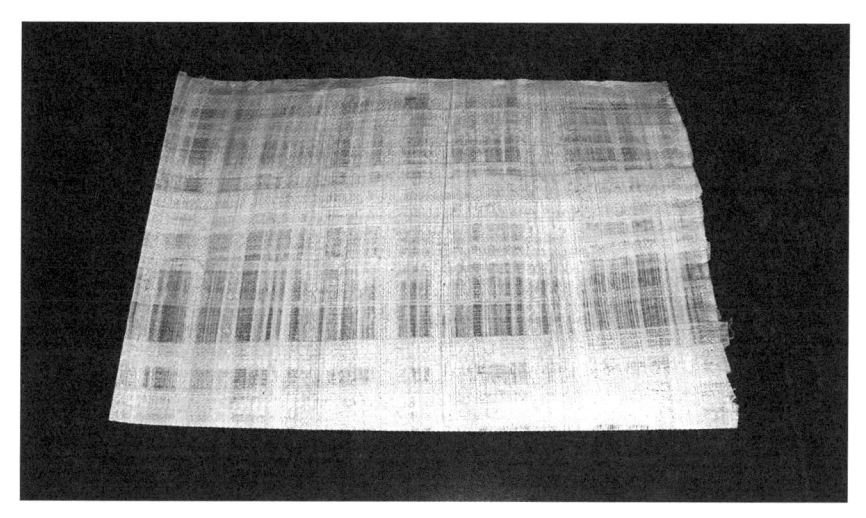

An example of a papyrus sheet used for writing ancient manuscripts.
(Courtesy of Randolph Richards)

Papyrus sheets were a standard writing vehicle for producing copies of biblical texts or other literary documents. Many ancient documents were produced on papyrus sheets that were sewn or glued together, normally with a flour paste. Papyrus plants were three-sided reeds grown alongside the Nile River in Egypt. Their stalks were cut into sections, and after the husk was removed, the pith of the plant was cut in strips that were laid side-by-side, first horizontally (the *recto* side facing up). Then the back side (*verso* side facing vertically) was placed against the horizontal side and pressed until they dried together. After that, these papyrus sheets could be used as writing materials: they were easy to write on, and colorful images could be painted or drawn on them. Some scrolls were inscribed on both sides (see Rev 5:1), though that was less common. Their "life expectancy" was about thirty years at most with moderate use, but some lasted considerably longer in dryer climates.

As writing techniques and technologies improved and longer scrolls were developed, major sections of the Hebrew Bible (or Old Testament) were able to be placed on one long scroll each (e.g., a scroll for the Law, one for the Prophets, and one for the Writings). Normally, the papyrus scrolls' standard length was approximately 3½ meters (about 11½ feet), but some scrolls could be much longer, especially in the case of parchment scrolls, which were as long as 22–32 feet. They could have been made longer still, but that would have made the scroll too large for easy use by the reader. The Law alone could occupy more than 30 feet of scroll space when the various pieces were sewn together. By the fourth century AD, it became possible to put all of the writings of the Old and New Testaments in one volume or codex, but Jewish communities still tended to keep the three parts of their Scriptures on separate scrolls. Parchment and papyrus manuscripts together comprised the vast majority of manuscripts before the third century, when the codex began to make considerable inroads in the Greco-Roman world.

The Codex

By the fourth century AD, the use of parchment was more common than papyrus, perhaps due to a shortage of the cheaper papyrus sheets, but by that time the use of the *codex* (pl. *codices*) had overtaken the use of the scroll in terms of popularity. This trend was perhaps a result of the relative ease of transporting the codices, as well as their enhanced accessibility: codices made it much easier to locate specific texts within a larger manuscript.

Because of the difficulty of transporting scrolls or rolls, the Romans (apparently) developed the concept of the codex, or tablet, as a new format for writing. Initially, such tablets were used for writing in schools and for private or less formal documents, but that quickly changed. The earlier form of the codex was essentially two pieces of wooden boards that could be bound together by leather straps; on the inside, wax was applied and used to write temporary lessons or messages. "Codex" is a Latin term that originally referred to the trunk of a tree and subsequently to a piece of wood (a block) that was split in order to form the two boards of the volume. After the wax had been used to convey the intended message, it was smoothed over and used again inside the two pieces of wood. In time, the use of wax gave way to the use of papyrus sheets, glued and/or sewn together in a book-like form akin to a modern book.

In its early stages, the codex was something like a notebook and used in a variety of ways for letters, legal transactions, receipts, etc. Some Roman writers, such as Martial (see below), circulated their writings in a notebook-like form, perhaps for easy portability on trips. The advantage of the codex was that several sheets of writing material could be tied together on one end, so that a writer could use both the front (*recto*) and the back (*verso*) of each page. These pages could then be read sequentially and quickly cited. These *codices* were made both from animal skins and papyrus sheets.

Papyrus, and subsequently parchment, sheets were incorporated into a codex first by taking a larger sheet, folding it in half so that both sides of the folded sheet (now equal to four pages) could be used for writing. Four sheets could be folded together and attached in the middle, forming a "quire" (the Old English equivalent to Latin *quaterni*, "set of four") producing sixteen sides or pages, trimmed along the outside edges to make the sheets uniform in size. This process of sewing quires together is very similar to how books are prepared for publication today. When multiple quires were sewn together, the result was that the codex manuscript could be expanded to include more books in one volume, thus creating a single, larger book. By the end of the second or early third century AD, codex technology had developed sufficiently so that one codex volume could contain the letters of Paul ($\mathfrak{P}^{46}$) or even the four Gospels and Acts ($\mathfrak{P}^{45}$).

From the early second century AD and thereafter, Christians showed considerable preference for the codex over the scroll for transmitting or copying their sacred Scriptures. This was at the same time when the vast majority of publications were in scrolls. Even in the third century, when the value and usefulness of the codex had long been recognized, only 20 percent of the total manuscripts produced were prepared in this fashion. On the other hand, from the earliest times, Christians overwhelmingly and almost exclusively preferred the codex over the scroll. In the fourth century AD, when codex technology had developed sufficiently to include all of the church's Scriptures, both Old and New Testaments were included in one volume. The church's complete Bible began to be published in one large volume of some 1,500 to 1,600 pages, as in the cases of Codex Vaticanus and Codex Sinaiticus, the two oldest known Christian collections of both the Old and New Testament Scriptures.

The codex had several obvious advantages over the scroll: it was more compact, easier to transport, about 25 percent cheaper to produce, and allowed readers much easier and faster access to particular passages. Consider how much more simple it is to number and turn pages than to unroll an entire series of books! Codices that were produced on parchment began to take priority over papyrus manuscripts in the fourth century and thereafter, although papyrus manuscripts continued to be produced until approximately the eight century. As we noted briefly above, some copies of the Scriptures were made on washed-out or rubbed-out parchment manuscripts (or palimpsests) that had been used earlier for other writings. The photo above of Codex Zacynthius (X 040) displays an example of this practice. The lighter color writing is the older washed away text. Again, the practice of reusing a manuscript was not unusual in antiquity, given the high cost of producing both materials and manuscripts. Although Christians began using the codex predominantly over the roll or scroll in the early second century, the rest of the Greco-Roman society made this transition largely in the late third and fourth centuries AD. But before we examine the church's preference for codices in more depth below, we should take a moment to review three important points about the changes that the codex introduced.

The potential for more books in one volume. The technological advances of the codex in the fourth century made it possible to include all of the writings of the Old and New Testaments in one large codex made from parchment. This does not mean that all Christians made the same transition to parchment manuscripts overnight, or that they all had a copy of all of the Scriptures in their local churches. For one thing, owning a complete copy of the Old and New Testament was quite expensive. It is estimated that it would take some sixty to one hundred animals to produce such a large parchment codex of the whole Bible. In addition,

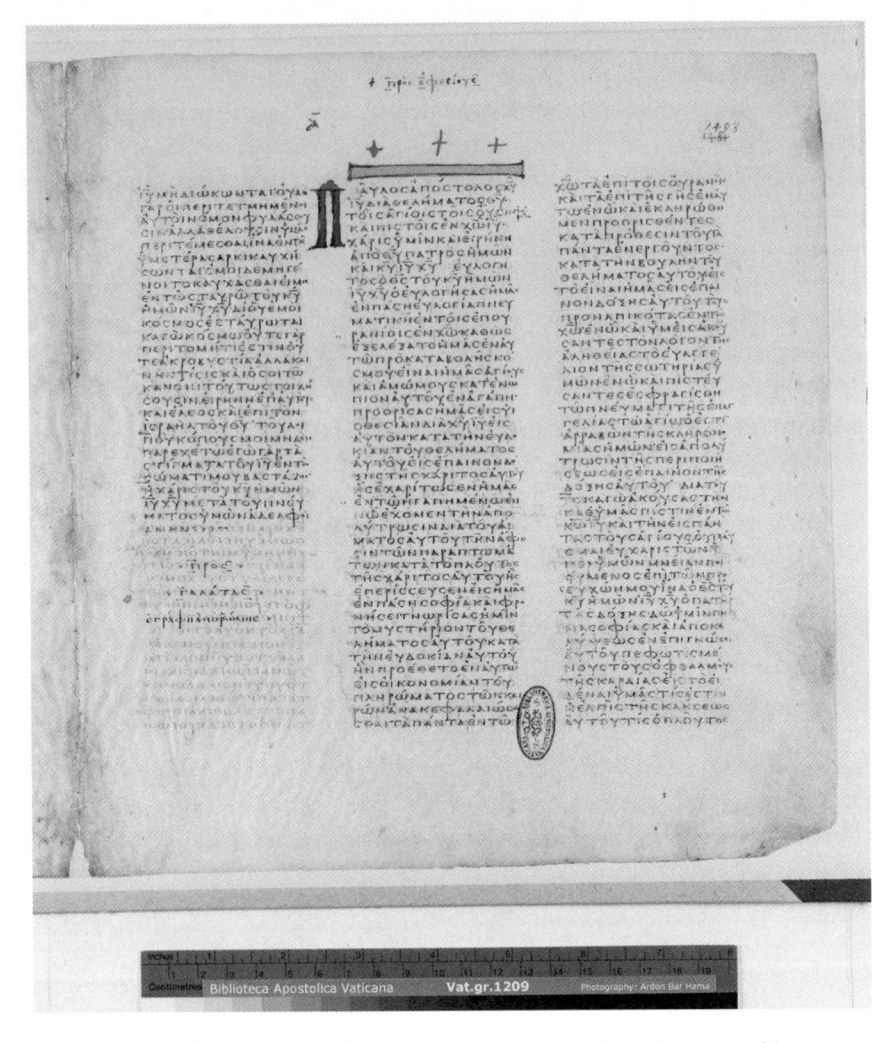

Codex Vaticanus (ca. AD 350) is one of the two oldest Christian Bibles containing both Old and New Testament books. This page shows the conclusion of Paul's letter to the Galatians and the first two columns of the letter to the Ephesians. (Courtesy of Biblioteca Apostolica Vaticana)

the expense for getting qualified professional copiers to reproduce the books of the Bible was prohibitive for most churches. As a result, most of the churches for many centuries continued to have only partial collections of their Scriptures produced by "literate amateurs." For the most part, even in the fourth and fifth centuries, all of the New Testament writings did not circulate in a single book. Sometimes only one or two Gospels and some letters were contained in those manuscripts that did circulate. There would not be a *widespread* publication of complete, single-volume Bibles for centuries, though this practice began in the fourth century at the instigation of Emperor Constantine (see the discussion of Constantine's role in the previous chapter). Still, the codex opened up the possibility of including all of the books in the Christian Scriptures in one volume, a prospect that likely also led to more decisions about which books to include in it and a more stabilized order or sequence of the biblical books.

Style A: Writing in capital letters. The first copies of the New Testament Scriptures were written in capital (majuscule) letters, with words running together without spaces between them (called in Latin *scripta continua*, "continuous script"). This practice, of course, made it difficult to decipher a number of the words and phrases in a text. To demonstrate an important facet of this problem that manifested both in the production and the deciphering of those manuscripts, we turn to a well-known example in English: the letters that spell "GODISNOWHERE" could mean either that "GOD IS NOW HERE" or that "GOD IS NOWHERE." *The context alone enables the reader to discern the actual meaning.* By the middle to late fourth century, Christians began using professional scribes more frequently to make copies of the Scriptures, and what they produced was generally of much better quality and more easily understood than before, but the continuous text without breaks could confuse even the most experienced of ancient scribes.

Style B: Writing in lowercase letters. By the eighth and ninth centuries, some copiers or scribes began to use lowercase (minuscule) rounded letters with spaces between the words, such as is familiar in most modern languages today. These manuscripts and their lettering are regularly called "minuscules" and sometimes "cursives" (referring to the practice of connecting letters together continuously, without breaks except between words). From the ninth century, and until the time when the printing press and moveable type were invented by Johann Gutenberg and he published the first printed Bible in 1456, lowercase parchment manuscripts of biblical books were regularly produced by hand, often with colorful imagery included in them (especially at the beginning of books and chapters, but sometimes in the middle of chapters). The colorful artwork often reflected the high value that the churches ascribed to these biblical manuscripts.

Early Christian Writing and Copying

Why did Christians prefer the codex instead of the scroll? The many possible reasons for this have been evaluated at length, but scholars do not agree on the matter. As we began to outline above, some have argued that the early Christians made use of the codex because of its economy; that is, codices were cheaper to make and many in the early churches were poor. This would have made better economic sense than continuing to use scrolls. (If the decision to use scrolls was for financial reasons alone, this would reflect obviously on the social condition of the earliest Christians.) Other sound reasons would be for the codex's compactness (i.e., it was easier to transport) or its convenience of use and ease of reference. But scholars generally conclude that none of the most obvious reasons fully answers the question of why the Christians, more than any other institution or constituency of the day, preferred the codex to transmit their sacred Scriptures. Perhaps they were seeking a different means of transmitting their sacred literature than the one used by their Jewish siblings (scrolls) with whom they were in regular conflict at the time. The practice may also go back to the apostle Paul, who, as noted briefly above, called upon Timothy to bring with him to Rome "the books and above all the parchments" (2 Tim 4:13). Is "books" here a reference to a codex? If the apostle Paul made use of "books," that may have set a precedent for others to follow, such that the content of Scripture (Paul) seemed to dictate its preferred vehicle.

Statue of Johann Gutenberg (1398–1468) from Mainz, Germany, who invented moveable type and the printing press. Gutenberg printed the Latin Vulgate Bible in 1456. (Creative Commons)

Photograph of a replica of the famous Gutenberg printing press at the Featherbed Alley Printshop Museum located in the lower level of the Mitchell House, in St. George's, Bermuda. (Aodhdubh at English Wikipedia)

This does not mean that these Christians took the codex's other advantages lightly, nor that we should do so. The argument for using the codex for transporting books more easily has antecedents: for instance, Martial, the Roman poet, advised his readers (ca. AD 80) to make use of the codex if they wanted to carry his poems on their journeys. His argument went as follows:

> You who want my little books [tablets] to keep you company wherever you may be and desire their companionship on a long journey, buy these, that parchment compresses in small pages. Give book boxes to the great, one hand grasps me. But in case you don't know where I am on sale and stray wandering all over town, you will be sure of your way under my guidance. (*Epigrams* 1.2, lines 1–7, LCL)

Like Paul's mention of a specific literary medium above, Martial indicated in his *Epigrams* that even the great poets' works were transported in this fashion; that is, on tablets. He mentions that Homer was transported this way ("Homer in parchment note books," 14.184) and that "Vast Livy, for whom my library does not have room, is compressed in tiny skins" (*Epigrams* 14.190). The codex

An example of moveable type used in printing prior to the advent of computer-generated fonts. The text in the plate reads (upside down and backwards), *The quick brown fox jumps over the lazy dog and feels as if he were in the seventh heaven of typography together with Her-mann Zapf, the most famous artist of the* . . . (Photo: Willi Heidelbach, Creative Commons)

was more *comprehensive* than the scroll and was capable of including more texts than several scrolls; but as we have seen, perhaps what became apparent with regular use of the codex was its manual convenience that allowed easy access and rapid referencing when teaching or debating opponents. Because Paul likely made use of the codex for its convenience and portability during his missionary journeys, and because his writings were among some of the earliest writings to be acknowledged as "Scripture," his example may well have instigated the use of the codex in early Christianity. When his letters were collected and circulated by his followers at the end of the first century, it is possible that the very form of transmission that Paul followed was repeated by others. The codex would have made it easier to circulate his writings in one volume. It may also have been used in the early churches for preserving lists of the sayings of Jesus, lists that preceded the written Gospel narratives as sources that early missionaries could use in advancing their mission.

The codex also tells us much about the early production of copies of Scripture. As codices became the standard form that Christians used in copying their

A page from the Gutenberg Bible. (Permission is granted by Claus Maywald of the Gutenberg Museum)

sacred writings, they initially were likely treated something like handbooks for everyday use. In these early stages of the copying of the Christian Scriptures, the copies were often poor in quality with many mistakes in them, no doubt because those who made the copies were, for the most part, amateur copiers and not professional scribes. It may also be that some of the early transcribers were not fully aware that they were transcribing sacred Scripture—the category and contents of which were still in flux—and as a result, they were less careful in their work. In addition to their mistakes, they also made frequent changes in the copies that they made, perhaps to clarify something that they thought was unclear in the text, or because they wanted their copy to reflect a current teaching in the church. For example, biblical scholars know well that the very last part of John 3:13 in many early manuscripts was added to show that Jesus was omnipresent, a trait that further confirmed his divinity.

In antiquity, there were generally two styles of writing: namely, the more literary quality of writing on the one hand, and the documentary style (that is, a less formal style of writing) on the other. The documentary style sometimes included abbreviations, unlike the literary style, and Christian copiers used this to their advantage in a way that simultaneously contracted and highlighted some of the most frequently used divine names and titles in Scripture. The early Christians tended to save time by abbreviating special sacred names, now called the *nomina sacra* (Latin for "sacred names"). They did this in many ancient Christian writings, but especially so in the copying of sacred Scriptures. The copiers would regularly contract the special name using generally only the first and last letters of that name and placing a short horizontal line over the letters to indicate the contraction. For example, the Greek word for Jesus (IĒSOUS) is often substituted with a simple IS with a short line drawn over the top of the abbreviated letters. The *nomina sacra* included fifteen names or titles, but some were more common than others, especially God (*theos*), Lord (*kyrios*), Jesus (*Iēsous*), Christ (*Christos*), and son (*huios*). Other common *nomina sacra* included the Greek words for Savior, David, Spirit, Father, mother, man, heaven, Jerusalem, and Israel. Well into the fourth century and later, these abbreviations were still used in Christian sacred Scriptures; for example, they are found throughout the mid-fourth-century Codex Vaticanus.

What is important here is that the use of such abbreviations in the early stages of copying the New Testament writings could mean that the earliest copiers were not conscious of copying literary sacred texts. Since abbreviations were not generally made in standard or formal books or scrolls of a literary quality, but more in tablets or notebooks such as the codex, this may suggest that in their initial use early Christians were still coming to terms with their own writings as sacred Scripture. As was mentioned earlier, the common practice of calling Christian writings "Scripture" *began* to take place around the end of the second century AD. Although abbreviations were common in secular documentary texts, they were rare in well-written literary texts. The use of *nomina sacra* probably points to the *practical* use of Christian writings in churches, since they generally were not high-quality written texts and were not generally valued as *sacred* or *scriptural* texts, even though they were regularly used in Christian instruction and worship. This documentary, or less formal, style of writing was characteristic of most of the papyrus New Testament manuscripts well into the fourth century, but the practice of using *nomina sacra* established in that earlier format continued on in the much more formal majuscule or uncial manuscripts of the fourth century and later.

In the fourth century, and apparently instigated at the command of Emperor Constantine (see the previous chapter), manuscripts of high-quality parchment and appropriate spacing began to be produced in the churches. Does this say anything about the views of the early Christians toward the literature that they had been reading in their churches? Unlike the much more meticulous style of transcription typical in the Jewish communities' treatment of their Scriptures, the Christians were generally less meticulous about manuscript preparation and production until after the time of Constantine's request for fifty copies of the Scriptures for use in churches in Constantinople. This is not to say that the empire's endorsement of Christianity alone caused Christians to change the way they reflected on and reproduced Scripture, but it was certainly *a* factor, though by no means the only factor, in shaping the canon and the treatment of its texts.

Well-known practices on the part of ancient Jewish communities illustrate the meticulous care with which they handled and copied their Scriptures. Paul Wegner (1999, pp. 78–79) has carefully summarized the practices as follows:

1. Only parchments made from clean [i.e., kosher] animals were allowed; these were to be joined together with thread from clean animals.
2. Each written column of the scroll was to have no fewer than forty-eight and no more than sixty lines whose breadth must consist of thirty letters.
3. The page was first to be lined, from which the letters were to be suspended.
4. The ink was to be black, prepared according to a specific recipe.
5. No word or letter was to be written from memory.
6. There was to be the space of a hair between each consonant and the space of a small consonant between each word, as well as several other spacing rules.
7. The scribe must wash himself entirely and be in full Jewish dress before beginning to copy the scroll.
8. He could not write the name Yahweh with a newly dipped brush, nor even take notice of anyone, even a king, while writing this sacred name.

While scholars do not agree on why the Christians adopted the codex instead of the scroll, its portability, Paul's use of the codex, and the gradual growth in acknowledging these writings as "Scripture" may account together for its use by the early Christians. That they continued to use the format *after* the recognition of the Christian writings as Scripture is likely a result of tradition and the precedent set by Paul and other early Christians. Again, the Christians' overwhelming use of the codex more than the scroll came at a time when the codex was not common (certainly not used for the preservation of important documents) in the rest of the Greco-Roman world. The large-scale substitution of the codex for the scroll in the production of literary documents began to take place in the Roman Empire only in the third and fourth centuries.

By the fourth century, then, when all of the Christian Scriptures from both testaments could be circulated in one volume, the codex with its inherent advantages, and the formatting that it encouraged, may have become significant factors in shaping the scope of the biblical canon. That is generally when most canon lists begin to appear.

Codex Technology and Canonical Choices

By the end of the second century, as we saw above, codex technology had progressed to the point where all four Gospels could be placed in one codex ($\mathfrak{P}^{45}$) and all of the letters of Paul could also circulate in one codex ($\mathfrak{P}^{46}$, approximately 200–212 pages). Before the fourth century, there were no manuscripts that contained all of the Scriptures and, to our knowledge, no *known* churches possessed all of the books that were later included in the Bible. Most churches even in the fourth century could not afford to make copies of all of their Scriptures, even when it became possible to combine all of the books in one large codex, and even though by that time there was widespread agreement on the general shape of the New Testament. At that point, it is especially important to recall which books were in the churches' sacred manuscripts.

There are no known manuscripts from before the year AD 1000 that contain all of the books of the New Testament and *only* those books. Even the earliest "complete" manuscript that contains all of the New Testament books, Codex Sinaiticus (ca. 375), also contains the Epistle of Barnabas and the Shepherd of Hermas (see the list at the end of the next chapter). Most of the 5,740 surviving New Testament manuscripts have considerably fewer books than we have in the New Testament today, and occasionally they contain some nonbiblical books.

The earliest surviving New Testament manuscripts were written on papyrus manuscripts (roughly second to eighth centuries AD) and have considerably fewer books in them than the later uncial or majuscule parchment manuscripts mentioned above. Only fourteen of the 127 known papyrus manuscripts have more than one book in them. Of those fourteen, some contain New Testament books alongside the nonbiblical books, as in the case of the famed $\mathfrak{P}^{72}$ papyrus manuscript (third to fourth century). It contains not only three New Testament books (1–2 Peter and Jude), but also several other books, including the Nativity of Mary, 3 Corinthians (purported to be further correspondence between Paul and the Corinthian church), the eleventh Ode of the Odes of Solomon (ca. AD 125), Melito's Homily on the Passover (ca. AD 170–180), a hymn fragment, the Apology of Phileas, and Psalms 33 and 34. All of these books were placed together without distinction in the same volume. What are we to make of this combination?

The books most frequently absent from the New Testament in these manuscripts are the same ones that Eusebius considered doubtful; namely, Hebrews, James, 2 Peter, 2–3 John, Jude, and Revelation, but sometimes also the Pastoral Epistles (1–2 Timothy, Titus), and often Philemon. This, of course, may reveal a lack of agreement on the scope of the New Testament in early churches, but it may reveal still more about the early churches' views of what was most practical and helpful for their congregations, and there is no guarantee that they were in agreement on this count. Since most of the early churches would not have had a complete collection of their Scriptures and likely could not have afforded such a collection, they may have selected those books that they believed were most useful to their local congregations. It is sometimes suggested that once an apostle (or other New Testament person) was believed to have written a given book, then everyone agreed that the book was inspired by God and concurrently added it to their canon of Scriptures. That, of course, is not the case.

Before we review the surviving manuscripts themselves in more detail, I should also mention one of the most neglected areas in the study of canon formation today. It has to do with the use of lectionaries (Scripture texts selected for reading in the church's worship calendar) in antiquity. Many churches still use lectionaries today, but those that survive from the ancient churches allow us to see the specific Scriptures that were read in those contexts and informed the faith of the early Christians, perhaps more so than other texts. These lectionaries seldom contain texts from outside of the core books (i.e., the Gospels and Pauline Letters) of the New Testament canon and seldom make use of the so-called fringe books in the canon mentioned above. The lectionaries are among the least studied ancient Christian texts, but their relevance is considerable when we think about the sacred texts that most influenced the early Christian churches.

Books in the Manuscripts

The surviving New Testament manuscripts are generally grouped in the following four categories.

Papyrus manuscripts. As we mentioned briefly above, the average lifetime of these manuscripts was about thirty years (but with less use could have lasted considerably longer), and almost all of those that have survived were discovered in the most arid climates (where they had better chances of being preserved due to reduced humidity) such as Egypt or the Judean desert.

The *127 known* (more are known but not yet cataloged) ancient, surviving papyrus Greek manuscripts of the New Testament books (roughly second to eighth century AD) range in size from only a few verses to those containing several books. All are fragmentary; that is, none are complete, though in many cases we can figure out what was intended since what is missing comes at the beginning or ending of the manuscripts, or the space missing can often be supplied from similar manuscripts. If we have a fragmented Gospel that begins, say, with Mark 1:11, it is a good guess that it also included verses 1–10 of the same chapter, since we have a multitude of manuscripts that contain those verses. The number of surviving papyrus manuscripts changes almost yearly, as more Greek papyrus manuscripts are discovered in museums, libraries, antiquarian collections, and archaeological sites in various parts of the world. Some of these manuscripts may not yet be catalogued and remain in boxes or trunks in museums, while others may be discovered in conjunction with other archaeological finds in the Middle East.

Fragmentary as they are, the surviving New Testament papyrus manuscripts are often missing important portions of their respective books, reflecting considerable damage and deterioration. Despite these setbacks, since these papyrus manuscripts are the oldest manuscripts that we have, they are thus very important in establishing the earliest texts and variant wordings of the New Testament books. The same applies to those manuscripts that contain not only New Testament books, but also books that were not later included in the church's New Testament. Such manuscripts, as we saw in 𝔓^{72} above, suggest that the early churches had not yet settled the scope of their New Testament when many of these manuscripts were prepared. In instances when a given manuscript can be dated with at least some precision, papyrus manuscripts present valuable evidence about the development of the text of the biblical book in question.

Uncial or Majuscule Manuscripts. Beginning in the fourth century AD until roughly the ninth century, there are presently 310 known parchment manuscripts of New Testament books that were prepared in uppercase or capital letters without spaces between the words. These manuscripts were generally prepared by professional scribes and have two, three, and even four columns per page. As noted above, the technology for producing a codex or book progressed to the point where it was possible to include the whole Christian Bible in one volume. It is here that for the first time we can see in one volume the recognized Scriptures of some churches. These manuscripts are invaluable for enabling scholars to see the development of the text of the Scriptures as well the specific books that comprised both their Old and New Testaments.

While these codices generally do not contain exactly the same books, they show that the "core" New Testament books—such as the Gospels, Acts, most of the letters of Paul, 1 Peter, and 1 John—were widely accepted as Christian Scripture, in the ancient churches. Other New Testament books, of course, were also included in the large manuscripts, as were some nonbiblical books, as we saw in Codex Sinaiticus's inclusion of the Epistle of Barnabas and the Shepherd of Hermas. The fifth-century Codex Alexandrinus contains Wisdom of Solomon, 1 and 2 Clement, and (oddly included in its New Testament) the Psalms of Solomon. Codex Vaticanus (mid-fourth century) omits 1–2 Timothy, Titus, Philemon, and Revelation. These and other manuscripts from the fourth to the ninth centuries let us know what books were *functioning as Scripture* in some Christian churches. While there is considerable overlap in their selections, as we can see in the lists and catalogues in Table 6 in chapter 7, there are also some key differences between these major codices, in both testaments.

Minuscule Manuscripts. There are some 2,877 surviving manuscripts produced in lowercase (minuscule) letters, with spaces between the words, that date roughly from the ninth to the fifteenth century. These are often of less value for determining the original text of the New Testament, but they remain critical because they show what books were most important to the churches at the time that they were produced. Like the manuscripts already profiled, they do not all contain the same books, though those that date from after the first millennium tend to show more stability and contain most of the New Testament books. During the time from which these minuscule sources date, we begin to see all of the books of the New Testament, and *only* those books, listed in these manuscripts. These sources also show how some texts of the Christian Scriptures have been changed or been modified over the centuries. As late as the eleventh and twelfth centuries, however, several manuscripts were produced containing nonbiblical books in them. For instance, in the twelfth century, the minuscule manuscript identified as Gregory 1505, which was discovered in the Lavra (Laura) Monastery on Mt. Athos in northern Greece, contains all of the books of the New Testament except Revelation, but it also concludes with a series of psalms and odes. As late as the fifteenth century, Armenian biblical manuscripts contained the apocryphal 3 Corinthians. And well into the fourteenth century, some Christians were still using Tatian's harmony of the Gospels. Tatian was a student of Justin Martyr in the second century, and his text was known as the *Diatessaron* ("through four," that is, a Gospel produced from the four Gospels), also called the "Gospel of the Mixed." Together, these manuscripts not only enable textual critics to trace the development of the New Testament text but also what books continued to inform the faith of the Christians at various stages of the church's history.

Lectionaries. As was noted earlier, lectionaries are selections of the Christian Scriptures that were read in worship services, beginning in the ancient churches. Most of the known lectionaries date from after the fourth century and are the most neglected of all of the biblical manuscripts. There are some 2,432 known lectionaries of New Testament passages; and while perhaps their greatest value is that they let us know what Scriptures most informed the church's preaching and teaching at the time they were written, they are also quite helpful in establishing the earliest text of the churches' Scriptures. If we can accurately date the lectionaries to a specific period, we can also determine what the text of the Scriptures was like in that generation. Like today, none of the lectionaries contains all of the books of the Bible, but they do tell us which Scriptures had the greatest and/or most frequent influence on the faith and practice of early Christianity. If one wants to know specifically which Scriptures most informed the faith of the ancient Christians, the lectionaries are fruitful sources to investigate; but unfortunately, few biblical scholars have given them their deserved attention thus far. Lectionaries, like the other ancient manuscripts above, offer us indispensable knowledge about which books informed the faith of the church at many stages of its history. In so doing, they also help tell the overall story of the formation of the church's Bible.

The Text of Biblical Manuscripts

As noted above, in the first three centuries of the church, literate but amateur copiers produced most of the copies of the church's Scriptures. Some of the copiers were more capable than others, but not infrequently they were unqualified for the task. Their role in reproducing the Christian Scriptures should not be minimized; although they produced many manuscripts with numerous errors in them, their dedication to making copies of the Christian Scriptures was an important feature in the expansion of the ministry of the early church, and perhaps in a few cases the survival of some texts that might otherwise have been lost. Nevertheless, the many changes to the biblical texts that these early copiers introduced cannot be ignored. Some of them continue to perplex biblical scholars today.

In the fourth century, professional scribes began to be employed to produce more accurate copies of the church's Scriptures, and the accuracy of the biblical manuscripts improved considerably, though all of those manuscripts were based on earlier copies of copies, and in them many significant variants survived in all subsequent manuscripts. In the seventh century and following, much of the task of making biblical manuscripts was delegated to monks in monasteries.

Until the invention of the printing press and moveable type in the mid-fifteenth century, no two biblical manuscripts were exactly the same. Textual scholars who devote considerable time to establishing the earliest possible text of the biblical books claim that there are some 200,000 to 400,000 variants in the

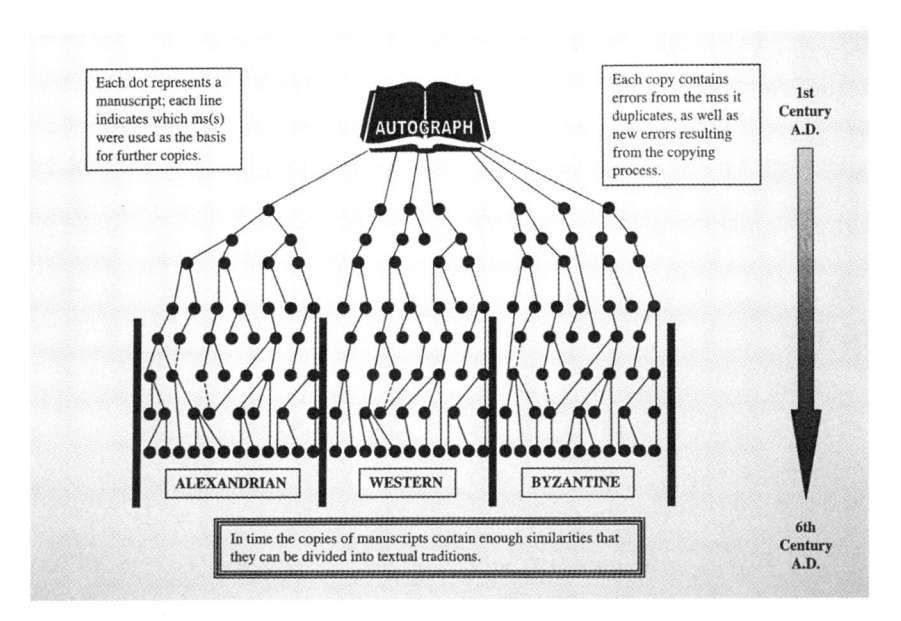

> Each dot represents a manuscript; each line indicates which ms(s) were used as the basis for further copies.

> AUTOGRAPH

> Each copy contains errors from the mss it duplicates, as well as new errors resulting from the copying process.

1st Century A.D.

ALEXANDRIAN | WESTERN | BYZANTINE

In time the copies of manuscripts contain enough similarities that they can be divided into textual traditions.

6th Century A.D.

This image illustrates how the early copies of the original texts of the Scriptures developed along various textual lines (or families of texts) and how those copiers who copied from these textual families both adopted whatever changes their predecessors had made to the biblical text and made further subsequent changes. This process of copying by hand (along with the inevitable errors and changes that sometimes occurred) took place from generation to generation until the invention of the printing press. Its moveable type for the first time made it possible to reproduce identical copies of a given text. (Courtesy of Paul Wegner)

existing Greek New Testament manuscripts. That means there are more variants than there are words in the New Testament! Most of these variants are *accidental* errors due to faulty eyesight, tired copiers, accidental omissions of words or lines of a text, and other such common errors, which we can easily correct by comparing the majority of manuscripts with the text in question, in order to discover which form of the biblical text is preferable.

On the other hand, there were a number of *intentional* scribal changes made to the biblical texts. Those were often intended to clarify what was believed to be the intended meaning of the Bible. Some of the scribes simply put "in other words" what they thought that the biblical text meant; in other instances, they wanted to make sure that the major teachings of their day were included in the biblical texts that they copied for church use. Some of these deliberate changes were clearly theologically motivated, as in the "Johannine Comma" (1 John 5:7–8; see p. 143 below for further information), but also in examples such as John 3:13b, Mark 1:1, Romans 16:7, and 1 Corinthians 14:33–36. Those theological motivations for intentional changes were generally intended as moves toward the earlier established orthodox Christian faith. Some of the early manuscripts reveal some doubt on the part of the copier about the authenticity of a particular passage, which is blocked off or otherwise identified as separate from the rest of the text, as many Bible publishers still do today with sections of text that are not well attested by the most reliable manuscripts. Some scribes chose to leave a blank space in a manuscript, suggesting that something was missing and that they did not have the rest of the text to fill in the gap.

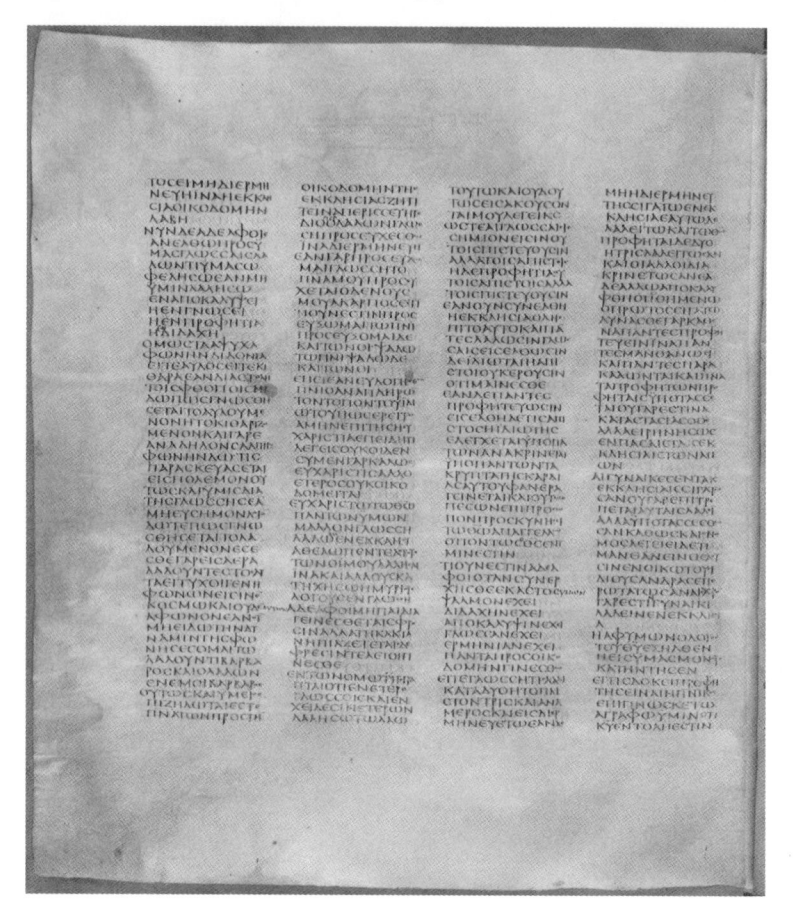

A portion of 1 Cor 14 in Codex Sinaiticus (ca. 375), containing one of the two oldest Christian copies of the Greek New Testament. In the fourth column, note a break in the normal flow of the text about halfway down the column and a second break in the normal flow of the text about three-quarters of the way down the column. Unlike the usual practice of writing without spaces or paragraph breaks in a column as elsewhere on this page, this paragraph shows that the uncertain copier separated the verses from the rest of the passage. The verses so copied are 1 Cor 14:34–35. Q83-f.4v [BL-f272v] for 1 Cor 14:5–37. (Reproduced by permission of the British Library)

This can also be seen in Codex Vaticanus, which leaves not only the rest of a column blank when a book is finished, but also an additional blank column that likely indicates that the copier thought that something was missing, as in the case of the ending of the Gospel of Mark (16:8). Many of the changes in the biblical text took place mainly in the second and third centuries, when the scriptural status of the New Testament books was not yet widely accepted, but some were introduced later as well. After the seventh century, most of the intentional changes disappeared, but those that do exist are not as many as some scholars have suggested.

As a result of the discoveries of many ancient biblical manuscripts in the last 130 years or so, biblical scholars have been able to establish a text of both the Old and New Testament that is effectively almost one thousand years closer to the original manuscripts than was possible before. The goal of reconstructing (as much as is possible) the most reliable text of what the original writers of the biblical books wrote comes about only by the work of many scholars who have taken on the complex and difficult task of sifting through the ancient manuscripts and comparing what they have in common and trying to account for their many differences. As a result of this process, we have discovered several important patterns:

1. There are three, possibly four, major *textual families* that have survived antiquity (Alexandrian, Western, Byzantine, but possibly also Caesarean). Some textual families were more accurate (Alexandrian) than others (Western and Byzantine); the Alexandrian texts generally reflect an earlier and more carefully prepared text of the New Testament books. There are no examples of the Byzantine text before the fourth century AD. The significance of this is that older translations of the Bible in English are based on this later text. By relying more upon the textual families that appear to have preserved the original text more accurately, many changes have been discovered, and scholars are convinced that they are closer to the original words in the biblical books than ever before. That said, none of these text-critical scholars would claim that they have now discovered the original wording of all of the books of the Bible. We may now be about as close as we can get to that goal, unless some additional, major discoveries are made.

2. After extensive comparison of the biblical manuscripts, scholars discovered that numerous variants or corruptions of the text had crept into the New Testament manuscripts over the centuries, and that the more reliable earlier manuscripts better reflected what the original writers wrote—with a few notable exceptions.

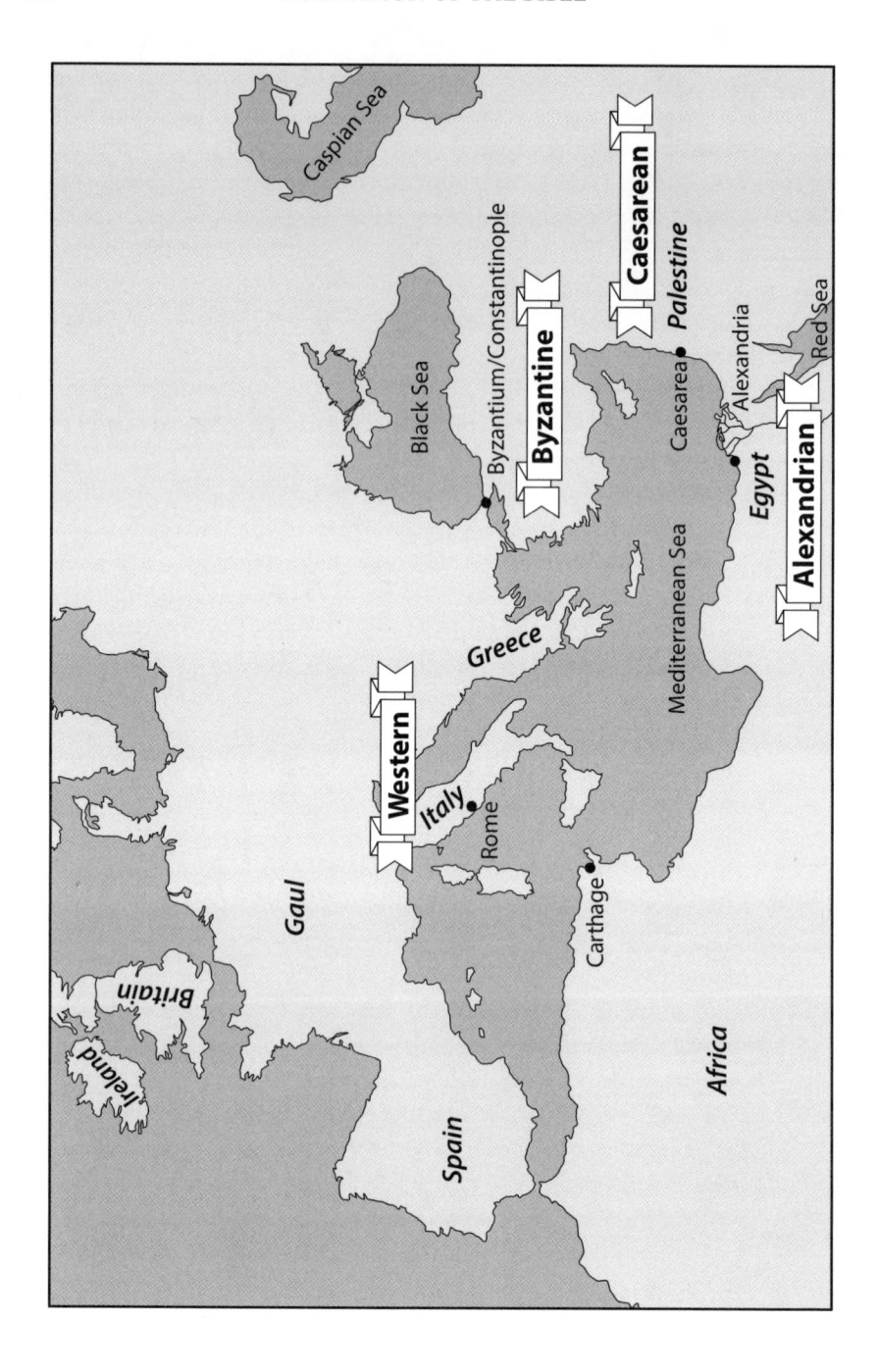

This map shows the locations of the various manuscript families that developed over the centuries from the copiers producing copies of the church's Scriptures.

3. As a result of the more recent discovery of many more ancient biblical manuscripts, all earlier translations—namely, those produced before 1993, are essentially out of date—an unfortunate consequence of reassembling a text closer to the biblical original than was possible earlier. With the publication of the most recent editions of critical, scholarly texts of the New Testament—the United Bible Society's 5th Edition of the *Greek New Testament* (2013) and the Nestle/Aland 28th edition (2012) of the Greek testament (called, ironically enough, by its Latin title, the *Novum Testamentum Graece*)—we draw closer yet to the original text of the New Testament, but it would be a mistake to believe that we have reached that goal. There are still some challenging and difficult passages to unravel, to which biblical scholars can offer tenuous, possible solutions, but certainty is not yet available.

Since almost all modern translations of the New Testament depend on these two modern texts of the Greek New Testament, translations dating before these editions are not as reliable or as accurate and do not accurately reflect the latest understanding of what the biblical writers wrote. A third Greek New Testament was introduced by Michael Holmes in 2010 that has some 540 differences with the two major Greek texts above (see his *The Greek New Testament: SBL Edition*, 2010), so it is clear there is still an element of uncertainty and debate about what the original text of the New Testament books looked like. Likewise, the more recent *Greek New Testament*, Tyndale House Edition (2017), is also a carefully prepared edition, but there are still some challenging and difficult passages to unravel, to which biblical scholars can usually offer only tenuous solutions, and certainty is not always possible. None of the present editions of the Greek text and none of the earlier biblical manuscripts that we now possess take us back to the first century when the New Testament writers wrote, but we need not be anxious about such ongoing critical discussion; again, *we are now closer to the original texts than ever before*—even if we are not there yet, but the core Christian beliefs are not now (nor earlier) in doubt!

Church pastors and a few biblical scholars today continue to make sensational claims, saying that we have the original text of the Bible and/or that none of the textual variants in the manuscripts that we possess affects any major Christian doctrine. That, of course, is an overstatement. There are several textual variants that *do* impact significant Christian doctrine (John 3:13, 1 John 5:7–8, Mark 1:1, and several others), but there are many other passages that are clear on such matters, so there is no need for alarm.

What can we say about the original text of the New Testament Scriptures? Christians the world over are anxious to know whether their Bible is trustworthy and whether it is based on the most reliable evidence. Because Christians base their faith, lifestyle, and hope in the Scriptures that they regularly read, they want to know if the texts deserve such trust. The answer, of course, is yes, but that does not mean that we know everything that we would like to know about the original text of the Bible. What we do know is that the Bible is very clear on who God is, how one establishes a relationship with God, what God has done for us in his Son, Jesus, and what the will of God is for our daily living. There are many questions for which we do not yet have fully satisfactory answers; but from the Scriptures, we get a pretty good handle on the most important ones!

The Greek New Testament and Modern Translations

The relationship between ancient manuscripts and modern translations of the Bible can be complex. Bible translators regularly face difficult choices about how to render words and meanings from one language into another. What we sometimes forget is that translators work with multiple manuscripts and must also make choices about what to include in their translations. In the pre-modern era, Desiderius Erasmus, the famed scholar of Rotterdam, produced the first modern Greek text of the New Testament in 1516, making use of two twelfth-century minuscule manuscripts found in the library of Basel, Switzerland. He later found and used four more manuscripts, none of which dated before the tenth century AD, which he used to produce subsequent editions of his Greek New Testament.

Desiderius Erasmus of Rotterdam (1466–1536) produced the first "modern" Greek New Testament in 1516 and in several subsequent editions. His Greek text became the standard text for translators of the New Testament, including those scholars who produced the King James Version of the Bible. (Painting by Hans Holbein the Younger, 1523)

It is well known that Erasmus's Greek version of 1 John 5:7–8 was reconstructed from the later Latin Vulgate and includes the words: "there are three that bear record in heaven, the Father, Son, and Holy Spirit." This passage, commonly called the "Johannine Comma," has no ancient Greek manuscript support. How, then, did it find its way into the King James Version of the Bible? Erasmus did not want to include it in his Greek text, but he gave in to pressure from others. He produced five editions of his Greek New Testament (1516, 1519, 1522, 1527, 1535), and subsequently the Calvinist Theodore Beza used Erasmus's 1522 edition as the basis for his *textus receptus* or "received text," which became the basis for the translation of the King James Bible.

Turning to the question of how such translational choices are made today, as mentioned earlier, there are currently three major, modern Greek New Testaments that are used in most of the translations of the Bible (the Nestle/Aland 28th edition, the United Bible Society 5th edition, and the Michael Holmes *Greek New Testament: SBL Edition*, and the Tyndale *Greek New Testament*). The biblical texts in the first two of these editions are almost exactly the same, even though they have different footnotes that support their respective texts of the New Testament. These modern Greek texts are all "eclectic" texts, that is, they constitute a *selective* text that uses the earliest and most reliable ancient Greek manuscripts to reproduce what the text-critical scholars believe is the earliest and most accurate text of the New Testament that is currently possible. What is not commonly acknowledged is that *there are no ancient Greek manuscripts that look exactly like these eclectic or selective texts* of the Greek New Testament that we have today. Likewise, there are no two ancient manuscripts that are exactly the same. The textual critics have constructed their respective texts of the New Testament by examining, comparing, and assessing a large variety of ancient biblical manuscripts. All modern translators of the New Testament Scriptures use these Greek texts for their translations, so these Greek texts are critical to the church today.

The most important ancient biblical manuscripts that scholars use to produce their Greek New Testaments are from the third to the fifth centuries AD. For example, one of the most important, early third-century manuscripts, a fragmentary text commonly known as $\mathfrak{P}^{45}$ (papyrus manuscript number 45), contains portions of the Gospels and Acts. Similarly, the earliest known fragmentary manuscript containing most of the letters of Paul, is commonly called $\mathfrak{P}^{46}$ and contains most of the letters usually attributed to Paul except for the Pastoral Epistles (1–2 Tim, Titus), and Philemon, but Hebrews is included. Of the space on the leaves that are missing from this manuscript, there is not adequate space to include all of the letters of Paul, especially the Pastoral Epistles. This is similar to the fragmentary Codex B (Vaticanus) that omits the Pastoral Epistles and Philemon. There are only two known manuscripts of the New Testament from the second century; both are highly fragmentary and each contains only a few verses from the Gospel of John; namely, 𝔓⁵² (ca. AD 125) and 𝔓⁹⁰ (roughly middle to late second century). All of the rest date from the third century and later.

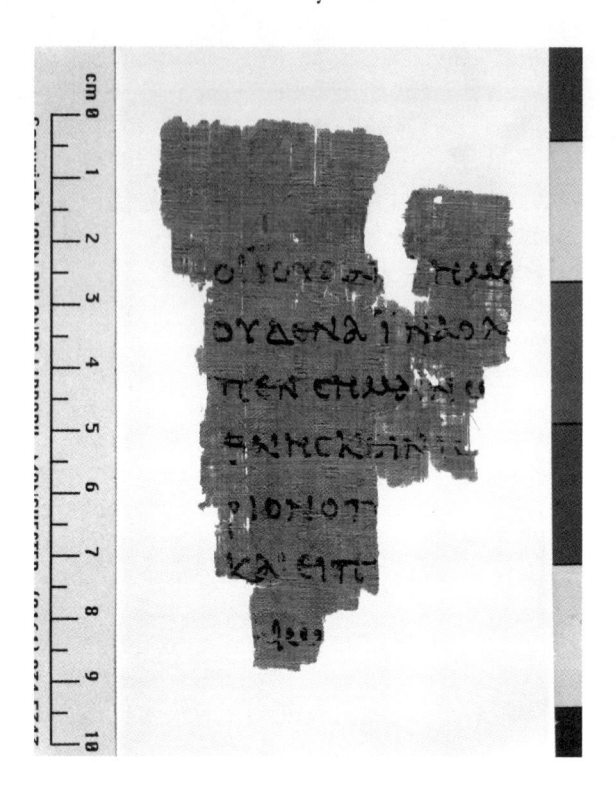

𝔓⁵² (ca. AD 125). This fragment of John 18:31–33 is the oldest known manuscript of any New Testament book. (Courtesy of John Rylands University Library, Manchester, England)

As we noted before, the most complete early Greek manuscripts containing all or most of the books in the New Testament are Codex Sinaiticus (ca. AD 375) and Codex Vaticanus (ca. AD 350). There are earlier manuscripts for parts of the New Testament, but they contain only a few books; the two most important exceptions are 𝔓⁴⁵ (fragments of all four Gospels and Acts, ca. early third century AD) and 𝔓⁴⁶ (containing most of the letters attributed to Paul, ca. AD 200). As close as these manuscripts allow us to get to the originals, there is always hope that other manuscripts will be found in some cave or other location by archaeologists or persons who happen upon them by accident. Future discoveries may answer some of our remaining questions.

The challenging work of text-critical scholars is essential to the church, but theirs is a task that receives little attention in most of our churches. If the past is at all indicative of the future of Bible translations, it is likely that in coming years, further changes will be made in future translations of the Bible based on additional manuscript discoveries or reassessments of the present evidence. Those who faithfully read their Bibles need not fear that something will be discovered that will negatively impact their faith, but readers should be advised that the work of establishing the earliest text of the Bible is a work in progress and will continue that way for the foreseeable future.

Translations

What Constitutes a Translation?

A Bible translation, in brief, is a careful rendering of the words of the Bible from the original languages (Hebrew, Aramaic, and/or Greek) into another language. It takes into consideration the various nuances of language, idiom, and culture, and offers meaningful equivalents in another language. A Bible paraphrase is different from a translation only in degree, not in kind. Paraphrases are translations that are less literal than the standard translations, but they also seek to present the full sense of the biblical text "in other words," in language that is easier to understand. They are generally directed to a lower reading level and phrased in more idiomatic and accessible language. Since exact word-for-word translation from one language to another is impossible and often makes little sense to readers even when approximated, translators regularly do their best to convey the full sense of the biblical text in equivalent *words*, without losing the original *meaning* of the biblical text. Those with more experience in reading the Bible and with some knowledge of translations often prefer the more literal translations such as the New Revised Standard Version, the New International Version, the Revised English Bible, the New Jerusalem Bible, or the more recent Common English Bible. These and other translations represent attempts to be faithful to the original language and meaning in engagingly readable English.

The Importance of Ancient Translations

The oldest translation of any portion of the Bible dates from the early third century BC and translates the Law or Pentateuch into Greek and was largely completed by the late second century BC. We discussed this translation earlier and acknowledged its value. It was copied and circulated in Jewish communities throughout the Greco-Roman world, and it also served as the Scriptures of the early Christian churches.

From the late second century AD, the early Christians also began producing translations of their sacred Scriptures. These translations include the Old Latin, Latin Vulgate, Old Syriac, Syriac Peshitta, Ethiopic, Gothic, Slavonic, and Armenian translations of the New Testament—though even the most well-known of these are rarely mentioned in churches today. None of these translations include exactly the same books of the Bible, and occasionally they include books that were not later included in the Bible. Apart from Jerome's Latin Vulgate, most of these early translations are of poor quality. They nonetheless reflect the early Christian perspective that the sacred Scriptures should be translated into the languages of the people that they were seeking to convert to the Christian faith. Church leaders realized how important it was for those who had become Christians to have the Scriptures in their own languages.

The Christians for whom these various translations were produced appear to have welcomed them as their sacred Scriptures and used them in their worship, instruction, and mission. So far as is known, no religious community ever thought that their Bible translation was uninspired or of less value than the Greek or Hebrew originals. Correspondingly, Christians of every language regularly accept their translations of the Bible as inspired Scripture; neither inspiration nor Scripture was limited to a particular language or culture. No Christians in antiquity claimed that the inspiration of their Scriptures was restricted to the original manuscripts or to the original languages in which the biblical books were written. As was true then, translations today vary in quality, but most (though not all) present adequately the core teachings of the Christian faith.

Early English Translations and the King James Version

John Wycliffe's translation of the Bible from Latin into English (1380–1382) is the first known English Bible.

John Wycliffe (1329–1384) (John M. Kennedy T., Creative Commons)

A number of English translations of the Bible were produced after that, and one of the most influential was that of William Tyndale, known as the Tyndale Bible (1526–1534), though he had not completed the Old Testament.

William Tyndale (1494–1536) produced the best-known English translation of the Christian Scriptures (New Testament) in 1526 (New Testament) and much of the Old Testament by 1534, but he did not complete it before he was executed in 1536. (Image from *Foxe's Book of Martyrs*; public domain)

This translation was followed by the Coverdale Bible in 1535, which was later revised and republished in 1539 as The Great Bible. John Rogers (1500–1555), who took the pen name Thomas Matthew, produced what became known as the Matthew Bible (1537), and he completed the Old Testament that was left unfinished by William Tyndale. In 1560, William Whittingham led some scholars to produce the Geneva Bible, which was a complete revision of the Great Bible. Matthew Parker produced the Bishop's Bible in 1568, and copies of it were placed in all churches of England between 1568 and 1606. The continual publication of English Bibles led two Roman Catholic scholars to publish an English translation of the Bible with notes supporting Catholic teaching. This translation was called the Douay-Rheims Bible (1582 for the New Testament and 1610 for the Old Testament).

Without question, the most remarkable and influential English translation of the Bible came with the publication of the King James Authorized Version of the Bible in 1611. Some fifty-four of the most talented and leading translators of the day were involved in the five-year project, translating the Scriptures under the mandate that it "had to be made of the whole Bible, as consonant as can be to the original Hebrew and Greek; and this to be set out and printed without marginal notes, and only to be used in all churches of England in time of divine service." (This quote is from Alister McGrath, *In the Beginning: The Story of the King James Bible and How It Changed a Nation, a Language, and a Culture* [New York: Anchor Books, 2001], 163–64.)

While many Christians today continue to use this King James Version (KJV), we now have biblical manuscripts that are hundreds of years closer to the original biblical text than was known when the KJV and all earlier English translations were published. That is, the King James Bible and earlier translations were all based on later and more recent biblical manuscripts. Although it was the best English translation of its time and for centuries afterward, it was nevertheless based on inferior manuscripts that were late in origin and contained many mistakes and corruptions of the text. Biblical scholars today have produced earlier and more accurate Greek New Testaments than was possible before, and all modern translators make use of them. For those who want a more accurate text based on the earliest known biblical manuscripts, I recommend one of the many good modern translations (a number of which are listed just below). This does not suggest that those who read the King James Version or its revised edition (NKJV) are in serious error for doing so. Many Christians came to their faith through the reading, preaching, and teaching of the Bible in the King James Version, and they have also grown in their faith through it. However, it is possible to get closer to the original text of both the Old and New Testaments than was possible before, and those who continue to read the King James Version would benefit considerably by also reading a modern translation. By doing so, they will see that some passages in the King James Version are later additions that were not a part of what the biblical writers wrote.

Which Translation?

I am often asked which translation of the Bible is the best one to read today. My response is frequently "the one you most enjoy and read most often!" There are some translations that reflect careful attention to the original languages better than others, generally offering more accurate translations and paraphrases of the biblical books. The following list of translations is not at all complete (there are many more!), but those listed are among the most accurate available today and are recommended for their quality in translation. Having said that, I should stress again that *no* translation is perfect and *none* can claim to be based on the original manuscripts. On the other hand, all of the most recent translations are much closer to the original manuscripts than any of the earlier translations. The best translations today are based on the best and earliest textual evidence and are prepared by competent translators. These include, but are *not* limited to, the following:

1. The most familiar or popular translations today that generally reflect careful scholarship and give attention to important text-critical scholarship include the Revised Standard Version (RSV), the New Revised Standard Version (NRSV), the New Revised Standard Version Updated Edition (NRSVue), the New International Version (NIV) or Today's New International Version (TNIV), The New English Bible (NEB), the more recent Revised English Bible (REB), the American Standard Translation (AST), the New Jerusalem Bible (NJB), and the new Common English Bible (CEB). The New American Standard Bible (NASB) is very literal and a delight to some beginning Greek students who wish to read something closer to a word-for-word translation, but the English lacks fluidity. The Common English Bible (CEB) reflects careful biblical scholarship and will find considerable approval from readers who want a modern English translation that is not overly loaded with technical notes or cumbersome language. Another fairly new translation, the English Standard Version (ESV 2008), is a fairly good translation as well. Its Study Bible edition is a hefty tome that reflects conservative biblical scholarship.

2. Paraphrases are free translations that tend to be fairly accurate in terms of the meaning of the biblical text, though they sacrifice some of the literal meaning of the original words. The more accurate ones include Today's English Version (TEV) and the Contemporary English Version (CEV). The *Living Bible* is the most published English paraphrase, but it does not reflect a careful reading of the biblical languages or the important critical notes in the standard Greek and Hebrew texts of the Bible. It nevertheless has had a good reception and generally avoids most controversies in translations. (An update to the *Living Bible* resulted in a more scholarly yet still modern version, the *New Living Translation* [NLT].) Some more free translations are not as carefully produced and often lead the readers in the wrong direction, including the *Amplified Bible* and the *Cotton Patch Version*.

For those who are unfamiliar with the Greek and Hebrew languages, *it is helpful to own at least two translations* of the Bible. It is often the case that one translation will help the reader understand the other.

Summary

Those readers who desire a better understanding of the formation of the New Testament canon as well as the text of the New Testament will want to know something about how the early writers and copiers of the church's Scriptures produced what they did. How careful were the early copiers and why did they use the codex instead of the more popular scroll? Did the size of a codex affect how the early Christians thought about the scope of their Scriptures? Since formal writings were all produced in scrolls in the first century, did that have an impact on how the early Christians viewed their religious texts? Did they initially think of them more as notebooks and nonprofessional documents that could be easily changed as occasion required?

In the first few centuries, those who copied the New Testament books felt quite free to make many changes in the biblical text, as we noted above. The vast number of them advanced Christian orthodoxy. When were these books recognized as sacred Scripture, and when (and why) did changes to the text of Scripture begin to be discouraged? There was widespread use of Christian writings almost from the time they were written, and many of those writings were regularly read in church worship and used in advancing the church's mission and catechetical needs.

By the end of the second century, several (though not yet all) of the New Testament writings were beginning to be called "Scripture," even though they had earlier been *used like* Scripture; that is, in an authoritative manner in the churches. As we saw, this was especially true of the four Gospels and most of the letters of Paul to churches. There was no consistent stabilization in the order or sequence of the books until it became possible to circulate all of the books of the Bible in one volume (fourth century AD), but even then there was a certain flexibility in terms of what books were included in these larger codices.

The choice of the specific books that actually made up the surviving biblical manuscripts is an important factor that is often overlooked by biblical scholars. The ancient manuscripts let us know what books most influenced the early Christian churches and (conversely) which ones did not! Long after church councils began meeting to discuss which books constituted sacred Scripture and could be read in the churches, many churches continued to use officially rejected books in their worship services. The various lists of Old and New Testament books (see lists in the next chapter) attest to this practice in the churches, but the later manuscripts also inform us about the evolving status of the church's Scriptures as well as major concerns or challenges they faced.

Since we know of no early churches that had the same books in their sacred collections that we have today, we can only wonder if the faith of the early Christians would have been much different if they had Bibles like the ones we have today. It is clear that the most important traditions about Jesus—along with the early church's core teachings about him—are presented in the New Testament writings, but several other writings also had some effect on the life and teachings of the early churches. Should we become more aware of them and learn what they have to contribute to our understanding of the early church and its mission in the world?

Finally, while the very words of the biblical books are important to Christians today, this was apparently not as important in the developing early churches. Our brief look at textual criticism suggests that the variety of texts in the biblical manuscripts was greater than what we who live on this side of the printing press often imagine. In the modern world, we have the ability to produce millions of copies of the Bible without one variant in its text, but in antiquity there were no two manuscripts exactly alike. All were hand-copied, and those who consider that to be a relatively easy task should try making just one copy of the Scriptures by hand! Scholars today debate whether there were some 200,000 (conservatively), 300,000, or even 400,000 variants in the wording in these manuscripts. Again, all of those options are more than the number of words of the New Testament! (There are also some acknowledged 900,000 variants in the surviving Hebrew manuscripts of the Old Testament.) Until the invention of the printing press, we had no two biblical manuscripts exactly the same. Most of the variants are of little consequence, are easily corrected, and do not affect Christian teaching or beliefs, but it is important to remember that some intentional variants were introduced by well-intentioned scribes trying to clarify the teachings of the church. A fixed text of the New Testament Scriptures was never physically possible, of course, until the invention of the printing press.

Interestingly, we are once again in a generation not unlike the time when the early transmission of the Bible took place, when the text of the Bible was more fluid. With the digitized transmission of the Bible now available on the internet and various other computerized venues, the ability to download and change the biblical text to suit one's fancy is once again changing, reflecting the current fluidity of the text in churches. This phenomenon is certainly more manifest now than when Christians carried their Bibles to church, and often in one translation alone! In many new paraphrases of the Bible today, changes to the meaning and wording of the biblical texts are quite common. The electronic age has allowed fluidity to happen once again, since well-intentioned teachers and preachers (not to mention authors!) can readily change the biblical text to readings "in other words" and interpretations. Many of these "other words" are regularly read in the churches that otherwise honor the Christian Scriptures. I suspect that members of those churches seldom know when a text has been changed to something else that supposedly clarifies its original meaning! In such contexts, the study of canon formation is as important and as urgent as ever before.

In the next chapter, we will focus on the how early church councils affected the contents of the biblical canon and also focus on the value of the ancient lists of the church's Scriptures.

Chapter 7

Councils, Catalogues, and Canons

Church Councils and the Biblical Canon

As we saw earlier, several individuals played a significant role in the formation of the Christian Bible, especially Justin Martyr, Irenaeus, Tertullian, Origen, Eusebius, Athanasius, Jerome, and Augustine. By the end of the fourth century, several prominent groups had played similar roles: three church councils had met at Laodicea (363), Hippo (393), and Carthage (397) to discuss, among other things, the scope of the Christian Bible—that is, what books were to be recognized as authoritative sacred Scriptures and read in the churches.

Although a number of Christians may think that these church councils actually determined which books were included in the Bible and which were not, it is more accurate to say that council decisions represented the books that had already obtained prominence and use in the various regions where the councils met, and that only in cases of dispute over the "fringe books" were such council decisions made. If church councils made any decisions at all about the scope of the biblical canon, they were only in regard to the books that were on the "fringe" of the collections that obtained recognition in some churches. This was not the case in the majority of the New Testament books that had long enjoyed widespread approval and use in the churches.

The following examples of church council decisions demonstrate what the views were in the communities surrounding those local church council meetings, which were represented by their respective bishops at the councils. Such decisions came only at the end of a long period of use in the churches and were *not* generally unilateral decisions "from the top." The local councils did not so much create biblical canons as they *endorsed* them; their decisions *reflected the state of affairs in their time*. In regard to the "fringe books" that did not reflect a majority of churches, the local church councils actually did make decisions that appear to have been based on what the *majority* view was at that time among the churches represented *at each council*. Interestingly, centuries after some church councils began to make such endorsements (see Pseudo-Athanasius, ca. sixth century, and the later Stichometry of Nicephorus, ca. 850), Christians were still using books in their worship and instruction that had earlier been condemned and rejected by local church councils. In light of this, it may be prudent to reflect on the influence and persuasiveness of councils: Why would earlier council decisions about rejected books need to be repeated centuries later if no one was using the so-called nonbiblical (rejected) books in their churches? It is safe to assume that what councils said was not always followed in the churches!

Among the several council decisions in the early church regarding its biblical canon, two are probably the most important. The first is the council held at Laodicea (ca. 360), which in its Canon 59 decided which psalms could be read in the churches. Canon 60 of the same council listed the books of the Old Testament canon (see the list in Table 4 in chapter 4 above). As it happens, these books are the same as those listed in the canon of Athanasius (367), except that Ruth is combined with Judges and Esther immediately follows. The council at Rome in 382 likely influenced the later councils at Hippo and at Carthage that accepted the decisions of Rome, as we see in the Carthage 397 and 419. It is most likely that the most important council decisions took place in AD 393, when the church council that met at Hippo in North Africa set forth a biblical canon similar to the one produced by Athanasius and affirmed by Augustine. Although the deliberations of this council are now lost, they were summarized in the proceedings of the Council of Carthage in North Africa in 397 and 419. This was apparently the first church council to make a formal decision on the scope and contents of the biblical canon, although the Council of Laodicea in 360 (mentioned immediately above) may have had some influence on it. Below we will list for easier comparison some of the collections determined by the church fathers of the fourth and fifth centuries, as well as some of those affirmed by church councils.

As a side note, it is also important to recall that decisions like those made by these councils have continued into the relatively recent past. As late as 1950, the Holy Synod of the Greek Orthodox Church authorized as part of its Old Testament canon several apocryphal books, including 2 Ezra, 3 Maccabees, and 4 Maccabees, which were placed in an appendix. The Old Testament of the Russian Bible of 1956 has the same contents as the Greek Bible, but 3 Ezra and 4 Maccabees are absent.

In the history of Christianity, then, the first Seven Ecumenical Church Councils, from the First Council of Nicaea (325) to the Second Council of Nicaea (787), all represent collective attempts to reach an orthodox consensus and to unify Christendom under the state church of the Roman Empire. All Seven Ecumenical Councils were established by a Byzantine emperor of the Eastern Roman Empire and all were held in that domain. Yet none of them dealt with the church's Scriptures; that is, with which books formed the church's Bible.

The Council of Trent

The Eastern churches appear to have been more conservative in their selection of writings for their Old Testament biblical canon than the churches in the West. This church council at the end of the process (for the Roman Catholic Church) was the Council of Trent. The first *ecumenical* church council to deal specifically with the scope of the church's Scriptures and other matters was held at Trent, and in twenty-five sessions between 1545–1563. In its fourth session on April 8, 1546, the church set forth its decision regarding the limits of the Old Testament canon and included the apocryphal books. The fourth session states in part:

> The holy, ecumenical and general Council ... following ... the examples of the orthodox Fathers ... receives and venerates with a feeling of piety and reverence all the books of the Old and New Testaments, since one God is the author of both; also the traditions, whether relating to faith or to morals, as having been dictated either orally by Christ or by the Holy Ghost, and preserved in the Catholic Church in unbroken succession.

This council affirmed the validity of both Scripture and unwritten traditions (church pronouncements) as sources of truth, as well as *the church's sole right to interpret Scripture*, an assertion of pivotal importance during the Reformation. It also affirmed the authority of the text of the Latin Vulgate for its Scripture, though it ordered a revision of it. The main thrust of the council was its repudiation of the spread of Protestantism and its affirmation of the books in its Scriptures. It also gave a decree on the books of the Old and New Testaments.

The list of Old Testament books affirmed at the Council of Trent is as follows:

> The five books of Moses (Genesis, Exodus, Leviticus, Numbers, Deuteronomy); Joshua, Judges, Ruth, 1–2 Samuel, 1–2 Kings, 1–2 Chronicles, 1–2 Esdras, Tobit, Judith, Esther (with additions), Job, Psalms, Proverbs, Ecclesiastes, the Song of Songs, Wisdom of Solomon, Ecclesiasticus (Sirach), Isaiah, Jeremiah, Baruch; Ezekiel, Daniel (with additions); the Twelve Minor prophets (Hosea, Joel, Amos, Obadiah, Jonah, Micah, Nahum, Habakkuk, Zephaniah, Haggai, Zechariah, Malachi) and 1–2 Maccabees.

The New Testament books are listed as follows:

> Matthew, Mark, Luke, and John; Acts, fourteen epistles of Paul (Romans, 1–2 Corinthians, Galatians, Ephesians, Philippians, Colossians, 1–2 Thessalonians, 1–2 Timothy, Titus, Philemon, Hebrews); 1–2 Peter, 1–2–3 John, James, Jude, and Revelation.

After listing the books, the document goes on to say, "If anyone does not accept as sacred and canonical the aforesaid books in their entirety and with all their parts, as they have been accustomed to be read in the Catholic Church ... let him be anathema" (trans. F. J. Stendebach). This decision was reaffirmed by the First Vatican Council (1869–70).

In the year 1559, the Reformed churches set forth their Gallican Confession (*Confessio Gallicana*) and affirmed again in the Belgic Confession (articles IV and V) of 1561 a biblical canon that excluded the apocryphal books that were included by the Roman Catholics. In England in 1562 and 1571, in the sixth of the Thirty-Nine Articles, the Church of England affirmed the use of the apocryphal books, but added that they were not to be used to set forth or establish the church's teaching. After listing the books that belong to the larger Old Testament canon and affirming the current Protestant Old Testament canon, the document concludes: "And the other books (as Hierome [Jerome] saith) the Church doth read for example of life and instruction of manners, but yet doth it not apply them to establish any doctrine" (trans. O. Chadwick). After this statement, the apocryphal books are listed.

Of Councils and Canon

It may be helpful at this point to integrate the council-oriented church history with some of the other significant moments in canon formation that we have already reviewed in previous chapters. In contrast to the ecumenical councils that never addressed the scope of the church's Scriptures, the local council at Trent in 1546 is similar to the decisions made earlier at the Synods of Hippo Regius in North Africa (393 and later expanded briefly in 397 and 419 at Carthage), but, as noted above, the acts of this council are now lost. A brief summary of those acts was read and accepted at the later councils at Carthage in 397 and 419. Augustine significantly influenced these councils, and he accepted the earlier list of Scriptures set forth by Athanasius in his AD 367 *Festal Letter*, discussed earlier. At the Council of Rome initiated by Damasus I in 383, there seems to be agreement with the biblical canon set forth at the council of Hippo, though the list published may be a sixth-century compilation. Likewise, Damasus I's commissioning of the Latin Vulgate in 383 was likely influential in fixing the biblical canon in the regions of the Western Empire; in 405, Pope Innocent I sent a similar list of sacred books to a Gallic bishop in Toulouse.

It appears that when bishops and councils spoke on the matter of canon formation, they were not defining something *new*, but rather they were reflecting and selectively sanctioning that which was already a matter of popular practice and circulation in their local churches. We might well recall at this point that the fourth century saw widespread agreement in the West concerning the twenty-seven books that make up the New Testament canon. By the seventh century in the East, with few exceptions, all of the books of the New Testament, including the long-debated book of Revelation, were accepted as canonical Scripture. In essence, the majority of churches in the East and West agreed on the scope of the New Testament canon by the middle to the end of the fifth century. Again, that does not mean that churches had no other notions about which books were their Scriptures; the nonbiblical books in the surviving biblical manuscripts suggest otherwise.

By way of review, the following is a list of those councils (and in one case, a decision by Innocent I that had an effect comparable to that of these council decisions) that dealt specifically with the scope of the Christian Scriptures.

1. Council of Laodicea (ca. 363). A local council of the church, in union with Rome, produced a list of books of the Bible similar to the list of Scriptures affirmed at the much later Council of Trent. This list was one of the earliest known church decisions on the scope of the biblical canon.

2. Council of Rome (382). A local church council under the authority of Pope Damasus I (366–384), which gave a list of books of the Old and New Testaments that is identical to the list that was later approved at the Council of Trent.

3. Council of Hippo (393). A local North African church council, again operating in union with and under the authority of the bishop of Rome, approved a list of the books that comprise the Old and New Testament canon. It is the same as that which was later approved at Trent.

4. Council of Carthage (397). Like the Council of Hippo, a local North African church council in concert with and under the authority of the bishop of Rome, approved a list of books comprising the church's Old and New Testament canon (again, the same as was later approved by the Council of Trent).

5. Innocent I (bishop of Rome, 401–417) in 405 responded to a request by Exuperius, bishop of Toulouse, with a list of canonical books of Scripture. His list was the same as that which was later approved by the Council of Trent. (See the list of Old Testament books in the list in Table 4 at the end of chapter 4 and the New Testament books listed in Table 6 in chapter 7 below.)

6. Council of Carthage (419). Like Hippo and the first Carthaginian council, a local North African church council, again in union with and under the authority of the Bishop of Rome, approved a list comprising the Old Testament and New Testament canons (same as that later approved by the Council of Trent).

7. Council of Florence (1441). An ecumenical council that gave a complete list of the Old and New Testament books. This list was later adopted at the Council of Trent. It was also at Florence that the so-called apocryphal books were first identified as "deuterocanonical" books; that is, as distinct from the "protocanonical" books (the thirty-nine books in the Jewish Scriptures and the Protestant Old Testament Scriptures that all Christians accept).

8. Council of Trent (1545–1563). This council was called primarily to respond to the perceived heresy of the Reformers. It is one of the most important councils in Roman Catholic Church history, since it clearly defined church beliefs that are current to this day about the scope of the church's biblical canon. The canon of the Old and New Testaments received final definitions: forty-six books in the Old Testament and twenty-seven in the New Testament (see list above). Both collections were and are held to be of equal authority. The Latin Vulgate edition of the Bible was also accepted as the authoritative edition of the church's Bible.

Protocanonical, Deuterocanonical, and Apocryphal Books

The term "deuterocanonical" has been used since the fifteenth or sixteenth centuries in the Catholic Church and Eastern Christianity to describe certain books and passages of the Christian Old Testament that are not part of the Hebrew Bible, or Jewish Scriptures; that is, the "protocanonical" books. The deuterocanonical books are regularly called the "Apocrypha" in Protestant churches. That term earlier referred to "hidden" books that were often read by new Christians or by those well advanced in their Christian journeys. Subsequently, at least by the late fourth or fifth centuries, individuals and churches began to refer to and even list nonbiblical books or *uninspired* books; that is, books whose message was considered false, books through which and through whose authors God evidently did not speak. Perhaps because "Apocrypha" had taken on such negative connotations, some in the Catholic Church at the Council of Florence began to speak of a "second canon" to identify the Jewish religious writings that were not a part of the "first canon" ("protocanonical") books.

As with many other council decisions that we reviewed above, these labels reflect earlier debates among churches and church leaders. Jerome, for one, evidently wanted to recognize only those books in the protocanonical collection, the books that would later be recognized as Scripture by Jews and Protestant Christians; but Augustine wanted to keep the "second canon" of Old Testament texts and argued persuasively in his day that these books should be read in the churches and therefore classified among the church's sacred Scriptures.

Which of these books are acknowledged today? The Roman Catholics regularly include in their deuterocanonical collection the following books: Tobit, Judith, the six Additions to Esther, 1 and 2 Maccabees, the Wisdom of Solomon, the Wisdom of Sirach (= Ecclesiasticus), Baruch (chapter 6 of which is the Epistle of Jeremiah), and the three Additions to the book of Daniel; namely, the Prayer of Azariah and the Song of the Three Young Men, Susanna, and Bel and the Dragon. Eastern Orthodox Churches include not only the deuterocanonical books that are in Roman Catholic biblical canons, but also 3 Maccabees, Psalm 151, and 2 Esdras (1 Esdras in the Catholic deutercanonical books is the same as 2 Esdras in the Orthodox Bibles. 2 Esdras in the Catholic Bibles is equivalent to Ezra and Nehemiah.)

The Ethiopian Tewahedo Church Bible has an even broader collection of Old and New Testament Scriptures than the Roman Catholic and Eastern Orthodox churches. Its biblical canon has eighty-one books and includes not only those books held by other Christians, but also several others: the Old Testament books include 1 Enoch, Jubilees, and *1, 2,* and *3 Meqabyan* (not to be confused with 1, 2, and 3 Maccabees); the New Testament includes two *Books of the Covenant,* four *Books of Sinodos,* an *Epistle to Clement,* and the *Didascalia* (not exactly the same as an ancient Western book by the same title). Even the list of books that make up the total of eighty-one varies somewhat, depending on which ancient or modern source one uses.

New Testament Canon Catalogues or Lists

The following collection of lists or catalogues of New Testament Scriptures by the early Christians reflects not only the significant similarities of sacred texts that informed ancient faith and practice, but also in several cases, the differences among them. We noted earlier that long after church councils met to deliberate such matters, some churches continued to use books that were earlier rejected by the majority. It continues to become clear that when one group of churches accepted a collection of sacred Scriptures, this does not mean that all churches everywhere did the same. We will start with some of the earliest lists and proceed to later ones to demonstrate this point. I encourage readers to compare the lists, their sequences, and even their groupings and labels, where applicable. The sequence or order of the New Testament books, like those in the Old Testament, continued to vary for centuries.

Table 6: Early Lists of Scriptural Books

The following tables have been adapted from my earlier tables published on the internet as provided by the kind permission of Continuum International Publishing Group.

In the following sub-tables, when "Paul" is noted without any of his letters named (e.g., Table 6.A.) the source has stated that all of Paul's epistles are among the texts accepted, but has not indicated which epistles are meant or how many of his epistles are probably meant, though the present thirteen epistles attributed to Paul appear to have been widely, almost universally, accepted, and Hebrews was thought to have been written by Paul, as well. If "Paul" is noted followed by a number (e.g., [13] or [14?]), the source has stated that all of Paul's epistles are among the texts accepted and also noted how many of his epistles are accepted. If the number following his name is 14, the source is including the Epistle to the Hebrews as Pauline. If there is a question mark, it is unclear as to which epistles were meant to be included. When the source actually names the epistles credited to Paul, the notation "*Paul*" is followed by a listing of the epistles credited to him in the order the source has listed them. This same pattern is followed for listings of the Gospels and the Catholic Epistles.

The lists are rendered in the order that the ancient sources listed the accepted texts and not in a fashion so as to make comparison simple. A careful reader will quickly grasp that the many sources, especially the early sources, were definitely not uniform in the order in which they listed the accepted New Testament books. The actual footnotes for each of the tables will appear at the end of the chapter.

A. Three *Possible* Early Lists Based on Eusebius

Irenaeus (170–180)[1]	Clement of Alex. (170)[2]	Origen (220–230)[3]
Matthew	Jude	Matthew
Mark	Barnabas	Mark
Luke	Apocalypse of Peter	Luke
John	Hebrews	John
Revelation	Acts	1, 2 Peter
1 John	Paul	Revelation
1 Peter	Matthew	1, 2, 3 John
Shepherd	Luke	Hebrews
Wisdom	Mark	Paul
Paul	John	

B. Lists of 4th-Century New Testament Collections of Scriptures

Eusebius[4]	Cyril of Jer.[5]	Athanasius[6]	Cheltenham[7]
Recognized			
Gospels (4)	Gospels (4)	*Gospels*	*Gospels*
Acts	Acts	Matthew	Matthew
Paul (14?)	*Catholic Epistles* (7)	Mark	Mark
1 John	James	Luke	Luke
1 Peter	1, 2 Peter	John	John
Revelation (?)	1, 2, 3 John	Acts	Paul (13)
Disputed	Jude(?)	*Catholic Epistles*	Acts
James	*Paul* (14)	James	Revelation
Jude	*Pseudepigrapha*	1, 2 Peter	1, 2, 3 John
2 Peter	Gospel of Thomas	1, 2, 3 John	1, 2 Peter
2, 3 John		Jude	
Revelation (?)		*Paul*	
Gospel of the Hebrews (?)		Romans	
Rejected		1, 2 Corinthians	
Acts of Paul		Galatians	
Shepherd		Ephesians	
Apocalypse of Peter		Philippians	
Barnabas		Colossians	
Didache		1, 2 Thessalonians	
Works cited		Hebrews	
by heretics		1, 2 Timothy	
Gospel of Peter		Titus	
Gospel of Thomas		Philemon	
Gospel Matthias		Revelation	
Acts of Andrew		**Catechetical Works**	
Acts of John		Didache	
		Shepherd of Hermas	

C. Lists of 4th-Century Collections

Epiphanius[8]	Apos. Canons[9]	Greg. of Naz.[10]	African Canons[11]	Jerome[12]
Gospels (4)	*Gospels*	Matt	Gospels (4)	*"Lord's Four"*
Paul (13)	Matthew	Mark	Acts	Matthew
Acts	Mark	Luke	Paul (13)	Mark
Catholic Epistles	Luke	John	Hebrews	Luke
James	John	Acts	1, 2 Peter	John
Peter	Paul (14)	Paul (14)	1, 2, 3 John	*Paul*
1, 2, 3 John	Peter (2)	*Catholic Epistles*	James	Romans
Jude	1, 2, 3 John	James	Jude	1, 2 Corinthians
Revelation	James	1, 2 Peter	Revelation	Galatians
Wisdom	Jude	1, 2, 3 John	**Approved to read**	Ephesians
Sirach	1, 2 Clement	Jude	Acts of Martyrs	Philippians
	Apos. Con.			1, 2 Thessalonians
	Acts			Colossians
				1, 2 Timothy
				Titus
				Philemon
				Hebrews
				1, 2 Peter
				1, 2, 3 John
				Jude
				James
				Acts
				Revelation

D. Lists of 4th-Century Collections

Augustine[13]	Amphiloch.[14]	Rufinus[15]	Innocent[16]	Syrian cat.[17]
		Canonical		
Gospels	*Gospels*	Gospels	Gospels (4)	*Gospels*
Matthew	Matthew	Matthew	Paul's epistles (13)[18]	Matthew
Mark	Mark	Mark	1, 2, 3 John	Mark
Luke	Luke	Luke	1, 2 Peter	Luke
John	John	John	Jude	John
Paul	Acts	Acts	James	Acts
Romans	*Paul (14?)*	Paul (14)	Acts	Galatians
1, 2 Cor	Romans	1, 2 Peter	Revelation	Romans
Galatians	1, 2 Cor	James	**Repudiated**	Hebrews
Ephesians	Galatians	Jude	(Books under the names of)	Colossians
Philippians	Ephesians	1, 2, 3 John	Matthias	Ephesians
1, 2 Thess	Philippians	Revelation	James the less	Philippians
Colossians	Colossians	**Ecclesiastical**	Peter+John = Leucian	1, 2 Thess
Titus	1, 2 Thess	Shepherd	Andrew = Xenocharides & Leonidas	1, 2 Timothy
Philemon	1, 2 Timothy	The Two Ways	Thomas & others	Titus
Hebrews	Titus	Preaching of Peter	Gospel of Thomas?	Philemon
1, 2 Peter	Philemon			
1, 2, 3 John	Hebrews (?)			
Jude	*Catholic Epistles (7)*			
James	James			
Acts	Peter			
Revelation	John			
	Jude (?)			
	Revelation (?)			

E. Lists of 4th-Century Collections

Muratorial Frag.[19]	Laodicea Synod[20]	Carthage Synod[21]	Eucherius[22]
Gospels	*Gospels*	Gospels (4)	
...	Matthew	Acts	Matthew
...	Mark	Paul (13)	Mark
Luke ("third book")	Luke	Hebrews	Luke
John ("fourth book")	John	1, 2 Peter	John
Epistles of John	Acts	1, 2, 3 John	Romans
Acts	*Catholic Epistles*	James	1, 2 Corinthians
Paul (churches)	James	Jude	Ephesians
Corinthians	1, 2 Peter	Revelation	1 Thessalonians
Ephesians	1, 2, 3 John		Colossians
Philippians	Jude		1, 2 Timothy
Colossians	*Paul*		Hebrews
Galatians	Romans		Acts
Thessalonians	1, 2 Corinthians		James
Romans	Galatians		1 John
Paul (individuals)	Ephesians		Revelation
Philemon	Philippians		**Missing**
Titus	Colossians		Galatians
1, 2 Timothy	1, 2 Thessalonians		2 Thessalonians
Jude	Hebrews		Titus
1, 2 *or* 3 John (only 2)	1, 2 Timothy		Philemon
Wisdom	Titus		2, 3 John
Revelation	Philemon		Jude
Apocalypse of Peter			
Forged (rejected)			
Epistle to the Laodiceans			
Epistle to the Alexandrians			
Others (?)			
Rejected			
Shepherd			
Works of Arsinous			
Valentinus			
Miltiades			
Basilides			
...			

F. Later New Testament Lists/Catalogues (5th, 6th, and 16th Centuries)

Gelasius[23]	Junilius[24]	Cassiodorus[25]	Isodore[26]	Trent Council[27]
Gospels	*Gospels*	*Gospels*	*Gospels*	Gospels (4)
Matthew	Matthew	Matthew	Matthew	Acts
Mark	Mark	Mark	Mark	Paul (14)
Luke	Luke	Luke	Luke	1, 2 Peter
John	John	John	John	1, 2, 3 John
Acts	Acts	Acts	*Paul*	James
Paul	Revelation	1 Peter	Romans	Jude
Romans	*Paul*	James	1, 2 Cor	Revelation
1, 2 Cor	Romans	1 John	Galatians	
Ephesians	1, 2 Cor	*Paul*	Ephesians	
1, 2 Thess	Galatians	Romans	Philippians	
Galatians	Ephesians	1 Cor	1, 2 Thess	
Philippians	Philippians	2 Cor	Colossians	
Colossians	1, 2 Thess	Galatians	1, 2 Timothy	
1, 2 Timothy	Colossians	Philippians	Titus	
Titus	1, 2 Timothy	Colossians	Philemon	
Philemon	Titus	Ephesians	Hebrews	
Hebrews	Philemon	1, 2 Thess	1, 2, 3 John	
Revelation	Hebrews	1, 2 Timothy	1, 2 Peter	
1, 2 Peter	James	Titus	Jude	
1, 2, 3 John	1, 2 Peter	Philemon	James	
Jude	Jude	Revelation	Acts	
	1, 2 John	**Missing**	Revelation	
		2 Peter		
		2, 3 John		
		Jude		
		Hebrews		

G. Uncial Manuscript Collections from the 4th & 5th Centuries

Vaticanus (4th c.)	Sinaiticus (4th c.)	Peshitta (SyrP) (5th c.)	Alexandrinus (5th c.)	Claromontanus (D; 5th–6th c.)[28]
Matthew	Matthew	Matthew	Matthew	*Gospels*
Mark	Mark	Mark	Mark	Matthew
Luke	Luke	Luke	Luke	John
John	John	John	John	Mark
Acts	Romans	Acts	Acts	Luke
James	1, 2 Cor	James	James	*Paul*
1, 2 Peter	Galatians	1 Peter	1, 2 Peter	Romans
1, 2, 3 John	Ephesians	1 John	1, 2, 3 John	1, 2 Cor
Jude	Philippians	Romans	Jude	Galatians
Romans	Colossians	1, 2 Cor	Romans	Ephesians
1, 2 Cor	1, 2 Thess	Galatians	1, 2 Cor	1, 2 Timothy
Galatians	Hebrews	Ephesians	Galatians	Titus
Ephesians	1, 2 Timothy	Philippians	Ephesians	Colossians
Philippians	Titus	Colossians	Philippians	Philemon
Colossians	Philemon	1, 2 Thess	Colossians	1, 2 Peter
1, 2 Thess	Acts	1, 2 Timothy	1, 2 Thess	James
Hebrews	James	Titus	Hebrews	1, 2, 3, John
Missing	1, 2 Peter	Philemon	1, 2 Timothy	Jude
1, 2 Timothy	1, 2, 3 John	Hebrews	Titus	Barnabas
Titus	Jude		Philemon	Revelation
Philemon	Revelation		Revelation	Acts
Revelation	Barnabas		1, 2 Clement	**Other works**
	Shepherd		Pss Solomon	Shepherd
	…			Acts of Paul
				Revelation of Peter
				Missing
				Philippians?
				1, 2 Thess
				Hebrews?

Table Notes

1. Eusebius, *Ecclesiastical History* 5.8.2–8 (ca. 320–330, Caesarea, Palestine). While Eusebius attributes this "canon" (*endiathēkon* = "encovenanted," or incorporated) collection to Irenaeus, it is probably Eusebius's listing of the references made by Irenaeus.

2. Eusebius, *Ecclesiastical History* 6.14.1–7 (ca. 320–330, Caesarea, Palestine). As with his attribution immediately above, while Eusebius attributes this "canon" (*endiathēkon*) collection to Clement, it is probably Eusebius's listing of the references made by Clement.

3. Eusebius, *Ecclesiastical History* 6.25.3–14. As we observed above, it is possible that this list is Eusebius's invention, based on a compilation of references to literature that Origen cited.

4. Eusebius, *Ecclesiastical History* 3.25.1–7 (ca. 320–30, Caesarea, Palestine).

5. Cyril of Jerusalem, *Catech.* 4.33 (ca. 350, Jerusalem).

6. Athanasius, *Ep. fest.* 39 (ca. 367, Alexandria, Egypt).

7. The Cheltenham Canon is also known as the Mommsen Catalogue (ca. 360–370, Northern Africa).

8. Epiphanius, *Panarion* 76.5 (ca. 374–377, Salamis, Western Syria).

9. *Apostolic Canon* 85 (ca. 380, Western Syria).

10. Gregory of Nazianzus, *Carm.* 12.31 (ca. 390, Cappadocia, Asia Minor, later ratified by the Trullan Synod in 692).

11. African Canons (ca. 393–419, Northern Africa).

12. Jerome, *Ep.* 53 (ca. 394, Bethlehem, Palestine).

13. Augustine, *Doct. chr.* 2.8 (ca. 395–400, Hippo Regius, North Africa).

14. Amphilochius, *Iambi ad Seleucum* 289–319 (ca. 396, Iconium, Asia Minor). The list concludes by acknowledging that some have questions about 2 Peter, 2 and 3 John, Hebrews, Jude and Revelation. (?) = doubted by some.

15. Rufinus, *Commentarius in Symbolum Apostolorum* 36 (ca. 394, Rome, Italy).

16. Pope Innocent, *Ad Exsuper. Tol.* (ca. 405, Rome, Italy).

17. Syrian catalogue of St. Catherine's (ca. 400, Eastern Syria).

18. Some add Hebrews to this and make it fourteen, but this is uncertain.

19. *The Muratorian Fragment.* While the majority of scholars contend that this was a late second-century AD fragment originating in or around Rome, a growing number hold that it was produced around the middle of the fourth century (ca. 350–375) and that it originated somewhere in the eastern part of the Roman Empire, possibly in Syria.

20. Synod of Laodicea, Canon 60 (ca. 363, Laodicea, Asia Minor).

21. Synod of Carthage, Canon 39 (397, North Africa). Revelation was added later in 419 at the subsequent synod at Carthage.

22. Eucherius, *Instructiones* (ca. 424–55, Lyons).

23. *Decretum Gelasianum De Libris Recipiendis et non Recipiendis* (ca. sixth century). This canon list is attributed to Pope Gelasius I (492–496), but it is more likely from the sixth century.

24. Junilius, *Instituta Regularia Divinae Legis*, Book I (ca. 551, North Africa).

25. Cassiodorus, *Institutiones Divinarum Saecularium Litterarum* (ca. 551–562, Rome).

26. Isidore, bishop of Seville, *In Libros Veteris ac Novi Testamenti Prohoemia* (ca. 600).

27. Council of Trent (*Concilium Tridentinum,* 1546).

28. Catalogue in Codex Claromontanus (D^p; ca. 500, Alexandria, Egypt).

CHAPTER 8

The Question of Authorship and Pseudepigrapha in Antiquity

It is often a surprise to those who begin their study of the history of early Christianity to learn that there were many writings produced in antiquity that were falsely written in the names of well-known figures of the past. This was a common practice well before the time of Jesus, especially in the Greco-Roman world and in ancient Judaism before the destruction of Jerusalem. "Pseudepigrapha" was a well-known term that was used to describe this practice that likely was penned around 30 BC. Dionysius of Halicarnassus (ca. 30 BC) spoke of the writings by those who wrote falsely in his name as *pseudepigraphoi*; that is, "falsely attributed writings." Eventually that designation was used by others to describe this common practice, which has ancient antecedents likely originating before biblical times. By the time of Jesus, the practice was so common that it was widely used in Jewish communities likely from the fourth century BC. Evidence of this can be seen in Jewish religious texts in late Second Temple Judaism (from the fourth century BC to AD 70). It is often surprising to new students of early Christianity when they find out that such writings were also produced and used by the early churches and were even occasionally cited as early Christian Scripture.

Sometimes it is difficult to distinguish between "apocrypha" (discussed earlier) and "pseudepigrapha" since both collections now have pseudonymous (i.e., written in a false name) writings in them. The term "apocrypha" was initially a reference to secret or hidden writings (Dan 12:4–9; 4 Ezra 14:45–47), but eventually it came to denote heretical writings that often were also pseudonymous writings. The general understanding of "apocrypha" among biblical scholars is the collection of books in the Septuagint that are not in the Hebrew Bible. Protestants call those books "apocrypha," but Catholic and Orthodox Christians use that term for heretical and rejected writings not to be read in churches. Those writings are often also pseudonymous writings. As noted earlier, not all apocryphal and pseudepigraphic books were written in false names.

For our purposes, I define "pseudepigrapha" essentially and broadly as *writings produced under a false name*. A pseudonym is a fictitious name or an assumed name, normally used by authors who choose to hide their identity to advance an unpopular perspective, to publish under the name of a well-known person to ensure its reception, for personal security, or for other reasons as we will see below. The practice of writing under a false name was more common from the late fourth or early third century BC. There were many Jewish writings produced in earlier well-known names such as 1 Enoch, the Wisdom of Solomon, and many of the writings known as the Old Testament Apocrypha and also the Old Testament Pseudepigrapha. Some of these date from the late fourth century BC and well into the first century AD. Most of them were produced from the third century BC to the second century AD. In the Christian churches, most of the pseudonymous writings were produced in the second to the fourth centuries, but some were written even later until there was broad agreement on the books that comprised the church's Scriptures.

Modern investigations of ancient pseudepigraphic texts focus mostly on those that were forged or wrongly attributed and more recently on the motivations for their production (see below), but that was not always the way they were viewed in antiquity. Not all pseudepigraphic writings are pseudonymous, which makes it more difficult to find a suitable name for the phenomena that we are describing. The practice of writing in another's name is commonly known as pseudonymity and its products as pseudepigrapha (singular = *pseudepigraphon*). It is often difficult to define this literature since it also overlaps with early Christian "apocrypha," which are also difficult to define because all of it was not pseudonymous. The Christian apocrypha is more commonly understood as literature written with the intent to deceive readers or as religious writings not included in the Bible. Some of these texts are not the same as those included in current lists of Old Testament apocrypha. Earlier distinctions are difficult to maintain in current research that focuses on a much wider collection of texts in both of these categories with the challenge of knowing when and how to limit such collections since date, genres, and names often vary. Several careful summaries of Old Testament pseudepigrapha and their understanding of Second Temple Judaism are found in Flint (1999: 2:24–66), Reed (2008: 467–89), Stuckenbruck (2010: 143–62), Tuckett (2015: 2–12), and in Collins, Evans, and McDonald (2020).

In Protestant Bibles that include the Apocrypha (or as Catholics call them, deuterocanonical texts), these writings are almost completely the additional books or portions thereof that are in the LXX but not in the Hebrew Bible and, following the example of Martin Luther, placed between the Protestant Old Testament and New Testament. Many of those texts are pseudonymous texts written under a false name; for example, Wisdom of Solomon, Psalms of Solomon, 2 Esdras, and others. From the fourth century AD, the term "apocrypha" was regularly used of doctrinally "heretical" or spurious texts. We should also observe that several of the Old Testament pseudepigrapha were either produced or rewritten and used by Christians. Given the presence of such writings among their Jewish siblings, it should not be surprising that some Christians also produced pseudonymous writings. Pseudonymous texts in the ancient Greco-Roman society as well as in Judaism and early Christianity are well known and their widespread use may have their origin, as suggested above, in the Greek era when pseudepigraphy was practiced by those wanting to sell books in the names of famous authors to kings wanting to establish libraries, as in the cases of Pergamum and Alexandria of Egypt (Elliott 1993; Metzger 1972; Rist 1972). I will focus initially on the production and use of pseudonymous writings in Judaism because of its influence on pseudepigrapha production and use in early Christianity.

Motivations

Why did some ancient authors produce writings in a false name? Scholars posit multiple motivations for it, but clearly much of it was intended to deceive readers in an attempt to honor an earlier beloved and admired teacher or mentor. The following are the most commonly listed motivations presented by scholars and I will list their names and dates here. Those interested in further details can consult the bibliography for more information. Jewish pseudonymous texts were commonly welcomed in many early churches (Clarke, 2002, pp. 440–68; Metzger, 1972; Rist, 1972). This fact is well established, but the motive for the production is where scholars are divided. Primarily, they are divided over whether pseudepigrapha were always discerned or detected by the early church fathers. Was the pseudonym written as something like a pen name to hide one's identity for sake of security from authorities, to honor one's esteemed model or teacher, as an act of humility, or simply to deceive readers to advance theological positions? Most agree that a majority of the known pseudepigrapha corpus was written to deceive readers.

Metzger (1972, pp. 5–12), for instance, lists several possible motives for producing pseudepigraphy in antiquity, classical history, Judaism of Late Antiquity, and early Christianity. *Some* of his examples include the following: (1) such texts were produced for financial gain, as in the cases of the libraries at Pergamum and Alexandria, paying for what they thought were acquired texts from earlier famed writers, but some persons were rewarded for producing pseudonymous copies in the names of famous authors. (2) Some pseudepigrapha were produced out of malice (Metzger provides several examples of this). (3) Some of it was produced out of love and respect for a venerable author or teacher from whom they had been taught or learned much. In this case, the text was produced in admiration and sympathy by a student wanting to honor his teacher. (4) Some of it was produced out of alleged, or real, modesty on the part of the author by attributing a work to someone better than themselves, or to God as in the famed case of Salvian writing to honor God in the name of Timothy, which means "honor of God." (5) Sometimes these writings were produced in the name of famed Attic writers modeling something after their works and were generally fictitious works (e.g., pseudo-Aristotle). (6) Creating epistolary texts attributed to famous persons, not only in classical names, but also in famed Jewish and Christian names (e.g., Epistle of Jeremiah and the Gospel of Peter) and Christian pseudonymous letters (3 Corinthians).

Aune (1983, pp. 109–10) lists four common explanations for the existence of pseudonymous texts in ancient literature: (1) they arose at a time when the biblical canon was already closed and well-known names were used to secure acceptance; (2) they were used to protect the identity of a writer who might be in danger if his or her true identity were known; (3) apocalyptic visionaries may have had visions from those figures to whom they attributed their work; and (4) the writer may have identified with a person of the past and written as that person's representative. He suggests that the first of these options is the most likely, but not without qualifications. He also concludes that "pseudonymity is functional only if readers accept the false attribution."

Finally, Charlesworth (1992, pp. 5:540–41 and 1997, pp. 2:768–75) lists seven categories of *Christian* pseudonymous literature including: (1) works not by the named author but probably containing some of the reputed author's own thoughts (Ephesians and Colossians; 2 Timothy and Titus); (2) documents written by someone who was influenced by another to whom the work is ascribed (1 Peter and maybe James); (3) compositions influenced by earlier works of an author to whom they are assigned (1 Timothy, 2 Timothy, Titus); (4) Gospels attributed to an apostle but deriving from later circles or schools of learned individuals (Matthew and John); (5) Christian writings attributed by their authors to an Old Testament personality (Testament of Adam, Odes of Solomon, Apocalypse of Elijah, Ascension of Isaiah); (6) once anonymous works (perhaps Mark, Luke, and Acts) now credited to some familiar New Testament persons (such as attributing Hebrews to Paul); and (7) compositions that intentionally try to deceive the reader into thinking that the author is someone famous (2 Pet 3:1).

Jewish Production and Use of Pseudepigrapha

The Jewish practice of producing and using pseudonymous texts may have begun even earlier with the Deuteronomistic history in the latter part of the seventh century BC, when Josiah's scribes discovered (or produced) the book of Deuteronomy in the name of Moses (Collins, 2018, pp. 163–81; cf. 2 Kgs 22:8–13). The same can be said about some of the psalms attributed to David, or proverbs attributed to Solomon. Pseudepigraphy is well represented in the famed nonsectarian scrolls in the Dead Sea Scrolls, with most of it dating from roughly 200 BC and circulating in Palestine in the time of Jesus, which continued until around AD 200 among the Jewish people. The production of Jewish apocalyptic texts in the name of a well-known predecessor was common in late Second Temple Judaism. Some texts now called "rewritten Bible" but more appropriately "rewritten scriptures"—such as the author of Jubilees who rewrites Genesis with his supposed revelation of the law to Moses during his forty days on Mount Sinai (Exod 24:18) were also common in antiquity.

The collection of Dead Sea Scrolls has provided multiple examples of Jewish pseudonymous texts that were brought to Qumran by their Essene residents. Some of those are regularly called "rewritten scriptures" that transformed earlier scriptural documents in the Hebrew Scriptures. These include, for example, the *Rewritten Pentateuch*, Jubilees rewriting Genesis, the Temple Scroll, 1 Enoch, Testaments of the Twelve Patriarchs (T12P), and others. These "rewritten" texts led readers to assume that the authors listed in the rewritten works were the authentic authors of those documents. Some Christians also rewrote portions of existing Jewish religious texts, as in 2 Esdras (4 Ezra) and Ascension of Isaiah, to transform them into texts discussion of the "rewritten" texts at Qumran.

Pseudonymous writings were commonly produced in late Second Temple Jewish writings and in early Christianity, and, as noted, some may be in the ancient Hebrew writings, perhaps as early as the late seventh century BC, as in the case of the production of Deuteronomy attributed to Moses. Did Moses write Deuteronomy or was it someone (or others) after him? The Jewish practice of producing pseudonymous texts likely began with the Deuteronomistic history in the latter part of the seventh century BC when scribes of Josiah produced or discovered the "book of the law" (likely Deuteronomy; see 2 Kgs 22:8–13). It was later affirmed that Moses wrote Deuteronomy (2 Chr 34:14; Deut 1:1; see Collins 2018: 63–181). There are also other examples of pseudonymous writings in the Hebrew Bible, likely Isaiah 24–27, as well as the later insertions in Daniel and Esther, some psalms attributed to David, and many proverbs attributed to Solomon.

The ancient practice of writing pseudonymously is seldom the same as using a pen name, as in the case of the well-known Mark Twain (born Samuel Clemens). Rather, we refer to cases in which a separate writer produces a document in the name of a known person (famous or influential) under a false name. The motivation *may* have been to deceive readers in order to have a wider distribution for the pseudonymous authors' views, but some of those writings may have stemmed from a desire to honor a renowned leader. For example, an author may have attempted to express a celebrated figure's views or to indicate that their views are in keeping with those of a well-known person. A useful list of the Old Testament pseudepigraphic texts is in Charlesworth (1985, pp. 836–40), and more recently in Bauckham, Davila, and Panayotov (2013).

Because pseudonymously written Jewish religious writings were widespread among Jewish communities in late Second Temple Judaism, it is important initially to focus on examples in that community before and during the time of

Jesus and his earliest followers. As noted earlier, pseudonymous writings were discovered at Qumran among the Dead Sea Scrolls including 1 Enoch. Several of these writings were also circulating among some early Christians and were presumed to be Scripture. By the fourth century, Athanasius set forth in his *Thirty-Ninth Festal Letter* (ca. 367) a list of the books that could be read in the churches. His Old Testament included all the books in the Hebrew Bible *except Esther*, but he also included Baruch and the Epistle of Jeremiah and likely also the additions to Daniel. He not only classified those books that were readable in churches as "canonical" Scripture, but he also listed a few others that were not canonical yet were quite popular among the people. He said that these additional books could be read privately by the young in the faith and for advancing piety. He identified these "noncanonical" (nonscriptural) writings as "readable" (Greek = *anagignōskomena*) texts because he thought they could be helpful for new converts. These writings included the Wisdom of Solomon, the Wisdom of Sirach, Esther, Judith, Tobit, the book called Teaching of the Apostles (Didache), and the Shepherd of Hermas. Most of these books were written pseudonymously.

This contrasts with those he classified as "nonreadable" (Greek = *mē anagignōskomena*); that is, they were "apocryphal" or heretical, spurious, and rejected books. Catholic tradition later adopted a larger collection of those "readable" books, which were later classified as "deuterocanonical" texts as noted earlier. These were largely those additional books circulating in the Greek Septuagint, but not in the Hebrew Bible. Orthodox tradition sometimes uses these books but only considers them to be readable and inspirational, not scriptural. Most Protestants regularly designate the deuterocanonical texts as "apocrypha" and exclude them from their Bibles, but some of the Protestant ecumenical Bibles do include them, following Luther's example and placing them between the Old Testament and New Testament.

Athanasius's *Festal Letter* was highly influential in churches in the East, but not all churches at that time accepted his whole list of Old Testament or New Testament canonical books. Many Syrian churches, as we saw earlier, did not welcome the minor New Testament Epistles (2 Peter, 2–3 John, and Jude) and Revelation until centuries later. The task of establishing the identity and scope of the so-called Old Testament apocrypha or deuterocanonical books has been long and challenging. This collection of Jewish religious texts dates *mostly* from 200 BC to AD 100.

Some pseudonymous texts were cited in the second and third centuries as or like Scripture by some early church fathers. First Enoch, for example, was cited as scripture by Tertullian (*De idolatria* 4.2–3), citing 1 Enoch 19:1, 99:6–7 and 1 Enoch 8:1 in *De cultu feminarum* 1.3 and 2.10; Clement of Alexandria, *Stromateis* 1.1.13; cf. *Eclogae propheticae* 2.1 citing 1 Enoch 19:3; Irenaeus, *Adversus haereses* 1.1.1; Origen (cited in Eusebius, *Hist. eccl.* 6.24–25) who quotes 1 Enoch 19:3 and 21:1 in *De principiis* 4.4.8; 1 Enoch 6:6 in *Comm. John* 6.25; cf.

Contra Celsum 5.52–55; and Rufinus, *Exp. Symb.* 36–38, in which he welcomes the reading of apocryphal writings and the opportunity to learn from them.

Christian Pseudepigrapha

The modern investigation of *Christian* pseudonymous writings began largely with Friedrich Schleiermacher in 1807 and subsequently F. C. Baur in 1835, who focused mainly on the Pastoral Epistles (1 Tim, 2 Tim, and Titus). They asked: Did Paul write them or did some of his followers? Baur argued that the production of pseudonymous texts in antiquity was to deceive readers, and after him several conservative scholars agreed with that assessment but denied its presence in biblical literature. They argued that it was always rejected in the early church (e.g., C. L. Mitton, Donald Guthrie, J. S. Candlish). More recently, several scholars have concluded that many of the earlier defenses against its use in the early churches are based more on theological arguments than on careful investigations or exegesis—namely, how could a book inspired by God and focused on divine truth originate in a lie or forgery? They also debate whether pseudonymous texts were included in the church's New Testament, a subject that divides current scholarship. Marshall (1999, pp. 79–89) has rejected Paul's authorship of the Pastoral Epistles *in their current condition*—especially 1 Timothy and Titus, but he nevertheless thinks there is sufficient authentic Pauline material in 2 Timothy to suggest that Timothy or Titus (or even both?) was the final author/editor of the corpus. He makes a strong case for the authenticity of the Pastorals and affirms their presence in the biblical canon.

Most biblical scholars now reject Pauline authorship of the Pastoral Epistles, though some acknowledge that authentic Pauline texts may be in them (e.g., perhaps 2 Tim 1:15–18; 4:5–21). Some scholars defend the practice of pseudonymous writing in the first century (Meade, 1986; Dunn, 1987, pp. 65–85; Aland, 1961, pp. 39–49). Since there are likely authentic Pauline traditions in the pastorals—namely, the rejection of Paul in Asia Minor (2 Tim 1:15–18), the manner of the apostle's death (2 Tim 4:6–8), and many of the closing comments to colleagues in 2 Timothy 4:14–22, also appear to be genuinely Pauline. His words to Titus may have a touch of authenticity in them as well (Titus 1:5–16). It would be easy to draw that conclusion.

We might ask whether 2 Timothy and Titus should be separated from 1 Timothy, which does not have much that is familiar from Paul in his acknowledged letters. If the author(s) of the Pastoral Epistles simply wanted apostolic sanction for Paul's views on organization and discipline in churches, and therefore attached Paul's name to their writings, what conclusion(s) should we draw about the Pastorals? Can they be sacred scripture for the church if there was deceptive intention in their construction? Since most of the important theological issues in the universally acknowledged letters of Paul (Romans, 1–2 Corinthians, Galatians, Philippians, 1 Thessalonians, and Philemon) are absent in the Pastoral Epistles (reconciliation, eschatology, "in Christ," justification by faith, the prominent role of the Holy Spirit, and a simple church organizational structure), can a case be made that the Pastoral Epistles in their current form were not originally written by Paul? Did someone who followed Paul perhaps write what he (or she) thought was what Paul would have said to address the issues later facing the churches?

Current biblical scholars also acknowledge that *early Christian pseudepigraphic texts* were inserted in several biblical books, reflecting pseudonymous authors portraying their own writings in the names of earlier well-known apostolic writings. They claim that some of these include *at the least* Mark 1:1b; 16:9–20; John 3:13b; 7:53–8:11; John 21; Romans 16:25–27; 1 Corinthians 14:33b–36; 1 John 5:7–8, and others as well. These insertions were not originally a part of the New Testament writings but were inserted later by copiers or scribes *generally* to advance later established orthodox doctrinal positions (Hull, 2011, pp. 84–85). Several pseudonymous books circulated in churches for a time and were produced in the typical genres in the present New Testament: gospels, acts, epistles, and apocalypses and mostly in the names of well-known church leaders (apostles, especially Peter, James, John, and Paul), but in some cases in the names of familiar Old Testament figures as in the case of the Ascension of Isaiah and portions of 2 Esdras (4 Ezra). There appear to be many parallels in genre, but generally with distinctions. Sometimes authors would use the first-person, include expanded narratives, and fill in lacunae missing in the canonical texts. Hull (2011, pp. 84–85) also focuses on the authorial aspect of these writings adding to or correcting differences in biblical texts (e.g., Chronicles vs. Kings and Matthew and Luke vs. Mark).

After a brief introduction, I will not only focus on the question of whether some pseudonymous works remain in the New Testament but also acknowledge that multiple insertions in the texts of several New Testament books also exist and that those insertions are passed along as the text of the original authors of those books. It appears that both orthodox and so-called heretical Christian groups inserted additional texts in biblical books to promote later views and teachings, which raises the question about whether such practices in antiquity should be judged by modern sensitivities.

For example, when Rufinus translated Origen's work he openly acknowledged that he sometimes changed it to make it cohere with the orthodoxy he thought was appropriate and to make Origen's writings more acceptable to his community. Remarkably, Origen himself welcomed several pseudonymous writings, which may provide an argument for the inclusion of the Pastorals in the church's New Testament canon. He accepted them not because of their authorship but because of their content (e.g., Susanna and others). By the mid to late fourth century, that argument began to change in favor of a rejection of known pseudonymous texts;

but by then, the widespread use and popularity of some texts later determined to be pseudonymous became difficult to exclude, especially 2 Peter, Hebrews, James, 2–3 John, Jude, Revelation, and likely some aspects of the Pastorals. Some pseudonymous texts continued to be welcomed by some church fathers longer than others, as in the cases of the Epistle of Barnabas and Shepherd of Hermas included in Codex Sinaiticus. For many centuries other later texts such as the Acts of Paul and Thecla, and 3 Corinthians continued to be read in some churches.

Scholars acknowledge that some unknown copiers of the biblical texts inserted a number of texts into both Old Testament and New Testament writings as they made their copies for various purposes (e.g., Isa 24–27 and also Second and Third Isaiah, Daniel and its later additions, Esther and its later additions, and the shorter Jeremiah in the LXX [sometimes the copiers included Baruch and the Epistle of Jeremiah], but the same is true as we saw above in Mark 16:9–20; John 3:13b; 7:53–8:11; 1 John 5:7–8; possibly 2 Thess 2:1–3; the end of Rom 16:25–27; and others). Most of the later textual insertions in New Testament texts were supportive of orthodox positions when the texts were copied.

The Growing Importance of Authorship

There are only a few certain statements about the importance of authorship in Christian writings much before the third century AD, though Paul does emphasize his own authorship in his writings when there were doubts about whether he had written a text or when others were written in his name (Gal 6:11 and 2 Thess 2:1–2). However, because the four canonical Gospels, Acts, Hebrews, and 1–3 John were all written anonymously, it is clear that authorship was not as important in the earliest stages of the church as it was later. Initially, the church's core beliefs or *regula fidei* that were circulating in the churches took priority over authorship. When the early church fathers cited the Gospels, they did not do so by the names of the authors of those Gospels in which Jesus' words are found, but rather by citing only the words of Jesus in them and not the specific Gospels (mostly Matthew) in which those words were found.

While the importance of apostolic authority is found in the first century and emphasized by Paul in his writings, it did not initially extend to the New Testament writings. Because Paul's authority was in question in the first century, he emphasized his apostolic authority in his letters (e.g., 1 Cor 9:1–2; 12:28; 15:3–8, 11; Rom 16:7; see also Acts 1:12–26). Generally speaking, however, that authority was *not focused on apostolic writing* until later in the second century (e.g., Justin, *First Apology* 64–67). Although the Gospels were doubtless read in the churches from the time they began circulating in churches, and although their authorship was likely known by many, the authority of apostolic writings was not noted until well into the second century, and it was the authority of Jesus cited in the Gospels rather than that of their authors. Emerging apostolic authority was soon attached to writings by the latter part of the second century, but not initially, as we see in their citations by the early church fathers. Later, the apostles or their disciples (Mark and Luke) became primary sources of authority in early Christianity. Apostolic authority of the canonical Gospels was likely known from the beginning of their circulation in churches (Evans, 2020, pp. 2–11), but it was the words and deeds of the Lord Jesus in them that were cited.

Scholars largely agree that several pseudonymous books or writings are in the biblical literature, and some contend that little more than a handful of the New Testament writings were written by the authors attached to them. Some scholars suggest that only nine of the twenty-seven New Testament books were written by those whose names are on them. However, that exceeds reasonable assessments of the New Testament writings, and such conclusions are regularly contested in scholarly essays. Nevertheless, several scholars continue to acknowledge that both the Old Testament and New Testament contain pseudonymous writings (Clarke, 2002; Flint, 1999; Metzger, 1972), and the primary question is how to identify and deal with it. While the early Christians did not invent this practice, they certainly produced pseudepigrapha and made use of it. So, if discovered, should it remain in the Bible?

This all raises the question of whether the early Christians ancients focused mostly on authorship as the final criterion for canonicity or the content of the writing. Najman and Peirano (2019) suggest that pseudonymous writings were produced and used in antiquity as a means of continuing the teaching of an earlier famed teacher when the issue of authorial origin was not as important as it later became. They acknowledge that this was not always the motivation for producing some pseudonymous writings. They insist that modern scholars often impose contemporary negative notions about pseudonymity anachronistically on ancient writings with the result that modern understandings of authenticity have obscured the dynamics of how such texts were viewed and welcomed in antiquity. They disagree that the distinctions between canonical and noncanonical writings that have been influenced by modern notions of pseudonymous writings do not reflect all uses of pseudepigrapha in antiquity. By way of example, they also cite Iamblichus (neoplatonist philosopher and student of Porphyry, ca. AD 245–325) who approved of such activity regarding writings produced in the name of the famed Pythagoras, saying:

> It was a fine thing that they [authors of pseudepigraphic texts] even attributed and assigned everything to Pythagoras and did not keep as their own any doctrines among those that they discovered except in rare cases; for there are in fact altogether very few people whose works are circulated with their own name attached to them.
> (Iamblichus, *De vita Pythagoras* 198.9)

Najman and Peirano also acknowledge that in antiquity unknown authors often imitated their exemplars or admired mentors by refinement and extension of what they believed was at the heart of the exemplar's intention. Attributing later writings to an earlier figure, they argue, was a way of extending and transforming that earlier person's work through the application and extension of the past and invigorating a new present. While not all current scholars understand pseudepigrapha this way, the understanding of how and why some of that literature was produced offers another possibility of how it might be considered now. It is important to look outside of the contemporary perspectives that lead to disputes over inspiration and other theological issues. In terms of the number of ancient *Christian* pseudepigrapha, there are more than eighty known *Christian* pseudonymous writings (see Evans, 2005, pp. 256–57) that are now referred to as "Apocryphal New Testament" or "Early Christian Apocrypha" or simply as "New Testament Apocrypha."

By the fourth century, churches regularly dismissed and rejected pseudonymous writings; but in the earlier church fathers, the focus was not so much on authorship as on the content of the writings in question. This was an important criterion for accepting the scriptural status of writings that formed the church's Scriptures. Before then, however, if a writing was determined to be heretical, then its authorship was regularly called into question, since it was asked how one with apostolic authority could write heresy. So, it was concluded that a writing with false teaching in it was falsely written in an apostle's name. Authentic authorship became more highly prized in the fourth century when notions of a fixed biblical canon of Scriptures that could be read in churches became more common in a majority of churches.

By way of example, it is well known that Origen in the third century denied that Paul wrote Hebrews and claimed that it was written anonymously, but he nonetheless welcomed its content. He concluded that "the thoughts are those of the apostle [Paul], but the diction and phraseology are those of someone who remembered the apostolic teachings and wrote down what had been said by his teacher" (Eusebius, *Hist. eccl.* 6.25.13). He concluded that God only knows who wrote Hebrews, so for him the issue of authorship was not as important as the content of the writing.

In the fourth century, it appears that most of the *known* or suspected deceptive pseudepigraphic writings were dismissed as forgeries—but were the church fathers at that time able to discern all the early Christian pseudonymous writings? Did they have access to Paul's other contested writings to compare with Paul's accepted writings? It is not clear that all church fathers would have recognized pseudonymously written writings. As recognition of the authority for apostolic authorship of written texts began to emerge, about mid-second century, many pseudonymous writings with apostolic names were produced in churches and some were initially and unwittingly welcomed as sacred scripture in some churches (e.g., the church at Rhossus that was reading the Gospel of Peter; cf. Eusebius, *Hist. eccl.* 6.12.3–6). The act of attaching apostolic names enhanced their reception as the church's Christian Scriptures.

However, the issue of authorship, or apostolic authorship in particular, does not appear to have been a significant factor even after the deaths of the apostles and until well into the second century when attributing apostolic authorship to pseudonymous writings began to emerge. The earliest references to the individual gospels, as we saw earlier, are few and initially the citation of gospel texts focused primarily on the words and actions of Jesus in them and not on their authors. While the sayings of Jesus in the Gospels were frequently cited by the second- and third-century church fathers, especially and more frequently in Matthew, the identity of the Gospels was not an important factor until later in the second century, beginning with Justin's *First Apology* (ca. 150–155). The composition of pseudonymous texts in apostolic names began to appear when early copiers and scribes began transmitting Christian writings in apostolic names. The question remains whether the authors of those pseudonymous texts intended to deceive readers by writing in the names of well-known prophetic figures (e.g., Enoch, Isaiah) or apostolic figures (Paul, Peter, John, James, Andrew, and others).

Biblical Writings and Pseudepigrapha

The crucial question here, however, is whether pseudonymous texts remain in the biblical writings. If a text was intended to deceive, how could it still be used or read in churches today? The question rightly emerges with the prevalence of pseudonymous writings in early Christianity and whether they were written by orthodox writers or so-called heretical authors. Again, that raises the question of the importance of authorship in the early churches or whether the content of a writing was more important to the earliest readers of the biblical literature.

The core teaching of the churches was circulating before there were written texts that advanced it. The subsequent writings that cohered with those early traditions and beliefs were welcomed initially without regard to authorship or the ability to discern it. The proclamation or gospel was the church's earliest tradition circulating in churches and over time was central to the selection of the books that would be included in the church's scriptures. Those teachings expanded from time to time to address emerging issues facing the churches, but they were not radically changed, and *regula fidei* was essential in the selection of books in the biblical canon. The criterion of orthodoxy determined which books would be acceptable despite disputed authorship. Most of the rejections over authorship focused on the heretical teachings in those documents; for example, the Gospel of Judas mentioned earlier in Irenaeus.

By the fourth century, whatever was believed to be pseudonymous was also rejected by the church fathers, but the questions remain: Did the church fathers recognize all of the pseudonymous writings that were circulating in the churches? Were some pseudonymous writings initially included into the church's Bible and wrongly believed to be authentic apostolic texts, yet wrongly remained in it? Modern scholarship has generally acknowledged that some pseudonymous texts were not recognized as such and were included wittingly or unwittingly in the church's sacred scriptures. Some of it was undetected in antiquity, although there were questions raised about many of the texts that were initially questioned and later rejected, but some of the disputed texts at that time (e.g., James, 2 Peter, 2–3 John, Jude, Hebrews, Revelation) were eventually welcomed as we saw earlier in Eusebius (*Hist. eccl.* 3.25). It is interesting that after citing Dionysius's questions about the authorship of Revelation (Eusebius, *Hist. eccl.* 7.25.22–27) and Origen's questioning of the authorship of Hebrews (Eusebius, *Hist. eccl.* 6.25.11–14), Eusebius acknowledges that both Dionysius and Origen still included in their New Testament the books whose authorship they questioned or rejected. Most scholars agree that Moses did not write Deuteronomy nor did Daniel the prophet write the biblical text attributed to him nor did Paul write Hebrews, but they were all welcomed into the church's Bible.

The anonymous texts—namely, the Gospels, Acts, Hebrews, and the Letters of John—perhaps should not be considered here since they do not claim apostolic authorship. However, despite not knowing or emphasizing their authorship, all were included in the Christian Scriptures. Regarding Revelation, of course, we see in the opening verses that it was written by "John," and the book is not necessarily a pseudonymous text since "John" was a popular name in the first century; there were several others also named John in antiquity, but the text was welcomed as if it were written by the apostle John. Interestingly, as we saw above, Dionysius denied that John the Apostle wrote Revelation, but he did not reject its scriptural status. The only question for him was about its authorship and evidently not its content.

The primary purpose of pseudonymous writing appears to have been twofold; namely, filling in gaps not included in the biblical texts and advancing theological positions which were primarily orthodox (e.g., 1 John 5:7–8; John 3:13b, and others) yet also nonorthodox ("heretical") positions. Both motivations, of course, are deceptive. Most Christian pseudonymous religious texts in names of apostolic figures appear to have been intended to present anachronistic? thinking in later documents and for later communities. Establishing authoritative beliefs in later churches doubtless was a motivation for some to produce such texts. Again, there is considerable evidence that shows that when such pseudonymous writings were detected, they were generally rejected by most church fathers and not included in their sacred scriptures. That appears to be the case especially from the fourth century and thereafter, but it also seems likely that the church fathers were not always aware that the writings they attributed to well-known persons were pseudonymous texts.

It is currently asked whether pseudepigraphy was a suitable venue for advancing Christian beliefs and whether such writings, if discovered in the biblical canon, should be excluded. It appears clear that some texts, whose authorship was unknown or disputed, remained in the church's scriptures because they had gained what is recently called an "irresistible momentum"; that is, because they were widely popular and long welcomed by many churches, excluding them later was no longer possible (Stuckenbruck, 2010, pp. 143–62). Whether Paul wrote Hebrews or the Pastoral Epistles was largely irrelevant because of widespread use in churches.

Given the above, does one welcome a book as Scripture based on its authorship, or is its content also a factor in the acceptance? Some anonymous texts were likely welcomed based on their contents—for example, the Gospels, Hebrews, 1, 2, 3 John, and Revelation written by John, but not likely the apostle John. It appears that some New Testament books were welcomed into the biblical canon because of a belief in their apostolic authorship (Pastorals, 2 Peter, Hebrews, Revelation, 2–3 John, and likely others). Some were welcomed likely because of their popularity among the churches despite their questionable authorship (Pastorals, Hebrews, 2 Peter, Revelation, and others). Eusebius acknowledges the widespread disputes over some New Testament books (*Hist. eccl.* 3.25), but despite Hebrews' questionable authorship it is likely that its valued content gave it the "irresistible momentum" (Origen and others) noted above, but eventually it was attributed to Paul likely to avoid its rejection. There were initial questions about the authorship of Hebrews in the 393 and 397 church councils at Hippo and Carthage, but by the 419 Council at Carthage, doubts were removed and Hebrews was attributed to Paul as that canon list suggests. Clearly, the insertion of apostolic names was not only useful in establishing the New Testament canon but important in advancing the use of pseudonymous texts in the ancient churches.

Some early Christians also welcomed the Gospel of Hebrews, the Gospel of Alexandrians, the Gospel of Peter, the Apocalypse of Peter, and others. Later, these were all rejected when it was believed that they did not transmit the church's core sacred traditions about Jesus, or that they were not faithfully transmitted, or were pseudonymous. However, eventually the core sacred teachings that focused on the identity of Jesus (Christology), his primary teachings, his activity (miracles), and fate (death and resurrection) were all transmitted in writing by some church fathers *before* there was a Bible. Those traditions were familiar in the church's teaching, preaching, singing, baptismal confessions, and eucharistic affirmations from their beginning, and they provided the boundaries of what was acceptable in the emerging scriptural canon. However, there was a continual production of pseudonymous texts in the second to the fourth centuries, mostly written in the names of well-known apostolic figures that some churches likely unwittingly welcomed as apostolic. The following is a listing of some of the most prominent Christian pseudonymous writings in the names of well-known persons in the New Testament.

1. Gospels:

The Protoevangelium of James
The Infancy Gospel of Thomas
The Gospel of Peter
The Gospel of Nicodemus
The Gospel of the Nazarenes
The Gospel of the Ebionites
The Gospel of the Hebrews
The Gospel of the Egyptians
The Gospel of Thomas
The Gospel of Philip
The Gospel of Mary

2. Acts (the first five of these are called the "Leucian Acts" and sometimes were circulated together):

The Acts of John
The Acts of Peter
The Acts of Paul
The Acts of Andrew
The Acts of Thomas
The Acts of Andrew and Matthias
The Acts of Philip
The Acts of Thaddaeus
The Acts of Peter and Paul
The Acts of Peter and Andrew
The Martyrdom of Matthew
The Slavonic Acts of Peter
The Acts of Peter and the Twelve Apostles

3. Epistles:

Third Corinthians
The Epistle to the Laodiceans
The Letters of Paul and Seneca

The Letters of Jesus and Abgar
The Letter of Lentulus
The Epistle of Titus

4. Apocalypses (revelatory writings like the book of Revelation):
The Apocalypse of Peter
The Coptic Apocalypse of Paul
The First Apocalypse of James
The Second Apocalypse of James
The Apocryphon of John
The Sophia of Jesus Christ
The Letter of Peter to Philip
The Apocalypse of Mary

Also, multiple extraneous pseudonymous *texts* inserted into the biblical texts were commonplace especially in the second and third centuries, many of which are well known to biblical scholars who address them in current critical commentaries. Some of these widely acknowledged insertions were noted earlier, and some of them include several Old Testament inserted texts as in the Daniel insertions and Esther insertions, likely Isaiah 24–27, and many others noted earlier. For more on the New Testament Apocrypha, see Burke and Landau (2016) and Burke (2020).

Pseudonymous Writings and the New Testament

The question of whether pseudonymous writings, if determined not to have been written by their attributed author, should remain in the Bible continues to be a point of scholarly debate. The arguments often begin from theological preference rather than historical inquiry. How can forgeries or fraudulent documents remain in the inspired Bible? The biggest question has to do with whether pseudonymous authors intended to deceive. Metzger (1972) suggests some of the authors may not have intended to deceive, but rather to honor the one in whose name the author added teachings supposedly from that earlier famed antecedent.

We have seen that the usual candidates include the Pastoral Epistles, Ephesians, Colossians, 2 Thessalonians, James, 2 Peter, and possibly also Jude and 1 Peter. In the case of 1 Peter, the question has to do with the letter's remarkably sophisticated Greek and style—uncommon among working-class persons from Galilee. But others respond that 1 Peter was written through a skilled secretary—namely, Silvanus (5:12)—similar to the case of Dionysius of Alexandria and his assessment of the book of Revelation or Origen's assessment of Hebrews.

Revelation is an interesting case because it makes no claim to have been written by the apostle John, though its author does name himself as "John" (Rev 1:9). It is likely that Revelation was included in the biblical canon over its competitors—namely, the Apocalypse of Peter and Shepherd of Hermas, because it was believed by a majority that the author identified as John was indeed the Apostle John.

From antiquity, the book of Revelation had a difficult time being received into the biblical canon, and even today the Orthodox Church, who finally welcomed it in their New Testament between the seventh and eighth centuries, does not read it in its liturgies. That, of course, rightly raises the question that if it is not read in church, how can it be considered Scripture or a part of the church's New Testament canon (Scanlin, 1996, pp. 300–12)? Today, as Dionysius noted earlier, we recognize that the style, content, and vocabulary of Revelation are considerably different from other writings attributed to John the Apostle—Gospel of John or 1 John or even 2–3 John, and it is seldom read in any liturgical texts in churches whether in the East or West. The Gospels, Acts, Hebrews, and 1–3 John were all written *anonymously* and not under a pseudonym, and the names that we now use for those works were later attached to them in the second century when apostolic scribal authority became more important following the deaths of the apostles and those near them.

We should also remember that it was not illegal to write pseudonymous texts in antiquity; but in practice when it became known, they were generally despised and rejected, especially in the fourth and fifth centuries AD when the major contours of the biblical canon were shaped, and especially if their contents were regarded as heretical.

For several centuries, both Jews and Christians accepted as Scripture many writings now identified as pseudonymous texts, but by the fourth century this began to change (McDonald, 2006, pp. 190–214, 230–32; and 2017, pp. 2:164–72, 327–35). Much of this literature was shaped and inspired by the language, metaphors, and symbols of the Old Testament or by the writings earlier attributed to pivotal early Christian leaders. The authorship attributed to Old Testament figures included names such as Enoch, Abraham, Shem, Moses, David, Solomon, Levi, and other Hebrew patriarchs, but Christian writings were also attributed to early apostolic leaders such as Peter, John, Paul, and James, as well as others who were in the apostolic community.

Conclusion

No one seriously denies the presence and influence of pseudonymous writings in antiquity. Its production and use were especially common in the Greco-Roman world, late Second Temple Judaism and early Christianity. Jews and Christians produced and used such texts and, in some cases, considered some of them as sacred Scripture. The ancient world did not have the same standards that moderns have regarding its production or use, at least in the early stages of its production and circulation in early Christianity. There is little evidence that the early Christians were sensitive to the ethical implications of pseudepigraphy that are current today. That thinking began to develop in later fourth century Christianity when the formation of the church's Scriptures became a more important feature of churches at that time. Some of the pseudonymous writings clearly advanced the doctrines of the majority of churches; e.g., *Apostolic Constitutions*. It may be that modern scholarship is imposing current ethical standards on early Christianity when the early Christians were not as aware that such activity was as unethical as we consider it today.

Although Tertullian clearly denounced pseudonymous writings, mostly when heresy was detected in them, the presence of such writings can be seen in other pseudonymous writings in Paul's name (2 Thess 2:2–3) in Paul's reason for writing in his own hand (2 Thess 3:17; cf. Gal 6:11) and in the fact that such deceptions were common in early Christianity. There were multiple examples of pseudonymous writings in antiquity, but they did not receive as much attention, especially if they advocated the church's core beliefs. The content was considered more important than authorship, but that changed significantly by the fourth century. Some of the New Testament writings made use of several pseudonymous texts that they believed were Scripture (e.g., Heb 1:2–3 and Wis 7:25; Jude 14 and 1 En. 1:9) and did so whether knowing it was pseudonymous or not.

It appears from the use and familiarity with Jewish pseudonymous texts that the primary question for the earliest Christians was whether the document was useful in their local communities for teaching and proclamation and whether it advanced their beliefs and sacred traditions. It should be remembered that the pseudepigrapha, whether Jewish or Christian, significantly outnumbered the books that comprise the church's Old or New Testament. The content of some of the pseudonymous writings was carefully monitored in churches and sifted *through* the church's core traditions, creeds, worship, teachings, baptisms, and eucharistic meals. In other words, content, usefulness, and coherence with community beliefs took priority over authorship until the larger church later made decisions about Scripture based on authorship and content (Augustine). By the fourth century, *most* known pseudonymous writings were rejected.

Again, Stuckenbruck's "irresistible momentum" idea reflects that some writings continued to be read as Scripture in many churches. I pointed out earlier that the later *Stichometry of Nicephorus* (ninth century AD) continued to reject pseudonymous writings that had been rejected four hundred or more years earlier. Why continue rejecting them if no one was still reading them? It also appears likely that a text that had complied with the church's sacred traditions and was useful to many local churches continued to be welcomed among the local churches' sacred Scriptures for centuries. That would also include 3 Corinthians in some Western as well as Syrian and later Armenian churches for centuries along with the Diatessaron. Some pseudonymous texts had a short life—that is, a "temporary scriptural status"—but others had widespread use in churches and were not rejected (except in the case of perceived heretical teachings). In response to the question, Did the early Christians welcome some pseudonymous writings as Scripture? the answer is yes, but the debate continues over which of the books are pseudonymous.

Perhaps it is best to conclude here by saying that regardless of whether the early Christians welcomed some pseudepigrapha for a time, it is important to remember that nothing was lost in terms of the church's core teachings, and nothing will be gained by deleting from or adding to the church's Scriptures. It is a settled issue for churches today whether Orthodox, Catholic, or Protestant.

Chapter 9

Epilogue

Did the Ancient Churches Get It Right?

In chapter 6, I asked whether Christians could trust their Bible? My answer was yes, of course, and now as I address the question of whether the church "got it right"—namely, whether they selected the right literature—the answer is still Yes! However, this does not mean that there are no remaining concerns or questions or differences to address. I should note that no writing was included in the New Testament or the Christian Old Testament that was contrary to the core teachings of the earliest churches on the identity and mission of Jesus the Lord. While there were differences for centuries over some books in their Scriptures, the boundaries for what was acceptable were well known centuries before there a closed biblical canon was formed. While some scholars focus more attention on the differences than is necessary, it is important to underscore that the vast majority of churches agreed on the core teachings transmitted in the churches from their beginning, and they agreed on those things despite many differences on other matters. The early Christians welcomed as their First Scriptures the Scriptures that they inherited from their Jewish siblings, though they were not yet in a final, fixed collection, even for the Jews, before they and the earliest Christians separated. The core books of their Scriptures were clearly those that are in the current Jewish Scriptures, the Christian Old Testament, though they also initially included other books that were nonetheless welcomed as sacred texts by many Jews in the time of Jesus. As we have already seen, this accounts for some of the differences in the Old Testament Scriptures in the early churches and even today. While all churches did not agree initially on all of the New Testament books, they did agree on the ones that eventually were acknowledged as sacred Scripture and that were also included in the Jewish Scripture collection. Though there remain disagreements on the scope of the Old Testament Scriptures, all churches welcome the books in the current Hebrew Bible, the so-called proto-canonical books, that remain in all Catholic, Orthodox, and Protestant church Bibles. However, there is nothing that should prevent all Christians from being informed by the same writings that informed the earliest Christians, as we have seen. Christians do not need to change their perspectives on which books comprise their Old Testament canon in order to be informed by the same writings that informed the faith of many in the early Christian churches.

There is almost unanimous agreement in the three major branches of the churches today on the scope of their New Testament Scriptures. Although the process of recognition took centuries to accomplish, all of the major churches have agreed that the New Testament writings that we have today are the best and earliest collection of Scriptures that carefully reflects who Jesus was and is, as well as what God has accomplished in and through him to bring hope, peace, and salvation to the world. The church in its collective wisdom has chosen to anchor its faith and teachings about Jesus the Christ—the the church's primary and final canon(i.e., the authority) of the church and its Scriptures—in selected writings that were written by those closest to Jesus, especially those believed to be his disciples. The books in the New Testament, with only a couple of possible exceptions (2 Peter and 1–2 Timothy), are the earliest Christian books that have survived antiquity and arguably reflect the faith of the earliest followers of Jesus. So, the answer to the question posed above is still the same. Yes, the ancient churches got it right! While the doctrines and traditions of the churches expanded over the years, the core or central teachings of the church that are essential for Christian identity have not changed.

The continuing validity and relevance of the biblical canon for the church may also have to do with another issue that is not historical in nature but theological: What should we do with our questions about the authority of the biblical text? That issue is also central to the whole idea that the notion of a biblical canon raises. Are we, at the end of the day, willing to hear and obey the message of the biblical canon that we adopt? Whatever conclusions we draw about the historicity and scope of the biblical books, do we receive these ancient books as canonical or authoritative texts that govern our lives today? More precisely, if we do not follow or obey the biblical message to inform and impact our beliefs and behavior, does a biblical canon have any value for us?

This is a different question from those that we ask of biblical scholars who are trained in the disciplines of critical investigation. Historical scholars do not necessarily accept faith and obedience as mandates for doing their critical inquiry, since that might interfere with their ability to do careful, independent research. Historians stand in judgment over the ancient texts that they examine and may even distance themselves—to the extent that they are able to do so—from the authority of those texts, but believers approach the biblical text differently, and this is an important matter for the church.

The historical methodology that developed from the time of the Enlightenment and following contends that the historian *as historian* is never subject to the texts that he or she examines, but rather is autonomous and distant from them. The ancient texts themselves do not compel the historian to accept its methodologies, assumptions, or conclusions. Historians seek to be objective in relation to the sources, even if such objectivity can never be fully achieved. Historians do not surrender their autonomy to the texts that they examine.

On the other hand, for those who are committed to the Christian faith and to a biblical canon, the situation is considerably different. If Christians recognize a biblical canon, there must come a time when they submit to its authority in their lives and in the church. That is the nature and essence of sacred Scripture. Those who accept a biblical canon will hear and accept their Scriptures' call to faith and obedience. Those who believe in God must answer to an authority that calls them to faith and mission. Believers will always ask if their understanding of the Bible is the correct one. They will also ask whether such matters as the Bible's views on divorce and remarriage, sexuality, homosexuality, and women in leadership roles in the church, are culturally conditioned and to what extent they are applicable today. They will also ask whether the authority of the Scriptures are inextricably linked to the patriarchal cultures that gave rise to the Bible in the first place, and whether the biblical teachings on such matters are sacred and applicable for all time. Historians, as historians, do not accept such authorities and could hardly be asked to do their task of examining humanity in its social environment with canonical restrictions, but those who are Christians approach their ancient religious texts with a different orientation.

When I was a pastor, persons in the church occasionally asked me for advice on what the Bible has to say about various matters, and whether we are obligated to follow its views on these matters or not. I often asked a counter-question: If my answer was yes, were they willing to follow those admonitions in the Bible? In other words, I asked them, would they be willing to accept the Bible's judgments on their behavior and act accordingly? If not, then, of course, the Bible would not function as a biblical canon for them; they would simply be asking historical and social questions that they might, or might not, choose to follow. Interestingly, some of those persons candidly admitted that they would *not* accept the Bible's views on certain issues if they differed from their own views, as in the case of divorce and forgiveness of spousal abuse. A woman once asked me about the Bible's views on sexual promiscuity and wanted to know what various texts really meant. She was not willing to allow the biblical texts to direct her behavior in that area, so while she had a historical curiosity about the Bible, this is far removed from an affirmation of the authority of the Bible in matters of faith and conduct. In such cases, *there is essentially no canon—the Bible has in a sense ceased to be Scripture for them.*

Our willingness to surrender to the will of God and do what the sacred Scriptures call upon followers of Jesus to do shows by definition that we *do* have a biblical canon. We do not have a biblical canon unless we are willing to follow its guidelines for ordering our lives. On the other hand, in the more conservative

Protestant churches where biblical literalism and submission to the authority of the Bible is a regular part of their faith perspective, it is not uncommon to find members of those faith communities accused, and even convicted, of crimes that the Bible condemns. In such cases, the Bible, while highly acclaimed, often does not function as canon among those who claim to affirm its authority. Unfortunately, it is not uncommon to find persons in churches that affirm the authority of the Bible and who practice behaviors forbidden in the Bible, such as discrimination or ignoring the needs of the hungry, the uneducated, the abused and oppressed in society. When that is true, all discussions about how we arrived at our current Bible, and what is and what is not canonical, are of little import and largely irrelevant. Those who follow the biblical canon only if or when it is convenient, and those who claim to honor Scripture while ignoring the heart of its message, essentially do not have a Bible canon.

On the other hand, as I hinted at above, there are several parts of the Bible that no longer seem as relevant today as they were before. For example, what should we do with some biblical texts that bar women from leadership roles (1 Tim 2:10–15; 1 Cor 14:33–35) or require women to wear coverings or veils in worship (1 Cor 11:2–16)? And what about issues of slavery (1 Cor 7:17–24 and Eph 6:5–9)? The Bible is a culturally conditioned book that must be translated out of its cultural moorings if it is to be relevant for the church today (recalling the criterion of adaptability from chapter 5). Is the patriarchal culture of antiquity in which the Christian faith emerged relevant to biblical interpretation today? Can we distinguish the universal Christian gospel from its ancient culture? Christians often do not agree on what constitutes a culturally conditioned tradition that can be discarded or ignored and what in the Bible is the will of God for today. Nevertheless, after the Bible's culturally conditioned message has been translated into our culture, how will it affect our living? Will it be relevant only when it is convenient or agrees with our prejudice or bias? In what sense is our biblical canon really a canon for us?

More than fifty years ago, a notable German New Testament scholar posed similar questions. He concluded that the essence of biblical faith is obedience to the call of God. Biblical faith, he claimed, abandoned all worldly securities and trusted one's self and future to an all-loving and wise God. For him, this God was revealed through both biblical revelation and the hidden activity of God in human affairs, and supremely in the cross. He argued that in the final analysis, faith cannot demonstrate to unfaith that what is at work is anything more than faith, but he nevertheless stressed that there is an assurance of faith that comes to the one who submits his or her life and security to God. Such trust, he argued, is not misplaced. He further argued that there was a kind of knowledge that admitted only the objective facts about the Christian faith (he called it "unknowing-knowing"). On the other hand, he claimed that there was also a special knowing grasped only by those who exercise faith in the God who comes to us in the preaching of the cross (a "knowing-knowing"). That kind of knowing is not available to a historian working as a historian, but comes rather to the one who exercises faith in God.

God is ultimately the true canon of faith for all believers to the extent that we are willing to submit ourselves to God's authority. If the biblical canon continues to call us to a life-transforming faith, offers to us an identity as the people of God, offers hope in this life and the next, and provides guidance for living today, then it has continuing validity.

Is There a "Canon within the Canon"?

Historically, Christians have generally agreed that the Bible is authoritative in all matters of faith and conduct and is foundational for their beliefs and instruction in living. Because the Bible has been so central in resolving matters of doctrine and conduct, questions about the Bible's origin cannot be insignificant matters. But does it matter how the Bible was put together or whether the books that are in the Protestant Old Testament Scriptures are different from those in the Roman Catholic or Eastern Orthodox Bibles? How important are the additional books in the Bibles of other traditions, and is anything lost in the Protestant tradition by not having them? Perhaps more importantly, what about the books in the Christian Bibles that are largely ignored in churches today, whether in the Old or New Testament?

Following up on the previous point for a moment, how normative can the Bible be if Christians ignore the admonitions of many of its books? It is not unusual for many Christians to say what their favorite part or parts of the Bible are, but neither is it uncommon to hear that they ignore (or have never even read) many parts of their Bibles, and that they concentrate instead on their favorite books. Are there any consequences for this? I regularly speak in academic settings, but also in many churches. In the latter, I hear church members acknowledge that they ignore many of the Old Testament books because they simply do not understand them; they focus mostly on the Psalms, a few of the Prophets, one or two of the Gospels and the letters of Paul. Since for them several biblical books are difficult to understand, they acknowledge that they put them on the "back burner," as in the case of books such as Leviticus, Hebrews, and Revelation. Christians regularly affirm all of the books in the Bible, but not infrequently read only a select few of them, and those are the primary books that influence their beliefs and conduct.

Biblical scholars have often dubbed the result of this practice as a "canon within the canon." Does it matter that many Christians ignore large segments of their Scriptures? This practice of having a "canon within the canon" often means that large segments of the Bible are left unknown and unstudied. On several occasions as I have been teaching Bible studies for church members, some reacted with disbelief when I mentioned some of the various laws and practices in the Old Testament, as in the cases of Deuteronomy 22:13–29, Judges 19–21, Psalm 109, and 1 Kings 1:1–4. "How could such things be in the Bible?" they ask. Not only are some of the laws and regulations in the Old Testament challenging for those reading them for the first time (indeed, many of them remain challenging after several readings), but there are also other challenging practices in the New Testament, as in the case of severe disciplinary practices (Acts 5:1–11). Interestingly, there can be a message in all of these passages that is important for those who acknowledge the two testaments as their Scriptures, but for those who do not regularly read them, they do seem strange indeed in our modern and distinctly different Western culture.

Those Christians who follow the liturgical calendar and use the standard lectionaries for their Scripture readings, preaching, and teaching in the church seldom realize that their lectionaries rarely include readings from all parts of their Bible: modern lectionaries seldom include all of the books of the Bible, even when followed over a number of years. Perhaps that is a good thing, since not all biblical books are necessarily of equal value for Christians today, and it is essential that a considerable amount of church instruction and proclamation focus on the life, teaching, and fate of Jesus, and the pivotal events of the Old Testament, such as the Exodus and God's preservation of his people Israel. Nevertheless, Christians who use lectionaries regularly affirm the whole Bible as their sacred book, even if they do not get around to reading all of it in worship or in the church's instruction. The lectionaries rarely include selections from the Chronicles, Nahum, Habakkuk, 2 Peter, 2–3 John, Jude, and Revelation. If they do, they include only selective portions of those books. Christians in more conservative churches often reject the use of lectionaries, but they like other Christians tend to ignore many parts of the Bible, even though they claim that the whole Bible is their final authority in all matters of faith and conduct.

Sometimes our own habits can be a factor that prevents us from keeping faith with the whole of the biblical canon. It is no longer unusual to go to a church, even a conservative church, and discover that many Christians there do not bring Bibles to church worship services. Pastors may inadvertently encourage this when they display their Scripture texts on video projection screens for the congregation. While this very popular practice brings all of the readers together to read the same Bible translation, the downside is that those who do not bring their Bibles to church seldom know the *context* of the passage selected for preaching or teaching.

I also occasionally chide pastors of such churches who proudly espouse biblical authority and claim to be a "Bible church," but often read less Scripture in their churches than the traditional mainline churches. The latter regularly read one or two passages in each of the Testaments, but some of the more conservative churches not infrequently read only one passage, often only a few verses long, in their worship services. Again, this makes it difficult for the congregation to know the broader context of those verses, and they have been given little chance to encounter God's word. As a consequence, the congregation will likely be unfamiliar with the context of the passage read. The context is an essential ingredient for reading Scripture with understanding.

Likewise, it is not unusual for some pastors to focus most of their attention on the Gospels and Paul and perhaps some famous stories in the Old Testament, while ignoring (purposely or not) the rest of the church's Scriptures. Lectionaries, canonically limited though they may be, often do a better job of getting to a wider sampling of the church's Bible than do those who select only their favorite Scriptures. For example, the late Donald Grey Barnhouse, former pastor of the Tenth Presbyterian Church in Philadelphia, reportedly preached Sunday after Sunday for some seven or eight years only on Paul's letter to the Romans. His successor, the late James Montgomery Boice, likewise followed the same practice and preached each Sunday on the Gospel of John for an even longer period than his predecessor did on Romans! These are admittedly rare examples, but they illustrate that some ministers affirm in principle the inspiration and authority of the whole biblical canon, but in practice are quite selective of the texts they utilize in their proclamation and teaching. The downside of this is a growing ignorance of the Scriptures that were intended to give to the church its identity and mission.

The Other Books: To Read or Not to Read

Over the last one hundred forty years or more, biblical archaeologists and others have discovered a number of books that were earlier included in Christian collections of sacred Scriptures but later excluded. After their exclusion, many of these ancient texts were lost, since the churches stopped making copies of them. Some of those that were lost and subsequently found include the Didache (or Teaching of the Twelve Apostles) and the Gospel of Thomas, 1 Clement, the Epistle of Barnabas, and many others. Should these books now be included in Christian collections of sacred books? This is not an easy question to answer, but it does raise questions about which books adequately or best reflect the faith of the church and its primary authority—Jesus.

Many of these books that were not finally included in the biblical canon have considerable value in helping us understand the context of Judaism in the time of Jesus as well as the context and even the interpretation of many passages in the New Testament during the development of early Christianity. Some of the earliest churches were quite familiar with books that were eventually excluded. In fact, they often made use of them in framing their theological positions as well as their codes of conduct and sometimes cited them as "Scripture."

Recently, the excluded books listed earlier have been getting considerably more attention in seminaries than was the case in previous generations. This is true regardless of the theological stance of the seminary or graduate school (liberal, moderate, or conservative). Many professors have discovered that several of the excluded books often provide useful information in advancing our understanding of the biblical books and the context of early Christianity. It is not necessary to expand the biblical canon in order to be informed by books that were ultimately excluded, even though some of them helped shape the faith of the earliest Christians.

Conclusion

Finally, there are many more discussions about the scope and even the validity of the biblical canon today than at any time in the last four hundred years. If the scope of the Bible were changed, as some Bible scholars have encouraged, would it make a significant difference in churches? What difference would it make in the churches' understanding of God, their identity, their community life, and mission if some books were taken away and others added? Would it be significant if passages that focus on the "end times" and the promise of Jesus' return, often called the Second Coming, were eliminated from the church's Scriptures? Questions about the shape of the Bible typically focus on questions facing churches today, even if many questioners have not fully considered the broader and long-term impact that changes to the shape of the biblical canon would have on further church divisions. As I have repeatedly affirmed in this book, it is not necessary to change the books and passages in the Bible in order to be informed by the same books that informed the faith of the earliest Christians. Those who read ancient books that are not in their Bibles often find gems that are useful and helpful in explaining other passages of canonical Scripture, and sometimes even inspirational as many in the early churches discovered.

I have said for many years now that there is no biblical or theological argument in the church's Scriptures for closing the biblical canon and that the ancient churches did not produce one—but they did provide both a catholic (i.e., books widely welcomed or used) and historical (books written by those closest to Jesus) argument for affirming the books that now comprise the New Testament. Those sacred books that were the earliest and closest writings to the primary events they describe and were more widely welcomed in churches are the ones that historic Christianity welcomed as the church's Scriptures. This historical argument did not prevent many churches from continuing to read books that had been excluded from their Scripture collections, but it did give these churches an argument that allowed them to prioritize the Scriptures that they believed best represented the faith of the earliest followers of Jesus, the character and saving work of Jesus himself, and the essential core of early church's teaching and faith.

Glossary of Terms Related to the Formation of the Canon

The following definitions will be useful for readers of this volume. They are technical terms that are important for understanding the story of how the church got its Bible. The use of the * before a term within a "definition" or "explanation" indicates that that term's meaning is also included in the glossary, either above or below.

agrapha (Greek = "unwritten"). The term refers to the sayings of Jesus not found in the canonical Gospels. The singular *agraphon* refers to individual sayings. At least some of these sayings are preserved in variants of ancient biblical manuscripts and in the writings of the early church fathers, as well as in some apocryphal Christian writings.

Amoraim (pl. of Hebrew *amora* = a "teacher" or "reciter."). These are rabbinic teachers from AD 220 through the talmudic period (AD 500–550). These teachers produced two commentaries (**gemara*) on the *Mishnah, often supplying references to the Jewish *Scriptures.

Apocalypse, apocalyptic (Greek = "revelation" or "disclosure"). This is a technical term that is used to identify visionary literature that directs attention to the end times. Apocalypses are sometimes called "tracts for hard times" and focus on revelations of the end times not earlier disclosed. Both Jews and Christians produced this genre of literature, the most popular of which is the book of Revelation in the New Testament. The term also applies to individual passages that fit this description, such as Isaiah 24–27 and Mark 13.

Apocrypha, apocryphal (Greek = "hidden"). Initially the term was used of writings that were included in the Old Testament writings *after* the books included in the Jewish *Masoretic text, which contains twenty four books that are the same books as the Protestant Old Testament *Scriptures. Roman Catholics sometimes refer to these writings as "Deuterocanonical Scriptures"; that is, writings in the second canon.

autograph. The term used in reference to the original manuscript of a biblical book that text-critical scholars seek to establish by comparing the ancient surviving manuscripts. None of the original manuscripts of the biblical books have survived antiquity.

baraita (Hebrew = "external"; pl. *baraitot*). A rabbinic oral tradition that was put in writing but not sufficiently known or approved to have been included in the collection of oral traditions that comprise the *Mishnah. It is not clear to what extent the *baraitot* were known or widely accepted in the second century AD.

BCE and CE. "Before the Common Era" and "in the Common Era." These are modern designations that scholars often use instead of the usual Christian BC (Before Christ) and AD (*Anno Domini* or Year of the Lord) in order to communicate more effectively with Jewish and other religious communities.

Bible (Greek, *biblion*, = "book," pl. *biblia* = books; sometimes "scroll" or "document"). This is the term that eventually came to refer to the collection of the Christian sacred *Scriptures.

canon or *kanon* (Greek = "a measuring rod," "standard," "rule"). Initially the term was used of a rod or rule to measure distances, but in time it came to refer to standards or guidelines in various areas of art, architecture, philosophy, and even literary standards for authors to follow. It eventually came to refer to the collection of sacred *Scriptures that make up the Christian *Bible.

codex (pl. codexes or codices, essentially a book form). As a successor to the ancient scroll, the codex presented writings in a book format. Initially codices were used as notepads and informal writing vehicles; but by the beginning of the second century, Christians generally adopted the codex for most of their writings. By the fourth century AD, most authors in the Greco-Roman world also adopted the codex format for their writings.

diaspora (Greek = "scattering" or "dispersion"). A technical term that was used of Jews living outside of the *Land of Israel. It was occasionally used of those Jews taken in captivity to Babylon, or the descendants of those generations, who remained outside of their homeland. (See also James 1:1 and 1 Pet 1:1, where this term appears with reference to Christians.)

ekklesia (Greek = "assembly" or "gathering"). This term is often used in the New Testament for groups of the followers of Jesus. It is sometimes modified with the words "of God" or "in Christ" or such like. This term is most often translated "church" in German (*Kirche*) and English Bibles. The term itself is neutral and was well known in the ancient world with reference to a given gathering or assembly. Christians may have used it to distinguish themselves from Jews who used the similar term "synagogue" (connoting a gathering-together) for their gatherings.

euangelion (Greek = "good news"). This word was initially used around the Greco-Roman world for good news or glad tidings, often for pronouncements of royal births, victories, and the like. The word "gospel" in English

Bibles comes from this word. It was used by Christians first to identify the message of what God has done in Jesus the Christ (Mark 1:1), but by the second century it was used generically to describe those Christian writings about Jesus now known as Gospels.

gemara (Aramaic = "completion"). The *Amoraim's additions to and explanations of the *Mishnah. Eventually these *gemara* became the two *Talmudim; namely, the *Bavli* and *Yerushalmi*.

geniza/genizah (Hebrew = "a hiding place"). A special room, normally at a synagogue, used to store old and/or decaying *Scriptures or portions of sacred texts. Even heretical literature, if it contained the divine names, was placed in a *geniza* out of respect for the divine names.

genre (French = "kind" or "type"; the derived adjective is "generic"). A kind of literature or art; used by biblical scholars in reference to the different kinds of literature that make up the *Bible, for example, prophets, *apocalypses, *gospels, history, letters, wisdom literature, and others.

Greco-Roman. This is a reference to the culture in the Mediterranean world from approximately the first century BC to the fifth century AD when Greek culture and Roman domination were inseparable and heavily influenced by each other.

Hagiographa (Greek = "holy writings"). A special designation for the third part of the Jewish sacred *Scriptures, also known as the *Ketuvim*.

Hellenistic. A term that roughly denotes the period from the fourth century BC to the fourth century AD, during which the influence of classical Greek language and culture spread throughout the Mediterranean world and influenced both Jewish and early Christian thought, as well as their *Scriptures; it also denotes this influence itself.

inscription. A writing carved on stone, wood, or metal.

Israel. *See* Land of Israel, below.

Judaizers. These were Jewish Christians who attempted to impose circumcision (as a rite of entry into Jewish identity and from there into Christianity) upon Gentile Christians and were known for their discrimination against Gentiles. See Gal 2:11–14; 3:1–5; Acts 15:1–5.

Ketuvim (Hebrew, "Writings"). The third of three divisions; namely, Law, Prophets, and Writings of the Hebrew *Bible. This collection included the later Old Testament books (Psalms, Proverbs, Job, Song of Songs, Ruth, Lamentations, Ecclesiastes, Esther, Daniel, Ezra, Nehemiah, and 1–2 Chronicles).

Land of Israel. It is difficult to identify adequately the name of Israel in antiquity since the modern designations such as Palestine and Israel, which were not used then (or were used differently), have political implications and are also anachronistic. I have decided to use throughout this volume the "Land of Israel," even when occasionally we are only talking about the southern part of Israel, Judah. As in the case of ancient Greece, it is difficult to find an appropriate designation for that land and its precise boundaries.

lectionary. A collection of selected *Scriptures or biblical passages (lections) that were (and are) read in Christian worship, usually in accord with the Christian liturgical calendar. Lectionaries date back to the early stages of the church.

Majority or Received Text. This name has been given to the collection of manuscripts of Byzantine texts of the Christian *Scriptures. These texts constitute the majority of the surviving biblical manuscripts, but there is no evidence of this textual tradition before the fourth century. The Byzantine texts constitute the majority of manuscripts. "Majority Text" is used similarly to refer to the Received Text.

majuscule. This term, along with *uncial, is the common designation for ancient manuscripts written in all capital letters and without spaces between the words. This includes Christian manuscripts from the second century through the ninth century. In the ninth and tenth centuries, lowercase letters began to be used, with spaces between the words in the manuscripts. These lowercase manuscripts are known as "minuscules." When the letters are joined together in the same word they are often referred to as "cursives."

Masorah (Hebrew, "tradition"), Masoretic, Masorete. The Jewish rules that govern the copying and transmitting of the biblical text. The Masoretes were Jewish copiers who stabilized the text of the Hebrew *Bible (i.e., according to these rules) and added *vowel points* so that words previously written only with consonants could be properly pronounced. Their careful preservation of the Hebrew text of the Jewish *Scriptures (the *Tanak*) dates from the seventh century. The most complete surviving Masoretic text of the Jewish Scriptures is the Codex Leningradensis (ca. AD 975), and it is based on the earlier Aleppo text (earlier produced in Aleppo, Syria) that was seriously damaged in 1947 and is partially preserved and now located in Israel.

Megillot. More specifically, *Hamesh Megillot* (Hebrew, "Five Scrolls"). A reference to the "Festival" books of the Hebrew *Bible written on scrolls and read on various Jewish holidays. The scrolls include Ruth, Song of Solomon, Ecclesiastes, Lamentations, and Esther.

Mishnah (Hebrew, "that which is repeated" or "repetition"), Mishnaic. The compilation and codification of Jewish oral tradition that dates from roughly the time of Jesus to Rabbi Judah ha-Nasi (roughly AD 10 to AD 200–220). It is referred to with the symbol *m.* and contains six orders, or divisions, with a total of sixty-three tractates. Some of the Jewish oral tradition is mentioned by Jesus in Mark 7:1–13. Many Jews believe that this is the "oral *Torah" that was given to Moses at Mt. Sinai when he also received the written law.

Nevi'im [Hebrew, "Prophets"]. The second of three divisions of the Hebrew *Bible, referring to its prophetic books, both the Former Prophets (Joshua, Judges, 1–2 Samuel, 1–2 Kings) and the Latter Prophets (Isaiah, Jeremiah, Ezekiel and the Twelve [Minor Prophets]).

nomina sacra (Latin = "sacred names."). There are several abbreviated names in the ancient Christian biblical manuscripts that generally include the first and last letters of the name with a line over the top of those letters to indicate that the word has been contracted. Initially the list of these abbreviated terms included such names as God, Jesus, Christ, Savior, and Spirit, but later included more than a dozen other well-known names in early Christianity, such as father, son, mother, and other popular names or designations.

Old Latin. The late second-century and later Latin versions of the *Bible that were produced before Jerome's fourth-century Latin *Vulgate translation of the Old Testament from the Hebrew Scriptures.

ostracon (pl. ostraca). Pottery or potsherd fragments used for nonformal writing material such as receipts and short messages, and traditionally for voting as well.

palimpsest (Greek = "rubbed again" or "re-scraped"). A manuscript that had its original writing erased by scraping and or washing so the surface could be resmoothed and used again for a new literary text.

papyrus (pl. papyri). A plant used in ancient times, especially in Egypt, to make writing material. Many documents written on papyrus have been found in Egypt and have helped to illustrate the language and customs of the Hellenistic world. The term is used of the manuscripts themselves and is also the origin of the English word "paper."

patristic(s). A reference to the early church fathers and the study of them. The patristic authors wrote from the second to the sixth or seventh centuries.

Pseudepigrapha (singular: pseudepigraphon), pseudepigraphic. Documents written under another person's name; that is, they are *pseudonymous*, literally "[under a] false name," writings. Ancient pseudepigraphic writings were typically produced under the name of a famous person, such as Enoch or Plato. Such writings were also common in Jewish and early Christian writings and typically written under famous biblical names or apostolic figures in the New Testament. Wisdom writings, for instance, were often attributed to Solomon and psalmic writings were attributed to David.

Qumran. Location of the remains of a Jewish Essene settlement near the Dead Sea, where in eleven nearby caves numerous biblical and nonbiblical texts, commonly known as the Dead Sea Scrolls (often abbreviated as the DSS), were discovered.

Received Text. The Received Text or *Textus Receptus*, the early editions of which were produced by Erasmus in 1519, 1522, 1527, and 1535, and which was later modified and corrected by Theodore Beza. This Greek text was the basis for the translation of the King James Version of the *Bible.

Scripture (Latin, *scriptura*, "writings," in Greek, *graphai*, "writings"). The reference that Jews and Christians use to designate their sacred writings, which Christians call their *Bible. The early Christians used "scripture" in reference to religious texts that were eventually included in the Bible, but also when referring to some religious texts that were *not* ultimately included.

Septuagint. The Greek translation of the Hebrew *Scriptures that was begun in 281–280 BC and was completed by around 100 BC. This translation is often symbolized by "LXX" (the Roman numeral 70), based on the tradition of the number of translators who produced it (rounded down from 72). It is not clear what books made up the Greek Old Testament in the time of Jesus, but it was the *Bible of the early Christian communities as well as the Scriptures of the *Hellenistic Jews in the *Diaspora.

stichometry. The practice of calculating and arranging the letters in ancient lines of a text and arranging lines to a page. This allowed for the reconstruction of a text and payment to those who copied the pages. The practice of stichometry is found in such ancient texts as the *Stichometry of Nicephorus* (ca. AD 850) that lists the books that were accepted and rejected as a part of the Christian *Scriptures.

Talmud (Hebrew, "learning"). The Talmud is the combination of the *Mishnah and its *gemara* or commentary. The rabbinic teachers from the third through the sixth century AD interpreted the writings of the *Mishnah and the *Tosefta, often adding biblical support for them and their interpretations of these traditions (*gemara*, Aramaic = "completion"). There were two major Talmuds (pl. *Talmudim*), largely produced between the fourth and sixth centuries, following the order of the Tractates in the *Mishnah. One of the two Talmudim originated in Palestine and is called the *Yerushalmi* (its symbol is *y.*) and the other one came from Babylon and is called the *Bavli* (its symbol is *b.*). Besides the books in the Hebrew *Bible (equivalent to the Protestant Old Testament, but in a different sequence), the sacred Jewish writings include the Mishnah, the Tosefta, and the two Talmudim.

Tanak. An acronym for the Hebrew *Bible based on the first letters of its three sections, *Torah* (Law), *Nevi'im* (Prophets), and *Ketuvim* (Writings), therefore TaNaK, or *Tanak*. The rabbinic term for biblical literature is *miqra* (Hebrew, "that which is read [aloud]") and expresses an important function of sacred literature; namely, that it was to be read aloud in the congregation.

Tannaim. (Hebrew = "teacher" or, "repeater.") These are the rabbinic teachers from roughly AD 10–200. The most famous of these teachers that overlapped the time of Jesus were Shammai and Hillel. The apostle Paul studied with one such well-known first-century rabbi named Gamaliel, who once came to the rescue of the early followers of Jesus (Acts 5:33–40; 22:3).

Targum (pl. *Targumim*; Aramaic = "translation"). Aramaic translations of and commentaries on the Jewish *Scriptures that were to be read in the synagogues after the reading of the Hebrew text of the Scriptures. By the fifth century AD, the most popular Targums were Targum Onqelos on the *Torah and Targum Jonathan on the Prophets, both written in the third century AD. The Targums are an important witness to the text of the Hebrew *Bible at an early stage.

textual criticism. The practice of scholars who study and compare ancient biblical manuscripts with the goal of establishing the most reliable text of the *Scriptures, that which is deemed closest to the original texts or autographs. There are many rules and guidelines that textual critics follow in establishing the earliest and most reliable text.

Torah. The Law, or the first five books of the Hebrew *Bible (Genesis, Exodus, Leviticus, Numbers, and Deuteronomy); the Torah (or Pentateuch) also constitutes the first of the three divisions of the Hebrew Bible (Law, Prophets, and Writings).

Tosefta (pl. *Tosafot*; Hebrew = "supplement" or "additions"). These writings are largely third- and fourth-century commentaries on the *Mishnah. Essentially, the Tosefta are those writings not included in the Mishnah. The symbol for Tosefta is t.

uncial (see *majuscule). This term designates biblical manuscripts written in capital letters with no spaces between the words. The majority of uncial manuscripts date from the second to the tenth centuries. Those uncial manuscripts written in the fourth century and following are generally on parchment instead of papyrus sheets.

Vulgate. Latin version of the *Bible translated by Jerome in the late fourth century and officially adopted by the Catholic Church in the sixteenth century, though used by the majority of Roman Catholic Christians for centuries before then.

Select Bibliography

The following is a collection of some of the important and (mostly) recent publications on the formation of the Christian biblical canon. This collection is not exhaustive, but does offer the reader a reasonable collection of sources that are quite helpful in exploring further the origin of the Bible in considerably more detail than I have been able to offer in this volume.

Adler, William. "Origen and the Old Testament Apocrypha: The Creation of a Category." Pages 287–308 in *The Old Testament Pseudepigrapha: Fifty Years of the Pseudepigrapha Section at the SBL*. Early Judaism and Its Literature 50. Atlanta: SBL Press, 2019.

———. "The Pseudepigrapha in the Early Church." Pages 211–28 in *The Canon Debate*. Edited by L. M. McDonald and J. A. Sanders. Grand Rapids: Baker Academic, 2002.

Aland, Kurt. "The Problem of Anonymity and Pseudonymity in Christian Literature of the First Two Centuries." *Journal of Theological Studies* 12 (1961): 39–49.

Aune, D. E. *Prophecy in Early Christianity and the Ancient Mediterranean World*. Grand Rapids: Eerdmans, 1983.

———. *The New Testament in Its Literary Environment*. LEC. Philadelphia: Westminster, 1987.

Barr, James. *Holy Scripture: Canon, Authority, Criticism*. Philadelphia: Westminster, 1983.

Barrera, Julio Trebolle. *The Jewish Bible and the Christian Bible: An Introduction to the History of the Bible*. Translated by W. G. E. Watson. Grand Rapids: Eerdmans, 1998.

Barton, John. *Holy Writings, Sacred Text: The Canon in Early Christianity*. Louisville, KY: Westminster John Knox Press, 1997.

———. *How the Bible Came to Be*. Louisville: Westminster John Knox, 1997.

———. *Oracles of God: Perceptions of Ancient Prophecy in Israel after the Exile*. London: Darton, Longman and Todd, 1986.

———. *The Spirit and the Letter: Studies in the Biblical Canon*. London: SPCK, 1997.

Bauckham, Richard, James R. Davila, and Alexander Panayotov, eds. *Old Testament Pseudepigrapha: More Noncanonical Scriptures*. 2 vols. Grand Rapids: Eerdmans, 2013.

Beckwith, R. T. *The Old Testament Canon of the New Testament Church*. Grand Rapids: Eerdmans, 1985.

Betz, Hans Dieter. "New Testament Theology: The Origins of a Concept." Pages 7–92 in *The Origins of New Testament Theology: A Dialogue with Hans Dieter Betz*. Edited by Rainer Hirsch-Luipold and Robert Matthew Calhoun. WUNT 440. Tübingen: Mohr Siebeck, 2020.

Blair, Edward P. *The Bible and You: A Guide for Reading and Understanding the Bible*. Nashville: Abingdon Press, 1953.

Bockmuehl, Markus. *Ancient Apocryphal Gospels*. Interpretation Resources for the Use of Scripture in the Church. Louisville: Westminster John Knox, 2017.

Bovon, François. "'Useful for the Soul': Christian Apocrypha and Christian Spirituality." Pages 185–95 in *The Oxford Handbook of Early Christian Apocrypha*. Edited by Andrew Gregory and Christopher Tuckett. Oxford: Oxford University Press, 2015.

Brakke, David. "Canon Formation and Social Conflict in Fourth-Century Egypt: Athanasius of Alexandria's Thirty-Ninth Festal Letter." *Harvard Theological Review* 87 (1994): 395–419.

———. "A New Fragment of Athanasius' *Thirty-Ninth Festal Letter*: Heresy, Apocrypha, and the Canon." *Harvard Theological Review* 103 (2010): 47–66.

Bruce, F. F. *The Canon of Scripture*. Downers Grove, IL: InterVarsity Press, 1988.

Burke, Tony, and Brent Landau, eds. *New Testament Apocrypha: More Noncanonical Scriptures*. Vol. 1. Grand Rapids: Eerdmans, 2016.

Burke, Tony, ed. *New Testament Apocrypha: More Noncanonical Scriptures*. Vol. 2. Grand Rapids: Eerdmans, 2020.

Campenhausen, H. von. *The Formation of the Christian Bible*. Translated by J. A. Baker. Philadelphia: Fortress, 1972.

Carr, David M. *The Formation of the Hebrew Bible: A New Reconstruction*. Oxford: Oxford University Press, 2010.

Charles, R. H. *The Apocrypha and Pseudepigrapha of the Old Testament*. 2 vols. Oxford: Oxford University Press, 1913.

Charlesworth, James H. "Foreword: The Fundamental Importance of an Expansive Collection of 'Old Testament Pseudepigrapha.'" Pages xi–xvi in vol. 1 of *Old Testament Pseudepigrapha: More Noncanonical Scriptures*. Edited by Richard Bauckham, James R. Davila, and Alexander Panayotov. Grand Rapids: Eerdmans, 2013.

———. *Odes of Solomon*. Missoula, Montana: Scholars Press, 1977.

———. *Old Testament Pseudepigrapha and the New Testament*. 2 vols. Cambridge: Cambridge University Press, 1985.

———. "Pseudepigrapha." Pages 540–41 in vol. 5 of *The Anchor Bible Dictionary*. New York: Doubleday, 1992.

———. "Pseudepigraphy." Pages 768–75 in vol. 2 of *Encyclopedia of Early Christianity*. Edited by Everett Ferguson. New York: Garland Press, 1997.

Childs, B. S. *The New Testament as Canon: An Introduction*. Philadelphia: Fortress, 1985.

Clarke, Kent D. "The Problem of Pseudonymity in Biblical Literature and Its Implications for Canon Formation." Pages 440–68 in *The Canon Debate*. Edited by L. M. McDonald and J. A. Sanders. Peabody, MA: Hendrickson, 2002.

Collins, John J., Craig A. Evans, and L. M. McDonald. *Ancient Jewish and Christian Scriptures: New Developments in Canon Controversy*. Louisville: Westminster John Knox, 2020.

Cross, F. M., Jr. *From Epic to Canon: History and Literature in Ancient Israel*. Baltimore and London: Johns Hopkins University Press, 1998.

Davies, P. R. *Scribes and Schools: The Canonization of the Hebrew Scriptures*. Library of Ancient Israel. Edited by D. Knight. Louisville: Westminster John Knox, 1998.

Davila, James A. *The Provenance of the Pseudepigrapha: Jewish, Christian, or Other?* JSJSup 105. Leiden: Brill, 2005.

deSilva, David A. "Pseudepigrapha." Pages 212–28 in vol. 2 of *The Oxford Encyclopedia of the Books of the Bible*. Edited by Michael D. Coogan. New York: Oxford University Press, 2011.

Donelson, L. R. *Pseudepigraphy and Ethical Argument in the Pastoral Epistles*. HUT 22. Tübingen: Mohr Siebeck, 1986.

Duff, Jeremy. "A Reconsideration of Pseudepigraphy in Early Christianity." *Tyndale Bulletin* 50.2 (1999): 306–9.

Dunn, James D. G. "The Problem of Pseudonymity." Pages 65–85 in *The Living Word*. Philadelphia: Fortress, 1987.

———. "Pseudepigraphy." Pages 977–84 in *Dictionary of the Later New Testament and its Development*. Edited by Ralph P. Martin and Peter H. Davids. Downers Grove, IL: InterVarsity Press, 1997.

Ehrman, Bart D. *Forged: Writing in the Name of God — Why the Bible's Authors Are Not Who We Think They Are*. New York: HarperCollins, 2011.

Elliott, J. K. "Apocrypha, New Testament." Pages 60–69 in vol. 1 of *The Oxford Encyclopedia of the Books of the Bible*. Edited by Michael D. Coogan. New York: Oxford University Press, 2011.

———. "The 'apocryphal' New Testament." Pages 455–78 in vol. 1 of *The Cambridge History of The Bible: From Beginnings to 600*. Edited by James Carleton Paget and Joachim Schaper. Cambridge: Cambridge University Press, 2013.

———— ,ed. *The Apocryphal New Testament: A Collection of Apocryphal Christian Literature in an English Translation based on M. R. James.* Oxford: Clarendon, 1993.

Evans, Craig A. *Ancient Texts for New Testament Studies: A Guide to the Background Literature.* Peabody, MA: Hendrickson, 2005.

————. "The Christian Apocrypha." Pages 145–66 in *Ancient Jewish and Christian Scriptures: New Developments in Canon Controversy.* Edited by John J. Collins, Craig A. Evans, and L. M. McDonald. Louisville: Westminster John Knox, 2020.

————. *Jesus and the Manuscripts: What We Can Learn from the Oldest Texts.* Peabody, MA: Hendrickson, 2020.

Farmer, W. R. *Jesus and the Gospel: Tradition, Scripture and Canon.* Philadelphia: Fortress, 1982.

Farmer, W. R., and D. M. Farkasfalvy. *The Formation of the New Testament Canon.* New York: Paulist, 1983.

Ferguson, E. "Canon Muratori: Date and Provenance." *Studia Patristica* 18 (1982): 677–83.

Freedman, D. N. "The Symmetry of the Hebrew Bible." *Studia Theologica* 46 (1992): 83–108.

————. *The Unity of the Hebrew Bible.* Ann Arbor: University of Michigan Press, 1991.

Frey, Jörg. "From Canonical to Apocryphal Texts: The Quest for Processes of 'Apocryphication' in Early Jewish and Early Christian literature." Pages 1–43 in *Between Canonical and Apocryphal Texts.* Edited by Jörg Frey, Claire Clivaz, and Tobias Nicklas. WUNT 419. Tübingen: Mohr Siebeck, 2019.

Fricke, Klaus D. "The Apocrypha in the Luther Bible." Pages 46–87 in *The Apocrypha in Ecumenical Perspective.* Edited by Siegfried Meuer. UBS Monograph Series 6. New York: United Bible Societies, 1991.

Gallagher, Edmon L. "Writings Labeled 'Apocrypha' in Latin Patristic Sources." Pages 1–14 in *Sacra Scriptura: How "Non-Canonical" Texts Functioned in Early Judaism and Early Christianity.* Edited by James H. Charlesworth and Lee Martin McDonald. London: T&T Clark, 2014.

————, and John Meade. *The Biblical Canon Lists from Early Christianity: Texts and Analysis.* Oxford: Oxford University Press, 2017.

Gamble, H. Y. *Books and Readers in the Early Church: A History of Early Christian Texts.* New Haven: Yale University Press, 1995.

————. "Canon, New Testament." Pages 852–61 in vol. 1 of *The Anchor Bible Dictionary.* Edited by D. N. Freedman. 6 vols. New York: Doubleday, 1992.

Gathercole, Simon. "The Alleged Anonymity of the Canonical Gospels." *Journal of Theological Studies* 69.2 (2018): 447–76.

———. "Other Apocryphal Gospels and the Historical Jesus." Pages 250–68 in *The Oxford Handbook of Early Christian Apocrypha*. Edited by Andrew Gregory and Christopher Tuckett. Oxford: Oxford University Press, 2015.

Grant, R. M. "The New Testament Canon." Pages 284–308 in vol. 1 of *The Cambridge History of the Bible*. Edited by P. R. Ackroyd and C. F. Evans. 3 vols. Cambridge: Cambridge University Press, 1976.

Gurtner, Daniel M. *Introducing the Pseudepigrapha of Second Temple Judaism: Message, Context, and Significance*. Grand Rapids: Baker Academic, 2020.

Guthrie, Donald. "The Development of the Idea of Canonical Pseudepigrapha in New Testament Criticism." Pages 15–39 in *The Authorship and Integrity of the New Testament*. Edited by Kurt Aland. London: SPCK, 1965.

Hahneman, G. M. *The Muratorian Fragment and the Development of the Canon*. Oxford Theological Monographs. Oxford: Clarendon Press, 1992.

Hannah, D. "New Testament Manuscripts: Uncials, Minuscules, Palimpsests and All That Stuff." *Bible Review* 6.1 (February 1990): 7–9.

Hirsch-Luipold, Rainer, and Robert Matthew Calhoun, eds. *The Origins of New Testament Theology: A Dialogue with Hans Dieter Betz*. WUNT 440. Tübingen: Mohr Siebeck, 2020.

Holmes, Michael W., ed. *The Greek New Testament: SBL Edition*. Atlanta: SBL Press, 2010.

Hull, Robert F. *The Story of the New Testament Text: Movers, Materials, Motives, Methods, and Models*. SBLRBS 58. Atlanta: SBL Press, 2010.

Hurtado, Larry. "Who Read Early Christian Apocrypha?" Pages 153–66 in *The Oxford Handbook of Early Christian Apocrypha*. Edited by Andrew Gregory and Christopher Tuckett. Oxford: Oxford University Press, 2015.

Jeremias, J. *The Unknown Sayings of Jesus*. 2nd ed. London: SPCK, 1964.

Johns, Loren L. "Do Mark 16:9–30 and John 7:53–8:11 Belong in Our Bibles? A Case Study in the Intersection of Textual Criticism and Canonical Considerations." Pages 83–105 in *Fountains of Wisdom: In Conversation with James H. Charlesworth*. Edited by Gerbern S. Oegema, Henry W. Rietz, and Loren T. Stuckenbruck. London: T&T Clark, 2022.

Jones, B. A. *The Formation of the Book of the Twelve: A Study in Text and Canon*. SBLDS 149. Atlanta, GA: Scholars Press, 1995.

Kahle, P. E. *The Cairo Geniza*. 2nd ed. Oxford: Blackwell, 1959.

Koester, H. *Ancient Christian Gospels: Their History and Development*. London: SCM; Philadelphia: Trinity Press International, 1990.

———. "Apocryphal and Canonical Gospels." *HTR* 73 (1980): 105–30.

Kraemer, D. "The Formation of the Rabbinic Canon: Authority and Boundaries." *Journal of Biblical Literature* 110 (1991): 613–30.

Leiman, S. Z. *The Canon and Masorah of the Hebrew Bible: An Introductory Reader.* New York: Ktav, 1974.

———. *The Canonization of the Hebrew Scripture: The Talmudic and Midrashic Evidence.* Hamden, CT: Archon, 1976.

———. "Josephus and the Canon of the Bible." Pages 50–58 in *Josephus, The Bible, and History.* Edited by L. H. Feldman and G. Hata. Detroit: Wayne State University Press, 1989.

Lightstone, J. N. *Society, the Sacred, and Scripture in Ancient Judaism: A Sociology of Knowledge.* Studies in Christianity and Judaism 3. Waterloo, Ontario: Wilfrid Laurier University Press, 1988.

Lim, Timothy H. *The Formation of the Jewish Canon.* New Haven: Yale University Press, 2013.

Mara, M. G. "Apocrypha." Pages 56–58 in vol. 1 of *Encyclopedia of the Early Church.* Edited by Angelo Di Bernardino. New York: Oxford University Press, 1992.

Marshall, I. Howard. *The Pastoral Epistles.* ICC. Edinburgh: T&T Clark, 1999.

McDonald, Lee Martin. *Before There Was a Bible: Authorities in Early Christianity.* London: T&T Clark, 2022.

———. *The Biblical Canon: Its Origin, Transmission and Authority.* Grand Rapids: Baker Academic, 2011.

———. "Canon." Pages 777–809 in *The Oxford Handbook of Biblical Studies.* Edited by John Rogerson and Judith Lieu. Oxford: Oxford University Press, 2006.

———. "Canon of the New Testament." Pages 536–47 in vol. 1 of *The New Interpreter's Dictionary of the Bible.* Edited by Katherine Doob Sakenfeld. 5 vols. Nashville: Abingdon Press, 2006.

———. *Forgotten Scriptures: The Selection and Rejection of Early Religious Writings.* Louisville: Westminster John Knox, 2009.

———. *The Formation of the Bible.* Volume 1: *The Old Testament: Its Authority and Canonicity.* London: T&T Clark, 2017.

———. *The Formation of the Bible.* Volume 2: *The New Testament: Its Authority and Canonicity.* London: T&T Clark, 2017.

———. "Hellenism and the Biblical Canons: Is There a Connection?" Pages 13–49 in *Christian Origins and Hellenistic Judaism: Social and Literary Contexts for the New Testament.* Edited by Stanley E. Porter and A. W. Pitts. TENT 10. Leiden: Brill, 2013.

———. "Identifying Scripture and Canon in the Early Church: The Criteria Question." Pages 416–40 in *The Canon Debate.* Edited by L. M. McDonald and J. A. Sanders. Peabody, MA: Hendrickson, 2002.

———. "The *Odes of Solomon* in Ancient Christianity." Pages 108–36 in *Sacra Scriptura: How 'Non-Canonical' Texts Functioned in Early Judaism and Early*

Christianity. Edited by James H. Charlesworth and Lee Martin McDonald. JCTS 20. London: T&T Clark, 2014.

———. *The Origin of the Bible: A Guide for the Perplexed*. New York: T&T Clark, 2011.

———. "Wherein Lies Authority: A Discussion of Books, Texts, and Translations." Pages 203–39 in *Exploring the Origins of the Bible: Canon Formation in Historical, Literary, and Theological Perspective*. Edited by Craig A. Evans and Emanuel Tov. Acadia Studies in Bible and Theology 6. Craig A. Evans and L. M. McDonald, series editors. Grand Rapids: Baker Academic, 2008.

———, and James A. Sanders, eds. *The Canon Debate*. Grand Rapids: Baker Academic, 2002.

———, and S. E. Porter. *Early Christianity and Its Sacred Literature*. Peabody, MA: Hendrickson, 2000.

Metzger, Bruce M. "Apocrypha." Pages 37–41 in *The Oxford Companion to the Bible*. Edited by Bruce M. Metzger and Michael D. Coogan. New York: Oxford University Press, 1993.

———. *The Canon of the New Testament: Its Origin, Development, and Significance*. Oxford: Clarendon Press, 1987.

———. "Introduction to the Apocrypha." Pages ix–xx in *The Oxford Annotated Apocrypha: Revised Standard Version*. Oxford: Oxford University Press, 1965.

———. "Literary Forgeries and Canonical Pseudepigrapha." *Journal of Biblical Literature* 91 (1972): 3–24.

Meuer, S., ed. *The Apocrypha in Ecumenical Perspective*. UBS Monograph Series 6. Translated by P. Ellingworth. New York: United Bible Societies, 1991.

Mroczek, Eva. "Hidden Scriptures, Then and Now: Rediscovering 'Apocrypha.'" *Interpretation* 72.4 (2018): 383–95.

———. *The Literary Imagination in Jewish Antiquity*. New York: Oxford University Press, 2016.

Najman, Hindy. *Seconding Sinai: The Development of Mosaic Discourse in Second Temple Judaism*. JSJSup 77. Leiden: Brill, 2003.

———. "How Should We Contextualize Pseudepigrapha? Imitation and Emulation in *4 Ezra*." Pages 529–36 in *Flores Florentino: Dead Sea Scrolls and Other Early Jewish Studies in Honour of Florentino García Martínez*. Edited by Anthony Hilhorst, Émile Puech, and Eibert Tigchelaar. Leiden: Brill, 2007.

———, and Irene Peirano. "Pseudepigraphy as an Interpretive Construct." Pages 331–58 in *The Old Testament Pseudepigrapha: Fifty years of the Pseudepigrapha Section at the SBL*. Edited by Matthias Henze and Liv Ingebord Lied. EJL 50. Atlanta: SBL Press, 2019.

Neusner, J., with W. S. Green. *Writing with Scripture: The Authority and Uses of the Hebrew Bible in the Torah of Formative Judaism*. Minneapolis: Fortress, 1989.

Oegema, Gerbern, ed. *The Oxford Handbook of The Apocrypha*. New York: Oxford University Press, 2021.

Oikonomos, Elias. "Deuterocanonicals in the Orthodox Church," Pages 17–32 in *The Apocrypha in Ecumenical Perspective*. Edited by Siegfried Meurer. UBS Monograph Series 6. New York: United Bible Societies, 1991.

Patzia, A. G. *The Making of the New Testament: Origin, Collection, Text and Canon*. 2nd ed. Downers Grove, IL: InterVarsity Press, 2011.

Reed, Annette Yoshika. "The Afterlives of New Testament Apocrypha." *Journal of Biblical Literature* 133.2 (2015): 401–25.

———. "The Modern Invention of 'Old Testament Pseudepigrapha.'" *Journal of Theological Studies* 20 (2009): 403–36.

———. "Pseudepigraphy, Authorship, and the Reception of 'The Bible' in Late Antiquity." Pages 467–89 in *The Reception of and Interpretation of the Bible in Late Antiquity*. Edited by Lorenzo DiTommaso and Lucian Turcescu. Leiden: Brill, 2008.

Rist, Martin. "Pseudepigraphy and the Early Christians." Pages 75–91 in *Studies in New Testament and Early Christian Literature: Essays in Honor of Allen Wikgren*. Edited by David A. Aune. NovTSup 33. Leiden: Brill, 1972.

Roberts, C. H. "Books in the Greco-Roman World and in the New Testament." Pages 48–66 in vol. 1 of *The Cambridge History of the Bible*. Edited by P. R. Ackroyd and C. F. Evans. Cambridge: Cambridge University Press, 1976.

Rothschild, Clare. "The Muratorian Fragment as Roman Fake." *Novum Testamentum* 60 (2018): 55–82.

———. *The Muratorian Fragment*. STAC 132. Tübingen: Mohr Siebeck, 2022.

Ryle, H. E. *The Canon of the Old Testament*. 2nd ed. London: Macmillan, 1914.

Sanders, J. A. "Adaptable for Life: The Nature and Function of Canon." Pages 531–60 in *Magnalia Dei: The Mighty Acts of God. Essays on the Bible and Archaeology in Memory of G. E. Wright*. New York: Doubleday, 1976.

———. "Canon, Hebrew Bible." Pages 837–52 in vol. 1 of *The Anchor Bible Dictionary*. Edited by D. N. Freedman. 6 vols. New York: Doubleday, 1992.

———. *From Sacred Story to Sacred Text*. Philadelphia: Fortress, 1987.

———. "Spinning the Bible: How Judaism and Christianity Shape the Canon Differently." *Bible Review* 14.3 (June 1998): 23–29, 44–45.

Schneemelcher, W., ed. *New Testament Apocrypha*. Rev. ed. 2 vols. Louisville: Westminster John Knox Press, 1991.

Schröter, Jens. "The Formation of the New Testament Canon and Early Christian Apocrypha." Pages 167–84 in *The Oxford Handbook of Early Christian Apocrypha*. Edited by Andrew Gregory and Christopher Tuckett. Oxford: Oxford University Press, 2015.

Stuckenbruck, Loren. "Apocrypha and Pseudepigrapha." Pages 143–62 in *The Eerdmans Dictionary of Early Judaism*. Edited by John J. Collins and Daniel C. Harlow. Grand Rapids: Eerdmans, 2010.

Stuhlmacher, Peter. "The Significance of the Old Testament Apocrypha and Pseudepigrapha for the Understanding of Jesus and Christology." Pages 1–15 in *The Apocrypha in Ecumenical Perspective*. Edited by Siegfried Meurer. UBS Monograph Series 6. New York: United Bible Societies, 1991.

Silver, D. J. *The Story of Scripture: From Oral Tradition to the Written Word*. New York: Basic Books, 1990.

Stevenson, J. *A New Eusebius: Documents Illustrative of the History of the Church to AD 337*. London: SPCK, 1957.

Sundberg, A. C., Jr. "Canon Muratori: A Fourth-Century List." *HTR* 66 (1973): 1–41.

———. *The Old Testament of the Early Church*. Cambridge, MA: Harvard University Press, 1964.

Swete, H. B. *Introduction to the Old Testament in Greek*. Cambridge: Cambridge University Press, 1914. Repr., Peabody, MA: Hendrickson, 1989.

Talmon, Shemaryahu. *Text and Canon of the Hebrew Bible: Collected Essays*. Winona Lake, IN: Eisenbrauns, 2010.

Theron, Daniel J. *Evidence of Tradition*. Grand Rapids: Baker, 1957. Repr., Eugene, OR: Wipf & Stock, 2009.

Tigchelaar, Eibert, ed. *Old Testament Pseudepigrapha and the Scriptures*. Bibliotheca Ephemeridum Theologicarum Lovaniensium 270. Leuven: Peeters, 2014.

Tuckett, Christopher. "Introduction: What is Christian Apocrypha." Pages 2–12 in *The Oxford Handbook of Early Christian Apocrypha*. Edited by Andrew Gregory and Christopher Tuckett. Oxford: Oxford University Press, 2015.

Wegner, Paul D. *The Journey from Texts to Translations: The Origin and Development of the Bible*. Grand Rapids: Baker Academic, 1999.

Wyrick, Jed. *The Ascension of Authorship: Attribution and Canon Formation in Jewish, Hellenistic, and Christian Traditions*. Harvard Studies in Comparative Literature 49. Harvard University Press, 2004.

Zeitlin, S. "An Historical Study of the Canonization of Hebrew Scriptures." In *Proceedings of the American Academy for Jewish Research* 3 (1931–32). Repr. 164–201 in *The Canon and Masorah of the Hebrew Bible*. Edited by S. Z. Leiman. New York: Ktav, 1974.